Selected Readings
in Movement Education

Edited by
ROBERT T. SWEENEY
East Stroudsburg State College

Selected Readings
in Movement Education

ADDISON-WESLEY PUBLISHING COMPANY
Reading, Massachusetts
Menlo Park, California · London · Don Mills, Ontario

This book is in the
Addison-Wesley Series in Physical Education

To Robert Bradley and
Brendan Aileen

Preface

Selected Readings in Movement Education was compiled because of the
need to provide relevant and current readings in movement education for
college classes in elementary school physical education. The articles included have been assigned to students majoring in physical education and
in elementary education. The text can be useful for those groups, as well
as for curriculum planners, preschool teachers, practicing physical educators, and college teachers preparing teachers of physical education.

Movement education has been gaining impetus throughout the United
States during the past two decades. Many factors have contributed to the
growth, which has seen its greatest surge in the 1960's. Federally funded
experimental programs have provided places to "try out" new ideas in the
framework of a reciprocal relationship between public schools and higher
education. Positions for elementary physical education consultants and
specialists have been created in national, state, and local associations and
at all educational levels in both private and public institutions. Conferences, conventions, publications, and commercial interests have all devoted
time, personnel, and finances to disseminating information about movement education, thus establishing an awareness of the theory. However,
the limited availability of in-depth material, the diversity of sources, the
differing concept foci of the various schools of thought, and other factors
make it difficult for the student or practicing physical educator to attain
solid understanding of movement education theory without undertaking a
considerable amount of investigation. Too often a teacher turns the
potpourri of convention programs, a few articles, and other isolated
materials into a curriculum without further examination of intent or

consequence. Curriculum change or revision for improvement demands decision-making based on logical hypothesis and a well-defined plan for initiation. Curriculum change in physical education requires no less preparation, quantitatively or qualitatively, than in any other curriculum area in our schools. It should be conducted in a planned, scientific manner.

This text is meant to aid in the beginning stages of that scientific process. The main purpose of the readings is to serve as a collection of data for future inquiry into the student-content-method-teacher schema within present and future physical education. Initiation of thought, direction to study through clarification of questions, definition of issues, selection of concepts, and motivation of readers to seek answers are all desired outcomes of the text.

The articles appear, in context, as they were prepared by their authors. Each article represents that writer's viewpoint concerning his stipulated topic. Some presentations are complete in themselves; others are parts of more extensive writings. Wherever possible, the complete work, i.e., the full article, the remainder of the book, etc., should be consulted. Additional writings by the same author should be read. The entries in the bibliography for each article should also be read to fully understand its background and meaning. In all cases, the reader of course should bear in mind the dates of publication. Several of the authors have gone beyond their included articles but have not as yet published their present thoughts.

The text is presented in four sections: (1) Theories of Movement; (2) Teacher and Methods; (3) The Question: What Is Movement Education? and (4) References. Materials within each section were selected for their relevance to that aspect of the overall topic of movement education. Some overlapping occurs, especially in Sections 1 and 2.

The editor wishes to express his gratitude to all authors for communicating their thoughts and for allowing them to be included in *Selected Readings in Movement Education*. He also thanks the copyright sources and all others involved in the publication of this text.

East Stroudsburg, Pennsylvania   R.T.S.
March 1970

Contents

Section 1

Theories of Movement

The articles grouped within this section have been selected for their comparison and contrast values as well as for their relevance to the overall topic. All are comparable in that they discuss movement education. Some articles show contrasting viewpoints concerning the same concepts, thus creating issues over the application of those concepts. Articles that are related, whether in national origin or in substance, are placed in close proximity.

The theoretical organizations of movement presented here establish our reasons for movement, that is, our student and program objectives. The implications for movement experience that can be derived from the theoretical organizations are innumerable, and they may be actualized through the individual interpretation of the teacher or student. Structured movement experiences, examples established by the theorist, may be found under the author's name in the appropriate section of the bibliography, which is arranged by subject matter.

The reader may benefit by conceptualizing the main concerns of each article. He may synthesize all the theories by making a grid or chart of the concepts mentioned within and between the theories. Further information regarding each identified concept should be sought in appropriate sources in sociology, psychology, philosophy, etc. This process of study should provide the student or reader with a skeleton or framework for his individual consideration.

1

Basic Movement Education with Simple Elements in Primary Schools

LISELOTT DIEM

In the field of physical education the primary schools all over the world are very insufficiently equipped. In Germany, for instance, 50 percent of the elementary schools have no gymnasiums for rainy and cold days. Also, there are very few swimming pools and playing fields surrounding the school buildings; there is not enough apparatus for hanging, climbing, etc.; there are not enough installations for jumping, running, and throwing, etc. In general, primary schools are not as well equipped and organized, or as well staffed with qualified physical education teachers as secondary schools. Why should this be?

STANDARDS AND IDEALS

It is generally recognized that ages 6-10 years are the important learning ages for motor skills, for all qualitative differentiation of movements, for improvement of coordination and sensing different movements, and for acquiring basic techniques. It is a fact that children like to experiment and in this way they get to know themselves very well—through self-movements, through moving themselves, and with others, and by running, jumping, climbing, dancing, etc. They test their abilities, their knowledge and their lack of knowledge, their potential and their restrictions; they express themselves individually through a variety of movement expressions and so increase their self-realization. With the beginning of school education at age 6, the child demonstrates great spontaneity, is willing to act, has a desire to exert himself in a playing group, and is eager to learn techniques. "How do you do this?" he asks. In this manner he starts to fix movement patterns and variations.

For example, the best learning ages for swimming, skiing, and ice skating are 6-8 years. The same ages are also very crucial for learning stunts and ball techniques. In summary, ages 6-10, the first four years of elemen-

From International Council on Health, Physical Education, and Recreation (ICHPER). Ninth International Congress, Seoul, Korea, July 28-August 2, 1966, pp. 100-105. Reprinted by permission.

tary school education, are the best years for the development of movement qualities—to learn *how* to move!

Unfortunately, in most cases the elementary classroom teacher is not prepared enough for these important tasks of teaching! The sad fact is that the teacher himself has not developed feelings for his own body movements and has no knowledge of the best teaching techniques because during his teacher training he was not given wide opportunities to learn qualitative differentiations of body movements. He was taught only recreational play instead of definite training methods, and so was never confronted with the challenging and creative task of stimulating young children in this direction. Throughout the world this is the reason why teaching elementary classes in physical education is so restricted. Highly qualified teachers are especially needed for this young age group and are seldom available just for the elementary level. It is interesting to note how the Olympic programs now try to influence this planning at the primary school level. They strongly encourage all nations to consider the best learning methods and motivate us to take advantage of the impressionability of young children in teaching sports. This Olympic trend and challenge should be accepted by us accordingly and should provide an impulse for the initiation and adoption of better standards in basic physical education. For instance, one will become a better musician if the opportunity is given to listen freely and extensively to music, and one learns early in life to differentiate sounds and rhythms; one will have a better understanding of languages if one learns early in life the specific modulations of different languages. Basic processes are learned unconsciously in early childhood by sensing, feeling, experimenting, imitating, and creating. A similar approach is necessary in learning movement.

If children are restricted during the first years of life in the various experiences of body movements they are bound to suffer in their total human development. For instance, a lack of movement may impair the capacity for speaking. It has been found in some cases that children whose speech has been affected by restriction of movement have regressed to the creeping stage of development. These children then can learn to speak only by special educative help. There is evidence too, that if children are restricted in free body movement they will lose their self-confidence and will therefore begin to fear most new learning situations. In most instances, they will always find explanations for their retreat (like some adults in similar situations) and consequently, will be hindered all of their lives in sensing themselves to the fullest extent and gaining the highest degree of self realization. To reemphasize: body movements are like languages—they are a naturally learned expression of man and must be acquired in all differentiations of performance, by sensing, by feeling, by watching, by trying, by experimenting, and by creating. This process will take place at the beginning by most young children unconsciously and spontaneously! Furthermore, self-movement leads to greater self-expression, to increased self-control, to better self-understanding, to progressive self-responsibility, to more independence, and to greater self-realization in becoming a whole person. But this development can only be guaranteed if there exists the proper assistance and competent leadership and if the necessary facilities are available.

Movement education means and includes the following basic elements:

1. The study of the specific phases of learning
2. The teaching of adequate play, task, and exercises for each phase
3. The acquisition of knowledge and understanding toward a greater self-realization through movement experiences and technical performance.

The learning phases for each child begin with *the first day of life,* and include the prenatal life. The fact is that before birth the baby is moving strongly and in a coordinated fashion—turning his head, bending and stretching his fingers and toes and moving his arms and legs. An active mother also helps the initial development of her child. Muscular contraction and relaxation applied at the right moment during childbirth facilitates a natural and less painful birth. This active approach during childbirth seems to be physically and emotionally of great benefit to mother and infant alike.

1. The first year is the phase of self-elevation.   As early as the first week of life the child tries to elevate his head which involves a third of the body weight. In the prone position the child tries this elevation as the best weight training for the development of the back muscles and as the best help toward final self-elevation. The child is born with strong back muscles and therefore the prone position is a natural help for training his abilities; in the back position the child does not have these early opportunities for self-help and self-exercise. The same is true during the bathing of the baby; the prone position allows free movement of arms and legs and helps the child toward early favorable water adaptation, water play, and the elements of swimming. The first months of a child's life are critical for the total development of various motor abilities as well as for the strengthening of emotional stability. This will help towards an increased sense of self-reliance and self-control.

2. *The second and third year is the phase of self-lifting.* The child learns progressively to handle and to manipulate his own body-weight: he tries to hang freely on father's hand, to pull and to push any movable object, to carry a baby car, to climb the stairs, to give resistance, to turn, to roll on the ground, to swing on bars, etc. And in all these efforts, the child learns by trial and error to spontaneously control his energies and forces.

3. *The third to the sixth year is the first phase of increased finer coordination.* The child advances to more difficult physical tasks and enriches his repertory of various movement-skills. He begins to play *with* other children. His ability for observation, imitation, and self-encouragement progresses. He starts to differentiate more consciously in terms of quick and/or slow movements, heavy and/or light movements, difficult and/or easy movements, up and/or down movements. These experiences of differentiations lead to a better control of his own movements in variations of space and time.

Every elementary school teacher should know these developmental stages and standards from infancy to beginning school age in order to build on the foundation of the previous movement experiences and to enrich and strengthen the repertory of an individual child's movements. The teacher should also be aware of individual limitations in the development of movements in accordance with a particular age. From three years up the child is ready and anxious to experiment in a group. The child wants to run, to jump, to climb, to swing, to twist, to balance, to roll, etc. Herein lies an ideal opportunity for a great variety of expression and experimentation. In considering some lesser known characteristics of this phase, psychologists have found that three-year-old children are ready for, and welcome competition, and they are inspired by some definite goals. Unfortunately, this natural desire in young children has not yet been recognized and utilized to any significant extent. There is more emphasis placed upon undirected play experiences. A directed learning process may be illustrated in teaching swimming. This activity ideally should start with three year old children in a warm, low-water-level pool. This early water experience will eliminate unnecessary fear and a long period of learning later on in a deep pool. The three year old child should *not* learn techniques but should learn *to feel at home in the water.*

4. The phase of six to eight years is the phase of experiencing and learning basic techniques. In this period the child compares and imitates the more specific elements of movement as he tries to jump up quickly and jump down without noise, to support his weight over an obstacle, to climb a moving rope or an iron bar, to swing from rope to rope—from one side of the *Ribitol* to the other, to stand on his hands, to throw a ball to a moving partner, to bend and to stretch the trunk, to perform various stunts, etc. The teacher will ask, "Who is able to try it?" and "Who can . . .?" Later on she will ask, "Why?" and perhaps suggest that it might be better to try it the way Mary did it and not the way David tried it. Then the teacher will ask David, after he has tried Mary's approach, "How does it feel now and which way is better?" School children learn by thinking about things, by reflection.

5. The phase of eight to ten years is the second learning-phase, the phase of finer differentiations and combinations in movements. For instance, in the field of languages a child progresses from the use of single words to whole sentences in a logical and creative manner. A similar process will take place with the combinations of movements in running and turning; in jumping and turning; in throwing and catching. All basic movements should be tried not only in various combinations, but also in different situations: with big, small, heavy, and light balls as well as with different apparatus for hanging and climbing movements; running barefoot on sand, grass or on a gliding floor; running up or down, etc. New situations give new impulses for coordination, for adaptation of one's own movement to different rhythms. Ball games or running games within the group provide the opportunity to react and adapt by a variety of movements in terms of space, time, and rhythm.

6. The phase of 10-12 years is the best age for performance progress. These are the years for experiences in competition with objective measurement, for mutual cooperation and team spirit in group activities, for learning apparatus activities and life-saving elements, etc.

These elements, if mastered in these areas, can be transferred to social situations as well. They can lend grace to social behavior and improve personal relationships. At this age, beginning football and basketball, relay races and dance composition are valuable team activities for learning the fundamentals of group cooperation.

7. In the phase of maturity from 12-15 years, the principles of coordinated movement performance and movement creativity are crystallized into a distinctive, personal style by the mastery of technique. In this phase, rather than learning anything new the student becomes aware of his personal responsibility for his individual movement behavior patterns and hence, for his personal life. The value of physical education is the degree to which principles of movement learned in school are transferred to personal life patterns after school, the degree to which the child assumes a personal responsibility for physical and mental health habits and continuation of movement.

Good physical education is not measured by the sum of exercises but by the sum of experiences which can be applied to living, to work, to recreation. Its value lies in the creation of movement intelligence, the desire to know the *how* and *why* of bodily function and movement which is necessary for a full and intensive life.

THE TEACHING PROCESS

The teacher does not give exercises; she gives opportunities for experimentation. Therefore, *"play"is the first step in this process.* Children (and adults) must have a lot of play activities for learning techniques for knowing themselves. Play allows freedom of action. You must decide if you must go in this or that direction in order to catch your partner; you must decide if you will throw in this or that corner to your team mate.

The second step is the movement task. "Who is able to run and turn around? Who will try to put the ball in the basket?" Spontaneity is expected as the response to these questions in addition to setting a specific goal. But the way is free for the child to make his own choice as to *how* to reach this goal. Only if this way is free in different directions can we speak of a "task." If there is only one way to move, there is no task because the exercise is fixed.

Now the exercise is formed. The teacher has chosen several different tasks for the pupils to perform. Each child must now learn the best technique for performing the task efficiently. This learning process shows three distinct phases:

1. *The naive phase.* This means that the pupil does not know anything about technique or about the goals behind different plays. He plays for pleasure, following an innate drive, but at the same time he unconsciously learns something about himself. He tries to run, to jump, to throw, to catch. All movements are done spontaneously in his own manner.

2. *The reflective phase.* This means that the pupil has been stimulated and motivated to reflect on his own movement performances and on those of his partners. He may wonder, "Why is Mary quicker than I in climbing? How can I be more successful in throwing the ball into the basket?" The questions of the *why* and *how* will give some progressive insight into one's own learning process.

3. *The self-learning phase.* This means that the pupil is ready to train himself; he is repeating a particular skill to its perfection.

In summary, all the above stated progressive steps and phases are repeated in the learning of every particular movement skill. It is of great importance to realize that the *play phases* in early childhood go hand in hand with the *learning phases.* Only well prepared elementary physical education teachers who know and comprehend all these learning steps and phases can be successful in guiding and leading children. As man, an intelligent being, learns through many experiences of his life, he also can learn through movement. The whole personality can be guided and a higher degree of self-realization can be achieved through movement education.

ELEMENTS OF SELF-REALIZATION

Finally, in the total process of physical education toward greater self-realization, four dimensions of self-realization through movement shall be specifically emphasized:

I am . . . through awareness of my physical potentials and physical abilities; through the knowledge of internal and external functional effects; and through training and healthful living, e.g., I am flexible, I am strong, I am coordinate, I possess endurance, or I am lacking all of these or some of them, but most of all *I am.*

I can . . . through knowledge of my movement experiences from which I can detect other potentials and abilities, e.g., I can run, I can jump, and turn, I can swim! This recognition will increase a feeling of self-confidence and self-understanding, and will open up additional experiences of I can; I can play in a group, on a team; I can dance with a partner!

I will . . . through the comprehension and knowledge of a successful learning process through repetition and vigorous training, as well as through the experience of joy resulting from accomplishment. I will jump and climb higher; I will run faster and wider; I will play with greater accuracy and concentration. This desire opens up avenues for self-initiative and will lead to greater accomplishments.

I create ... through the knowledge and realization that I can create various individual expressions of movements; that I can use my own insight and my own fantasy to accomplish an aesthetic and effective movement. I create a new dance; I create a new exercise on an apparatus; I create a new strategy of a particular ball play!

It must be understood that especially the last two dimensions of self-realization—I WILL and I CREATE—can only be put into action if the child has acquired elementary skills, the same basis as for expressions of the arts or languages.

THE TURNGARTEN

The *turngarten* offers an ideal setting for the simple self-constructed elements for physical education. The *turngarten* is the result of a need for self-help and the product of progressive reflections for more meaningful and successful elementary movement experiences. This *turngarten* provides the pupils with opportunities for constructing apparatus, allows children freedom for experimentation during and after school hours, and provides opportunities for self-training as well as for the regular lessons.

2

Principles of Movement Education for US

ROBERT W. FREEMAN

WHAT CAN YOU DO?

What can you do in two hours of physical education class per week to help children become more physically fit and keep them fit for a lifetime? The answer seems to be, "not much" except motivate them to *move*. "Start them moving when they are young, help them to enjoy the experience, and they will move for the rest of their lives—if they have a good ex-

Reprinted by permission of the author and YMCA, Chicago, Ill.

perience." The robot class of "Line up," "count off," "100 Jumping Jacks," etc., in most cases falls short of a good experience.

In place of the robot class, children need to be exposed to, inspired, motivated and challenged by an imaginative leader. The leader's activities must be so interesting that the child prefers exploring the challenges of these activities to sitting down and watching television.

"Let's Play!" should be the cry from the children in their backyards and playgrounds; at that time the children commence with the activities the teacher or leader has introduced at his gymnasium or playfield.

The activities introduced are merely an extension of the child's natural play as well as sport fundamentals. The class may begin with children doing the things they would naturally do while playing. The leader's job is to help the children explore new ways and variations of their play activities.

Instead of the very directed method (explanation, demonstration, execution), the leader using the movement education approach may say, "Show me how you get over that low horizontal bar." The leader may then ask, "Why does Johnny get over the bar so easily?" "Let's all try it Johnny's way." It is important to point out that every child should be able to perform the activity even if the apparatus must be adjusted or if the leader has to assist the child through the activity. No child should leave the class having completely failed!

Steinhaus states in his preface to the American Edition of Liselott Diem's book, *Who Can,*

The child is challenged to perform a task but is not told exactly how to do it. He must create his own solution. To Mrs. Diem the mastery of effective and economic use of the body in all kinds of movement is one of the tasks of developing into a healthy, mature human being. This conviction must be shared by every true physical educator. It is noteworthy that Europe's leading woman physical educator has independently perfected a concept of education that fits so naturally into the newer American concept of *Development Tasks* that the Havighurst school of the University of Chicago has successfully introduced into general education. [1] *

The equipment used in Movement Education programs is relatively inexpensive and may be classified into two groups: hand apparatus (balls, wands, skip ropes, magic rope, hoops, etc.) and heavy apparatus (low horizontal bar, vaulting boxes, mats, climbing ropes, and benches).

---

* Numbers in brackets are keyed to the bibliographical references at the end of this chapter.

It is important that the class have a sufficient amount of hand apparatus available in order that each child has his own ball, wand, etc. How can we help a child learn to throw and catch when he does not have a ball? It is also interesting to note that when each child has his own ball he is too busy to ridicule the less skilled, and the less skilled are allowed to progress at their own rate, free of the fear of ridicule.

MOVEMENT EDUCATION FOR US

Presently there are two widely accepted approaches to Movement Education: the German play-exploration approach, and the English movement-exploration, somewhat dance-oriented, approach. Here in the United States we tend to be more familiar with the English approach, possibly for the simple reason that we read English more readily than we read German.

While *Movement Education for US* is admittedly more German-oriented, it is most definitely an attempt to meet the physical education needs of the children of *our* country. We have some unique problems stemming from our affluent society and our approaches to the education of our people. The author has attempted to take these into consideration.

At the present time, our physical education programs seem to be very much sports-oriented with a heavy emphasis on physical fitness. It has been this writer's experience that our male physical educators are more willing to accept the movement education approach because of its direct application to organized sports.

The modern American educator's thinking tends to be more psychologically oriented than that of his European counterpart. The American educator finds movement education acceptable because of its concern for the individual and his development of "feelings of adequacy." In the Association for Supervision and Curriculum Development's 1962 yearbook, *Perceiving, Behaving, Becoming,* p. 100, we read, "It is the function of our schools to produce an ever larger number of adequate personalities. This is our reason for being, the charge of our society." [2]

1. Extension of the child's natural play, the foundation of movement education

As part of their research for the development of the German Movement Education approach, its founders observed children at their natural play and developed programs for the physical education class that would further challenge the child at his own play.

Many of us have independently explored various ways of motivating children to *exercise* at home on their own but have been frustrated by the children's lack of interest in our proposed "homework" *exercise program.* We found the children playing or watching television, rather than doing our professionally prescribed exercises. Prescribed exercises do not seem to be an effective approach.

But if we can motivate children to participate in *vigorous, physically active play,* then it appears that we have come upon a practical approach to what we claim as our unique contribution to education—*physical fitness.*

2. Sport fundamentals in a play atmosphere

Fundamentals in ball handling, track and field, tumbling and gymnastics are presented in ways that challenge the child's imagination and interest. With and without apparatus, the children explore activities which promote the development of efficient, well-coordinated movements.

Professor Liselott Diem states in her book, *Who Can,*

The more surely a child masters a movement, the more skillful he becomes and the more fun it is for him to "play" with this movement. Spontaneously the child invents his own variations. While jumping rope he introduces turns. He skips while bouncing a ball. He runs forward and backwards. Every new activity demands a different adjustment. Thus, movement is perfected: coordination is refined, running becomes faster, jumping lighter and springier, higher and farther; climbing is more dexterous; and catching more sure. In this way, out of a growing confidence in movement there emerges an awareness of the body as a wholly integrated being. From enhanced confidence in movement there comes a joy in group action and movement with a partner, and the striving for excellence in competition and organized games. [1]

3. Inexpensive equipment

Basically we use equipment that can be found around the home or in the neighborhood playground. It is important that enough hand apparatus (balls, wands, skip ropes, etc.) be available in order that each child has his own piece of equipment. "How can a child learn to throw and catch a ball unless he has one!"

It is of course ideal when there is enough heavy apparatus (horizontal bar, climbing ropes, vaulting boxes, mini tramps) available so that more than one child can be active at a time.

4.   Use of educationally sound methods

a.   Develop feelings of adequacy by providing opportunities for each child to experience some degree of success in every session.

Professor Irma Nikolai, German teacher of movement education, states, "No child should ever leave the class having failed completely, even if it means lowering the apparatus or physically carrying the child through the maneuver."

b. *Motivate the children* by recognizing small achievements, and giving encouragement, in an atmosphere of love and trust. This assumes the absence of threats, shaming embarrassment, and high-level competition that results in continual failure.

c. *Include the child in problem solving.* This method requires the instructor to present a task so that it can be understood by the children. The instructor must overcome the temptation of solving the problem for them. He must be willing to recognize any method the child uses to solve the task. For example, if the desired task is to kick a momentary handstand, the instructor may ask, "Who can place their hands on the floor and kick their feet up over their head?" The children's solutions to this task may be many and varied. One child may lie on his back, with hands on the floor, and lift his feet up to a candle position or bicycle position. Recognition of the child's success in completing the task is necessary, even though the result was not the stunt the instructor intended.

5. *Love*

Love, in this sense a concern for the individual, is probably the most important single principle in the effective application of movement education. Without love the whole program can become nothing more than a collection of meaningless activities that could even lead to frustrations on the part of both teacher and student.

It is important to mention that the material presented here should be considered as a "take-off point." Your job is to challenge the children with these or similar activities and then further challenge them to develop new ideas and variations of their own. Your objective is to help them to discover their own creative ability and hopefully instill within themselves the desire to continue to pursue these and other activities at home alone or with their playmates.

Your success will be determined largely by the type of *atmosphere* in which you present these activities. We have found that a *friendly, encouraging* atmosphere most effectively produces the desired results. *Do not* be afraid to show the children you are their friend, (not necessarily their buddy, but rather an adult friend). And *do* treat them the way you would like to be treated.

You, the teacher, leader, instructor, have two powerful factors in your favor; first, the children, for the most part, are anxious to show off to you, and second, young children have a fantastic sense of fairness. Use this show-off factor in your method of presentation. Very challenging words are, "Show me how you can . . . ." It is important that you *recognize* their accomplishments of your challenges.

The second factor, "sense of fairness," is a most powerful disciplining tool. When a discipline problem arises, point out to *all* the children that those misbehaving are being unfair because "we must wait for them to join us; they are wasting *our* time." If the majority of children have found your program interesting and fun, group pressure should take care of the discipline problems. Or perhaps the discipline problem is an indication that your programs aren't really very interesting; and the programs, or your method of presenting them, need variation.

A SUGGESTED APPROACH

1. Free time

As soon as the children enter the gymnasium or playfield, they should be encouraged to participate in free play, rather than sit down and wait for the entire class to assemble. During this free-play time, hand apparatus should be available for the children to play with as they wish. The instructor should be available; he now has a few moments to encourage and assist the more poorly skilled, and to observe in general the level of the entire class.

2. Warm-up

When all the children are present, the activities on the forthcoming pages, especially hand apparatus and partner activities, can be used as warm-up. (Note: this takes the place of the formal-lineup, calisthenic-type warm-up.) The author believes that formal calisthenics have relatively little value for children in grades K through 6 when the desired results can be obtained through the above means.

3. The Lesson

Kindergarten through third grade programs should include:

a. Big-muscle activity—running, hopping, jumping, crawling, balancing, rolling, carrying, swinging, climbing, throwing and catching.

Robert W. Freeman   15

b. Simple activities—allow much time for self-discovery, as in simple obstacle courses, etc.
c. Challenges to imagination—imitate animals, invent new ways of doing things.
d. Beginning of doing things with a partner.
e. Opportunities to become aware that others are in the room or play area and to be able to do their activity without colliding with others.
f. A minimum of standing around and waiting in line.

Fourth through sixth grade programs should include:

a. Reinforcement of the big-muscle activity and the beginning work for developing finer muscle control.
b. Continued development of basic skills—ball handling, balancing, climbing, etc. The fourth through sixth grader still needs the freedom to explore these activities without the constant pressure of a standard set by the teacher.
c. Opportunities to do things with partners—competition and cooperation with the partner, the beginnings of team work.
d. An awareness of and introduction to adult sports. They are often willing and anxious to participate in formal sports. Avoid sports that require a high degree of organization. This early team experience should not be hampered by complicated rules.
e. Adventure and daring activities. Children at this age have a wonderful, adventurous, daring spirit which should be challenged by obstacle courses, gymnastics and tumbling, etc. These children have a little more patience than K through third graders. They are willing to listen to directions and wait their turn in line. It is recommended, however, that the teacher still avoid lengthy explanations or waiting of turns. These children are still "little people of action," and when something gets boring, they invent their own "action," which the teacher calls misbehavior—and we have discipline problems.

REFERENCES

1. Liselott Diem, *Who Can,* Frankfurt am Main, Germany: Wilhelm Limbert, 1964.
2. Arthur Combs, Chairman, 1962 ASCD Committee, *Perceiving, Behaving, Becoming.* Washington, D.C.: Association for Supervision and Curriculum Development, a department of the National Education Association, 1962.

3

Developmental Movement: Developing a Point of View

MUSKA MOSSTON

In view of the current national concern about the poor physical condition of our young people, particularly those of elementary and high school age, it becomes necessary to assess our physical education program and the subject matter as it has been taught in schools during the last several decades. Since one of the objectives of physical education is physical development, it is necessary to clarify the meaning of this objective and its *real* place in the execution of our program. This is not to say that the traditional concomitant social and emotional learnings have no place in our work, but we should recognize the fact that we, the physical educators, are the only ones who deal specifically with the physical development of the child. Although the chemistry teacher or the history teacher may recognize the physical development objective, he cannot do anything about it in the laboratory or the lecture room. It is the physical educator who has the training, the facilities, and the time to reach this objective. The problem remains one of subject matter, subject matter which involves human motion.

Human movements are infinite and purposeful. Bringing a fork loaded with meat to the mouth is purposeful. Taking a walk through the woods, swimming across the pool, shooting the ball through the hoop—all are purposeful movements. Over the years physical educators, coaches, choreographers, and therapists have proposed many purposes for human movements and selected specific movements to accomplish these purposes.

HUMAN MOVEMENT CATEGORIZED

Through the history of physical education, various values have been attached to human movements. These values seem to fall into three categories: *assigned value of movement, functional value,* and *intrinsic value.*

Assigned value belongs to the domain of the dancers and the choreographers who attribute a feeling, an idea, or a mood to the performed movement. These values are determined by the decisions and imagination

Reprinted from Muska Mosston, *Developmental Movement*, Charles E. Merrill Publishing Company, 1965. Reprinted by permission.

of the individual dancer and by the culture of a given society (as in interpretation of social or folk dancing). Another example of assigned value is in the case of the competitive gymnast who has to adhere to an assigned code of beauty and "good form" determined by a restricted group of gymnasts. (Pointed toes in performance become nearly second nature to a gymnast.)

The functional value belongs to the domain of the coach. The player, coach, and game are under the jurisdiction of a specific measurable purpose and a tight set of rules. These determine the value of a given movement.

The third category, the intrinsic value of movement, is consonant with the developmental concept presented here. It is concerned with the contribution of movement to the intentional development of physical attributes such as strength, agility, and balance. These values are designated as intrinsic since they are devoid of culture and individual mood or personality. A set of push-ups will help develop the shoulder girdle and arms of an American fifth grader or a French adult, a basketball player or a swimmer. Rope skipping with high knee raising will promote the agility of *any* individual who does it.

THE DEVELOPMENTAL CONCEPT

The contributions of these movements are universal since the criteria of this view are based on the principles of physiology and kinesiology. The materials presented here are within the reach of most students and are treated progressively, step by step, which will help the student realize the developmental nature of his work. A jump can be viewed in many ways. It can be used as a competitive movement (high jump) which sooner or later excludes the mediocre student and the beginner and becomes the possession of the topnotch competitive athlete. Or the jump can be recreational as in the variety of games or in random play. In this presentation, the jump is treated as a tool for gradual and intentional development. There are simple jumps and more complicated ones, easy and more difficult leaps. By gradual presentation of the variety of jumps, the development of agility and strength will be achieved systematically. The student will be able to see that there are *specific* objectives which he can attain on his level. It is not proposed that this developmental subject matter ought to replace the traditional sports and games in the program. On the contrary, these activities must be combined with games for the all-round development of the individual.

Let us explore the meaning of the *developmental concept.* Anyone who participates in an activity starts from some initial level of achievement and success.

The problem that confronts the teacher is whether he can present the individual student with materials arranged so that success will be met at each step of the way.[1] Let's take an obvious example: the high jump. Teaching the high jump to a student requires a minimum starting height and a decision concerning the intervals of raising the bar. The structure of the high jump event illustrates the developmental concept. A student can start at height X and gradually move on to height $X + a$, $X + b$, $X + c$, and so on. The intervals a, b, c can be small or large depending upon the developmental rate of the individual's agility, leg strength, and mastery of the technique. The developing factors here are the height intervals. The step-by-step addition of height induces better performance, and the size of the interval encourages success along the way.

Another instance is weight training. In order to develop strength in the forearm and the upper arm one might do curls with a given weight. Here again, one must consider the starting weight, the intervals of added weight, and the number of repetitions with each weight. The structure of weight training illustrates the developmental concept. The developing factors here are the weight, the number of repetitions, and perhaps the speed of performance. If the magnitude of these factors can be determined for the performer, a carefully designed program will help him develop and reach his objective of increased strength in his arms.

DETERMINING THE DEGREE OF DIFFICULTY

These two examples suggest that an essential aspect of development is the increasing degree of difficulty in the task.

We are confronted now with two fundamental questions:

1. Can we apply this idea of development to any movement?
2. How do we determine the degree of difficulty so that we can arrange our subject matter in a gradual sequence?

These questions will be answered with a physiological discussion and a kinesiological analysis in the beginning of each chapter dealing with the development of a specific attribute (strength, balance, agility, flexibility, and endurance).

---

[1] For a discussion on success and motivation in learning, see Jerome S. Bruner, *The Process of Education* (New York: Random House, 1960).

Figure 1

Figure 2

An example of calculating the degree of difficulty is given below:

The position: Forward tilt—straight trunk, arms are along the side of the trunk (Fig. 1).

Purpose of this position: Development of strength in the muscles of the back and rear of the pelvic girdle.

The problem: Which position is more difficult to maintain, Fig. 2 or Fig. 3?

Solution:

Step 1. The straight tilted trunk (b) represents a lever that tends to rotate around an axis (A) due to the gravitational force (f).

Step 2. In order to remain in this position groups of muscles with the force of X_1 must be working to maintain the position in Fig. 2 and perhaps with force X_2 to maintain the position in Fig. 3.

Step 3. If $X_1 = X_2$ then there is no difference in the degree of difficulty between the two positions.

Step 4. We want to determine which statement is true:

$$X_1 = X_2$$
$$X_1 > X_2$$
$$X_1 < X_2$$

Figure 3

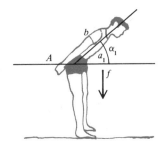

Figure 4

Step 5. The only observable difference between the two positions is the angle of the trunk's tilt (α), the angle between the trunk and the horizontal line passing through the axis (A).

The length of the trunk (b) remains constant for the *same* individual.

The gravitational force (f) remains constant for the same individual.

Step 6. Now we have to determine the relationship which exists among the three factors involved in this position: b, α, f.

Step 7. We need to introduce an additional factor—the force arm (a), which is the perpendicular distance from the axis (A) to the line of force (f).

Step 8. The relationship of a and f is expressed as follows:

1) $M_1 = a_1 \cdot f$ (See Fig. 4.)
   M_1 = the moment of force for Fig. 4 which tends to rotate the trunk in the same way.
2) $M_2 = a_2 \cdot f$ (See Fig. 5.)

Step 9. $a_1 = b \cos \alpha_1$, and $a_2 = b \cos \alpha_2$
   Substitute in (1) and (2) of Step 8.

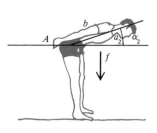

Figure 5

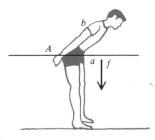

Figure 6

Step 10. $M_1 = b \cos \alpha_1 \cdot f; M_2 = b \cos \alpha_2 \cdot f$
Since b and f remain the same for the same individual, the only difference is in the cos of the angle α.

Step 11. The smaller the angle, the larger the cos. Since α_2 is smaller than α_1, $\cos \alpha_2$ is larger than $\cos \alpha_1$
∴ (from Step 10)
$b \cdot \cos \alpha_2 \cdot f > b \cdot \cos \alpha_1 \cdot f$ or $M_2 > M_1$

Step 12. Let's go back to Step 2.
The muscles that will maintain the position in Fig. 3 (X_2) will have to resist M_2, and the muscles which will maintain the position in Fig. 2 (X_1) will have to resist M_1, since $M_2 > M_1$.

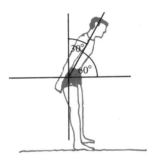

Figure 7

Step 13.   Conclusion: $X_2 > X_1$, or:
It is harder to maintain the position in Fig. 3 than in Fig. 2. Fig. 3 is of higher degree of difficulty.

From this relationship we learn that the degree of difficulty depends upon changes (increase or decrease) in any of the following factors:

1. Changing the angle of the trunk's tilt. Indeed, the lower we tilt (approaching the horizontal) the harder it "feels." If we tilt to $60°$ from the horizontal line we can calculate:
$X = b \cdot f \cdot \cos 60°$
$\cos 60° = 0.5$
$\therefore X = b \cdot f \cdot (0.5)$

By tilting only $30°$ from the vertical position the resisting muscles will have to work half the amount of the tilt to the horizontal position. At the horizontal tilt position:

$$X = b \cdot f \cdot \cos 0°$$
$$\cos 0° = 1$$
$$X = b \cdot f \cdot 1$$

$\alpha = 0°$

Figure 8

2. Changing the length of the lever (b). Indeed it is harder to perform a tilt with arms raised above the head.

Figure 9

3. Changing the force (f) by adding weight. It is harder to perform the tilt by placing a medicine ball (or any other weight) behind the neck.

4. Any combination of *A*, *B*, and *C*.

Figure 10

SELECTING MEANINGFUL CATEGORIES

Our next major issue involves a view concerning classification of human motion. The question at hand is: What concept shall guide us in the selection of the movements to teach in our classes? Indeed, the question of what to teach is a primary problem for the curriculum builder and the teacher. In sports the WHAT is dictated by the structure of the game or the athletic event. In teaching hockey it is necessary to teach how to hold the stick and how to swing it under various conditions. Thus the game itself determines the teaching materials and their classification. Any teacher who prepares a program in hockey will include this phase in the planning and the teaching. It is inconceivable to have a basketball unit without lessons in the various passes. An essential part of soccer is the "stop and go" phase; without the ability to stop the ball from any direction and immediately start with the ball in a desired direction, the soccer game is not in full bloom. The teacher of soccer will design lessons to teach the student just how to stop the ball and how to continue running with it. Techniques may vary, but all will teach this phase of soccer, for it is determined by the structure, requirements, and purposes of the game.

Now—what do we do with the infinite variety of human movements, how do we determine which one to choose, and how do we classify them into workable units?

A review of the contributions of leaders in the area of movement classification reveals three major directions or emphases:

1. An activity direction (jumping, running, etc.), which includes exercises of classical forms of athletics. This direction also includes the "natural movement" school.

2. Anatomical direction, which includes exercises for single or several parts of the body. It might also be called "position" gymnastics.[2]

3. Physical attribute emphasis (development of strength, endurance, etc.).

These emphases were accomplished by the use of the body, light apparatus, or heavy apparatus. Often the systems employing these directions showed a degree of inconsistency or perhaps a deliberate mixture of directions.[3]

---

[2] Note that in European literature, particularly Scandinavian, the term gymnastics refers to calisthenics, free exercises, and the like and is not confined to the heavy apparatus.

[3] See the chapter, "The Battle of the Systems," in Arthur Weston, *The Making of American Physical Education* (New York: Appleton-Century, 1962).

A SHORT HISTORICAL SURVEY OF
MOVEMENT CLASSIFICATIONS

An example of the first kind of system is that of the German Guts Muths (1759-1839) who offered the following classification in his book *Gymnastik für die Jugend* (1793):

> Jumping, running, throwing, wrestling, balance exercise, climbing, carrying, pulling, dancing, marching, military exercises, bathing and swimming, exercise in summoning the fire brigade, watching, fasting, reading aloud and reciting, training the organs of the senses.[4]

Guts Muths' gymnastics were introduced to Denmark by Nachtegall (*circa* 1800) who divided his own materials into seven schools: the introductory school, the running school, the jumping school, the climbing school, the swimming school, the school of military exercises, the school of mixed exercises.

Perhaps another example of the first direction can be found in present day British schools. The excellent publications *Moving and Growing*[5] and *Planning the Programme*[6] clearly illustrate the view of the "natural movement" school which decries the "artificial" movements of other systems. The natural movement system includes a variety of jumps, runs, hanging, climbing, and so on with and without the use of the mobile and stationary apparatus. These two publications, which describe children's growth through movement, replaced in 1952 the previously compulsory *Syllabus of Physical Training for Schools* issued in 1933.

In the domain of the anatomical direction Ling is the king. Pier Henrik Ling (1776-1839) who founded the Royal Central Institute for teachers in Stockholm, divided his gymnastics into four main divisions: educational or civil gymnastics, military gymnastics (weapons exercises), medical gymnastics, aesthetic gymnastics (ballet and mimic art).

According to Thulin,[7] Ling classified the exercises as follows:

1. Arm, leg, head, and trunk movements without apparatus and with or without support. Also called: free standing exercises.

2. Heave-exercises, climbing, twisting, spanning, balance exercises, jumping and vaulting—all with apparatus.

---

[4] Guts Muths, *Gymnastik für die Jugend.*
[5] London: H.M. Stationery Offices, 1952.
[6] London: H.M. Stationery Offices, 1953.
[7] J. G. Thulin, *Gymnastic Handbook* (Lund, Sweden: Sydsvenska Gymnastick Institutet, 1947).

Ling's classification dictated the lesson structure of the Swedish system for many years. The Swedish rule required all muscles and joints to be exercised in each lesson and in a set order.

Johannes Lindhard (1870-1927), who was a professor at the Gymnastic Physiological Laboratorium of the University of Copenhagen, maintained in *The Theory of Gymnastics* that

> The relation between gymnastics and physiology is as yet too uncertain for physiology to be made the basis of classification. The exercises may, however, be classified according to the objects aimed at. . . . We seek to discipline the student in order to teach him self-discipline. . . . We try to develop courage and resourcefulness. . . . This is achieved partly by detailed work systematically dealing with each separate part of the apparatus of motion. . . .[8]

Accordingly, Lindhard classifies his materials in four main groups:

1. Exercises the chief object of which is to discipline, rouse, educate in the general sense of the word:
   a) Order exercises
   b) Exercises of deportment
   c) Walking exercises

2. Exercises the chief object of which is a systematic training of muscles and joints.
   Corrective exercises
     Starting positions
     Exercises:
   a) Head and neck exercises
   b) Trunk exercises
   c) Arm exercises
   d) Leg exercises

3. Exercises the chief object of which is the development of the nervous co-ordination.
   Balance exercises

4. Exercises that aim in the first place at developing strength, endurance, and resolution.
   a) Marching

---

[8] Johannes Lindhard, *The Theory of Gymnastics* (London: Methuen and Co., Ltd., 1939), pp. 42-43.

b)   Running
c)   Jumping
d)   Games and sports

Lindhard concludes that "it will often be very difficult to refer a certain exercise to a definite group, for no exercise has so single a purpose that its place in the system is unquestionable."[9]

K. A. Knudsen (1864-1944), who was the chief gymnastics inspector of all elementary schools, secondary schools, and colleges in Denmark at the turn of the century, exalts Ling's achievement in his invention of the form-giving exercises.

Knudsen describes Ling as follows: "He had anatomical insight and he had an artist's sense of beauty and harmony. His form-giving exercises show his abilities as an artist, as a sculptor not in marble but in flesh and blood."[10]

Knudsen offers the following main divisions:

1. Order exercises.

2. Form-giving exercises, the main object of which is to mold the body into a harmonious development of its different parts by eradicating faults and producing suppleness. They are mass exercises, and are divided into the following groups: leg exercises, arm exercises, neck exercises, and trunk exercises.

3. Exercises of skill. They further neuro-muscular co-ordination and affect the organs of respiration and circulation. They develop bodily strength and endurance and several of them may further qualities such as courage, energy, and presence of mind. These are divided into the following groups: balance exercises, heaving exercises, marching and running, jumping and vaulting, agility exercises.

A most detailed work on movement combining the anatomical classification with balance, agility, and vaults (*Gymnastic Handbook,* 1947) was done by Major Thulin, who was the principal of the South Swedish Gymnastic Institute at Lund. He also published the *Gymnastic Atlas* (1938), which contains 8,500 pictures to explain the exercises, positions, and movements described in his handbook.

---

[9] *Ibid.,* p. 44.
[10] K. A. Knudsen, *A Textbook of Gymnastics* (London: J. and A. Churchill, Ltd., 1947), I, p. *vii.*

A major contributor to the third direction (development of physical attributes) was Niels Bukh (1880-1950), the principal of the Gymnastic High School at Ollerup, Denmark.

Although his book *Primary Gymnastics* offers the body region as a primary classification and his sub-divisions are "mobilizing, strength-building and agility promoting exercises," Niels Bukh in his daily work put great emphasis on agility. He states that

> The physical aim of gymnastics is to regain and maintain man's natural suppleness, strength, and agility, so that these powers may have an opportunity of developing bodily beauty and harmony, and effecting purposeful action. Skeletal stiffness should give place to mobility, weakness of the musculature to strength, and awkwardness to agility.[11]

Bukh's materials are characterized by energetic swift movements of parts of the body and a great deal of bending and twisting, done to a rather vigorous rhythm.

To these he added running, vaulting, and jumping exercises "which in special degree promote agility and involve the strong use of the whole body."

This historical survey is by no means an exhaustive study of views concerning movements; however, it does highlight the major influences that have been in effect all over the Western world during the last century and a half. (It does not include the dancer's views.)

THREE-DIMENSIONAL VIEW OF MOVEMENT CLASSIFICATION

The present materials represent an integrated concept of three dimensions of movement classification. One dimension is the matrix of *physical attributes* (strength, agility, flexibility, balance, rhythm, endurance, and others).

The second dimension is the anatomical divisions of the body. It focuses on the *part of the body* or region which is being developed by the given movement (the shoulder girdle, the lower leg, etc.).

The third dimension involves the *kind of movement* which is used to develop the desired attribute in a particular part of the body (bending, leaping, turning, throwing, etc.).

---

[11]*Primary Gymnastics* (London: Methuen and Co., Ltd., 1941), p. 16.

The relationship of the three dimensions is inherent in the very nature of movement. Obviously, whenever we move, a part of the body, or the whole body, is involved. Repetition of the movement due to life needs or performance aspiration results in development of some physical attribute, from the finger dexterity of a violinist to the combination of qualities required of a ski jumper.

Any movement can be analyzed and classified by this three-dimensional view of movement. This awareness can help the teacher, the coach, and the student select the movement or series of movements to accomplish a stated objective: "He needs more strength in his leg to improve his take-off"; "she needs to improve her coordination in order to be more graceful"; "an inflexible pelvic region curtails the accuracy of this diver." What movements can we use to overcome these deficiencies?

Let us examine the three-dimensional diagram. Let point X represent a one-foot-high hop. The anatomy involved is the leg; the kind of movement is a hop or jump; and it relates to the development of strength (in the leg). Suppose point X represents alternate arm swings and circles. The diagram shows the relationships of the shoulder, the swing, and the development of flexibility (at the shoulder joint).

In order to present this three-dimensional scheme in a workable fashion, it was necessary to establish preferences in classification for the purpose of organizing the materials. This preference is based upon the fact that a child responds well to stimuli regarding his ability and achievement. A child can understand the questions: "How fast can you run?" "Are you strong enough to pull this rope?" "Can you stand on your head?" "Can you climb up that rock?"

The child does not need to think, "Now I am developing strength in my abdomen by raising my leg high during the climb." He just enjoys the *presence* of strength and agility by accomplishing his objective. However, the teacher must be aware of the contribution of the movement to the child's development, its place on the scale of degree of difficulty for the child, and its role in the growth pattern of the child.

The classification of movements here is done for developmental purposes—the *intentional* development of physical attributes which would otherwise remain undeveloped or at best be left to chance. The categories of physical attributes included in the present materials are agility, balance, flexibility, strength, and endurance. Rhythm is treated here as an integral and necessary part of all movements in any attribute development. Materials to develop various body regions and the whole body are presented in

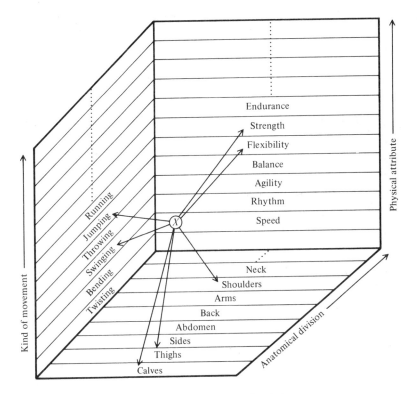

Fig. 11 Three-dimensional view of movement classification.

each category. For the performance of these movements four approaches are offered:

1. Movement designed for the individual student using the body as an "instrument"
2. Use of inexpensive apparatus
3. Use of a partner
4. Related simple games

In each approach, directions for variations and problems to solve are offered. The variety of movements increases motivation and can be applied to large classes in the public schools. These materials take advantage of one excellent apparatus which we all possess—the human body. Each chapter includes a definition of the physical attribute with a discussion of its principles of development. Current physiological research and kinesiological knowledge has been applied to the material.

Recognizing the developmental concept will aid the teacher and student in preparing a program of instruction which may take the following steps:

Step 1. Determine your objective, based on the knowledge of your students' needs.

Step 2. Determine the *present* level of performance in a specific physical attribute. This can be done by observation, trial and error, or by measurements. This step can be done by the student himself once he learns the concept of development.

Step 3. Select the movements which are proposed to develop the attribute.

Step 4. Program the movements for the class, the smaller group, or the individual.

4

Agility Development
RUDY MUELLER

The program that follows is designed to develop one specific physical attribute, known as agility. Agility enables one to move his body through space for short distances quickly and in a controlled manner. A person could have strong leg muscles and/or be very fast and yet not have a high degree of agility. To be agile, he must develop the ability to integrate a fine combination of muscular strength, body-part coordination, body balance, kinesthetic awareness, and speed into a series of fluid movements.

Vertical agility (up, down, and up again) involves a starting position, takeoff, flight, and landing. Lateral agility involves a starting position, locomotion pattern, change of direction, control of the line of balance, and a postural arrangement. Each of the components of vertical or lateral agility takes on additional significance when one is designing specific agility activities.

In any agility movement there is an additional element, which Mosston [1] identifies as *touch and go*. The concept of touch and go refers to the immediate takeoff after landing, for which maximum suppleness and fluent motion are required. The ability to spring instantly is the result of a unique coordination of muscles in the landing and takeoff sequence, and the spring is executed with a minimum of pause or delay between the two acts.

Each of us possesses a degree of agility, the improvement of which is the aim of this program. This attribute can be developed by participation in *agility work.* [2] To ensure continued development, the degree of difficulty of the activities must be periodically increased. The degree of difficulty should be such as to present a challenge, but it should not discourage or defeat the performer.

One changes the degree of difficulty by manipulating the components of the activity. In vertical agility one can change the starting position or the base, manipulate the center of gravity, or devise a different postural arrangement. One may overload the flight by manipulating the flight motion (i.e. turning), changing distance, establishing new postural arrangements, etc. In the landing one can change the base, posture, location, and center of gravity. As one goes through the suggested agility activities, he can identify the one or more components that have been overloaded.

The identification of the components of an agility movement and the comprehension of the degree-of-difficulty concept make it possible for anyone to design an infinite number of activities.

Organizationally, the activities can be a common experience to all, time-controlled, statistically recorded, completely individualized, self-directed, or the instance can be discovered by the learner. The organization depends on the teacher's philosophy concerning the *teacher-student transaction.*

I would like to share with you several other observations about the agility program.

1. The motivational level of students seems to be very high. I believe that condition exists because the experience is very intense for a relatively short period of time. The performer feedback about his accomplishment is immediate and highly visible. The design of the activity ensures a degree of success, and the periodic changing of the specific activity holds the student's interest.

2. One could evaluate the results of such a program by recording its effect on certain standardized agility tests or self-devised tests more congruent with the definition of agility as described in this paper.

3. One could also conduct an ongoing evaluation by counting and recording the number of "touch and go" sequences a person does in a given time span.

4. Another recommendation is that one have a control factor, either quantitative or qualitative, other than fatigue. The number of repetitions, sets, or time limitations are examples of quantitative control; prescribed postures, body position, and touch and go, of qualitative control.

5. Students feel, on reflection, that agility has a positive effect on one's self-concept. This effect is particularly true when a student is discussing how he feels about his new physical ability in the area of agility. There is a need for additional information to verify this observation.

AGILITY ACTIVITIES

The following are some of the activities that have been used to promote agility.

1. Single-tire drill: Place one foot in and one out of tire on floor. Jump up into tuck position and land, switching feet. Touch and go.

2. Bench drill (on Swedish box): Place one foot on bench and one on floor. Push off top leg and switch leg positions to opposite side of box. Touch and go.

3. Triangle slide drill (with three tires or dummies): Starting at rear tire, do defined locomotion pattern to left forward tire and then to right. Repeat pattern back to first tire. Repeat entire sequence in opposite direction.

4. 180° double-tire drill (with tires tied together next to each other): Place one foot in each tire. Jump, turn 180°, and land with one foot in each tire. Touch and go.

5. Diagonal rope drill (with 15-20' rope tied 4' high at one end and slanting to floor, where it is held down with 25 lb weight plate): Stand with side to rope and, starting at low end, jump sideward. Jump from side to side, progressing up the rope until you've gone as high as possible. Jump backward down the rope. Touch and go.

6. Four-tire drill: Starting with two feet inside left rear tire, jump forward into next tire, jump sideward, backward, and sideward, finishing in original tire. Touch and go.

7. Crazy leg drill (with two tires tied together next to each other): Start by putting right foot in left tire; bring left leg forward and step into right tire. Continue, alternating legs and using touch and go.

8. Straddle-jump drill: Stand with one leg on each side of tire. Jump into air and touch toes. Return to straddle position. Touch and go.

9. Double tire, front and back (two tires placed a foot apart): Stand in one tire facing the other. Jump forward into the other tire and back again. Keep body fully extended during flight.

REFERENCES

1. Muska Mosston, *Developmental Movement,* Columbus, Ohio: Merrill, 1965.

2. Donald R. Hilsendager, Malcolm H. Strow, and Kenneth J. Ackerman, "Comparison of Speed, Strength, and Agility Exercises in the Development of Agility," *Research Quarterly,* **40,** No. 1 (March 1969), 71-76.

5

A Brief Theory of Movement Education

JOAN TILLOTSON

Movement Education Defined

Movement education is that phase of the total education program which has as its contribution the development of effective, efficient, and expressive movement responses in a thinking, feeling, and sharing human being.

Exploration Defined

Exploration is a "child-centered" approach or method of teaching which allows for individuality, creativity, spontaneity, and self-discovery.

This article was written in 1966. Reprinted by permission of the author.

Problem Solving Defined

Problem solving is a teacher-guided method or approach which involves the following procedure: (1) presenting the problem; (2) providing time for exploration with guidance; (3) refining and selecting solutions to the original problem; and (4) demonstrating for evaluation, analysis, and discussion. The process is then continued for development of more complex movement patterns.

Movement Education Aim

The *aim* of movement education is to develop an awareness of the self in the physical environment, the body and its capabilities, and the components of movement responses of each child in every class. This aim will be attained most meaningfully through the use of exploration and problem-solving experiences.

A movement emphasis for all sports, games, rhythms, and gymnastics starts with providing experiences for each child to become alert and efficient in his use of the space in which he moves, whether it be on the playground, in the gymnasium, in the classroom, or at home. Opportunity for children to explore the space available to sense the relationships possible in his work with others, with equipment, and with the physical play space is essential. Guided practice in "space moving" should be one of the first activities for all children in their physical education classes and should continue to be practiced daily.

Because body capacities are so varied, each child must be exposed to all of the possibilities for bodily movement. Children know that they can move their bodies through space by locomotor actions of running, leaping, jumping, twisting, falling, and rolling, as well as moving in one space. Exploring the many untried possibilities for movement and refining known movement patterns should be encouraged daily, not only as ends in themselves, but toward sports, games, rhythms, and gymnastic activities.

A thorough study of movement includes concentrated analysis of any movement itself. Such analysis emphasizes understanding that each action performed demands the use of three elements: (1) space—direct straight-line action and indirect biplane action; (2) time—fast or slow speed; and (3) force—strong or light effort. Emphasis is also placed on smooth, controlled performance regardless of the movement pattern. Providing tasks which encourage practice with the elements of movement and progress to refinement of movement patterns is essential in a movement-oriented physical education program.

Placing the emphasis on movement education through exploration and problem solving first and then applying movement problems, patterns, and tasks to game situations constitute the basic theory of a movement-oriented physical education program. Movement experiences as ends in themselves should be presented daily in our classes. However, application of those movement experiences needs to be made daily for the children to understand the purpose of the tasks: the "why" of movement training. Space awareness transfers simply into any of our tag games; body capabilities are essential in skills performances (dodging, throwing, stunts, apparatus, swimming—to name only a few); and analysis of movement elements is necessary for the analysis of any skill, whether it be in jumping, kicking, rope climbing, or driving a car.

Experiences in movement education through exploration demand concentration on individuality. Thus, all things being equal, each individual child solves a given task within his own capabilities, under the alert guidance of the teacher. He progresses at his own rate of speed through unique motivational devices designed by the teacher with the help of the students.

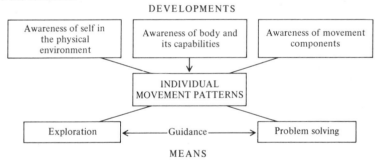

DEVELOPMENTS

| Awareness of self in the physical environment | Awareness of body and its capabilities | Awareness of movement components |

INDIVIDUAL MOVEMENT PATTERNS

| Exploration | ←——Guidance——→ | Problem solving |

MEANS

SUGGESTED HINTS FOR TEACHING THROUGH EXPLORATION AND PROBLEM SOLVING

Guidelines in Understanding Children

1. Be sensitive to children as individuals who have ideas of their own.

2. Be alert to the children as they are trying to tell you something by their random movement patterns and spontaneous verbal comments.

3. Be alert to behavior changes of children as you observe them in your classroom or as they participate on the playground, in the gymnasium, or in the cafeteria.

4. Encourage individualization through praise and suggestions.

5. Notice the wide range of individual differences and learn to accept and nourish them!

Guidelines in Understanding Movement and Its Contribution

1. Be secure in the knowledge that movement is the basis for all human activity: to move well is to live well.

2. Observe children in the light of a movement vocabulary.

3. Be eager and willing to experiment with all the possibilities for active movement participation.

4. Work toward development of efficient movement patterns, recognizing that control of the basic elements of movement will lead toward efficiency.

5. Recognize that all movement patterns are composed of three basic elements:

   Speed: represented by fast and slow tempos and varying degrees of time between these two extremes.

   Space: represented by direct and indirect actions, by high, low, big, and small actions, and by varying degrees of "space" between these extremes.

   Force: represented by heavy and light actions and varying degrees of strength between these two extremes.

Guidelines in Planning Movement Experiences

1. Set an atmosphere that is conducive to work: warm, personal, and full of understanding, knowledge, and skill.

2. Start with familiar activities and move to unfamiliar ones; repeat activities often: children enjoy and learn much from repetition.

3. Exploration is an important part of learning; it is dynamic, purposeful, and inventive.

4. Use effectively the interplay between free exploration and guided comments.

5. Problem solving leading toward development of movement response is a prime key toward learning experiences.

6. Guide the children through planning problems based on your increased understanding of children and movement.

7. Plan problems that will stimulate and excite the children to move; emphasize moving well.

8. Lead from one problem to another quickly and smoothly; keep in mind the sequence of problems.

9. Allow for plenty of time for children to solve problems within their capabilities.

10. Use words and phrases that are directive at times and less directive at other times, being sure the words and phrases are meaningful to the children.

11. Provide challenges that are difficult enough for individual children to accomplish over a short period of time. Simple problems can develop into two-, three-, and four-part patterns or more, depending upon the individual child solving them.

12. Concentrate on three basic concepts and direct children's movement patterns toward: awareness of themselves in the space provided; awareness of their bodies and their unique capabilities; awareness of the simple analysis of movement according to the speed, space, and force of the move.

13. Concentrate on one basic movement element during one particular lesson; develop this element through movement problems and through game situations.

14. Plan observation sessions for the children. These sessions will encourage good movement development and will assist in their analysis and understanding of their own patterns as well as those of others.

15. Evaluate at the most opportune time and with a sincere, serious spirit.

Guidelines in Evaluation of Desirable Outcomes

1. Is respect for individual's worth instilled through your methodology?

2. Is respect for equipment instilled?

3. Are self-respect and self-control fostered?

4. Is alertness gained through listening, moving, and thinking?

5. Is there a carry-over of movement practices evident from problem solving of individual problems into game, rhythmic, and stunt activities?

6. Is there a keener sense of kinesthetic awareness apparent through movement practice?

7. Are the children conscious of safety actions?

8. Do individuals think for themselves?

9. Do children recognize qualities of movement in other children?

10. Can a child take an idea given by one child and use it so that his movement pattern is improved?

Program of Movement Education for the Elementary Public School Children of Plattsburgh, New York

JOAN TILLOTSON AND STAFF

PHILOSOPHY

Because the atmosphere is quiet, serious and individualized;

Because children work within their own capabilities and at their own rate of speed;

Because children solve problems and tasks designed so that each can gear his responses to and within his own range of experience and understanding;

Because each teacher uses his own judgment in guiding each child, being primarily concerned that all children are learning each day;

Because each individual teacher is responsible for the maintenance check on all equipment and within his own discretion adjusts the equipment for safe use;

All children work safely, purposefully, and with maximum control.

Our common philosophy inherent in the apparatus activities of our schools' physical education program can be stated simply:

Provided with the atmosphere conducive to individualized learning and provided with adequate safety rules and regulations, each child will assume responsibility of progressing within his own rate of development with guidance by the teacher.

This program was set forth in 1967-1968. Reprinted by permission of the author and her staff.

SAFETY RULES AND REGULATIONS

The following safety rules and regulations have been accepted as basic, minimal, and adequate for physical education classes. (*Note:* More advanced apparatus activities which take place after school use the same basic rules but will vary according to the difficulty level of the individual children and their current needs.)

1. Only one person at a time is on a single piece of equipment. (Exceptions: Swedish window ladder, cargo net, Lind climber, low balance beam, and other exceptions set up by individual instructors.)

2. Individuals are working *alone* unless problems dictate otherwise. (*Alone* means not touching others or giving assistance in any way.)

3. A quiet atmosphere is imperative. The teacher's voice should be audible at any time. Only constructive chatter is allowed and only if problems so dictate.

4. Mats are to land on, not to stand or sit on. This rule eliminates the hazard of children's moving into the path of someone coming down off a piece of equipment and into another child. It means that children do not stand on a mat while waiting for turns to use equipment.

5. When resting, the floor, not mats or apparatus, is used. Thus the concept is established that when mats and equipment are used, they are used constructively at all times.

6. Children will assist in moving equipment only within the discretion of the individual instructors and basic school policies.

SUPERVISION

At *no* time do children use the apparatus or equipment without supervision.

A variety of apparatus and/or equipment is used in one class period. This provides children with more opportunities for maximum participation and creates a relaxed and unhurried atmosphere, which is more conducive to learning in a safe environment. Under such conditions, the need to rush, to push, or to work too closely to others and to have long periods of inactivity (all potential creators of problems) is eliminated.

The teacher continually moves about the area helping students with their choice of activity or with solving the problem which was presented by the teacher. Children receive assistance or are spotted by the teacher, depending upon each child's individual readiness and need.

As the children move from one piece of apparatus to another, they are purposeful and quiet. They chat constructively only when such behavior is dictated by certain problems to be solved. The "quiet work atmosphere" may be established by the use of any of the following forms of class organization:

1. Individuals move from piece to piece as directed by the teacher.
2. Individuals move from piece to piece at their own discretion.
3. Children move with partners and work with partners on a designated problem as directed by the teacher.
4. Children move and work with partners on a designated problem at their own discretion.
5. Small groups move from piece to piece as directed by the teacher.
6. Small groups move from piece to piece as they collectively decide.

Because the teacher is aware of individual differences, he is alert to those who might be a distracting influence to the rest of the class and works individually with them toward development of a seriousness of purpose. At the same time, the teacher gives words of encouragement to those whose movement responses are unique, to those who need encouragement to experiment with new ideas, and to those who need to refine their movement pattern. The teacher creates an environment conducive to sound, purposeful work through discussion sessions with the total class, rest periods, demonstrations and analysis by the children, and reenforcement of rules and regulations necessary for safe work.

7

Some Thoughts on Movement Education

HAYES KRUGER

I think of movement education as the central theme of good physical education, in which developmental activities, skills, knowledge, and concepts reside on a core of basic movement experiences and concepts.

The development of skills depends upon intelligent practice or training. Understanding is demanded for the former while coaching is required in the latter. Each skill is a highly specific motor pattern. Nonetheless, in sports, gymnastics, aquatics, and dance particularly, there are concepts, basic principles, and mechanics of movement rooted in the understanding derived from developmental movement education that enable the learner to proceed more intelligently and with greater self-reliance than is possible when each skill is taught solely as an independent motor pattern.

The elements of basic movement are *space, time, force, and flow.* All movement has a spatial quality. It may be *forward, backward, sideways, up, down,* or in *some combinations of directions. High, medium,* and *low level,* as well as the range of the movement, further describe its spatial relationship. *We explore* and thus experience the extremes of these ranges of movement, and we express them as *large or small, far or near, away from or close to.* The *movement* response to the verbalized problem presented by the teacher enables the child to *contrast the differences* and thus to develop wider capacity for movement possibility as the concepts of personal and general space gradually grow.

If we are able to disregard what we observe the body doing in the way of movement, we can better focus our attention either on where it is moving in relation to the available *space* or on what the relationship of the body parts is. No matter how the body is manipulated, it must be supported, except in brief periods of flight, such as in a leap or during a dismount from apparatus. In any case, the movement has a spatial relationship to the supporting area. Going over or under apparatus, hanging from it, or supporting oneself on it are functional ways in which movement takes place other than on the floor. And last, when an object is manipulated during a body movement it also has spatial qualities, no matter what is being done with it or to it. A ball being dribbled is at a particular level, moving within a specific range and in a particular direction, and it may range from near to far in relation to the body. *Awareness of the spatial potential* is important to the *total learning process.* Remembering that this potential is related to the perceptual awareness as well as the kinesthetic awareness of the child enables the teacher to present additional related problems, to develop discussions from observations by children of children, and to lay the foundation for analysis that becomes the basis for further exploration. *Stretching, bending, twisting, turning, pushing, pulling, swinging, and many locomotor movements that transfer the body's weight to many different body parts are an outgrowth of the child's efforts to find many ways of moving.* The ways of moving can be dealt with in a number of more limited problems as an outgrowth of a more general problem. As children move, they are showing the teacher what they know. If they don't move on hands and feet, perhaps they are not aware that they can or should, or perhaps they are still copying some-one who always gets the "right" answers. Presenting a problem that in-volves movement at a low level takes care of that situation very nicely. There are many "correct" answers at this stage.

As movement-oriented teachers observing the young child at play as well as the skilled player, we can see in each case how much of the spatial potential is being realized. If we are perceptive enough, we can see many of the conceptual as well as many of the physical limitations that must be overcome in order to maximize the movement possibilities. The good coach does so as he observes his players, and he reorganizes his practice sessions accordingly. The good teacher must do so to help children develop greater awareness of their own movement potential.

Time is a relative element that describes a movement in terms of its speed. Fast movement is contrasted with slow movement. Speed increases, decreases, or remains the same. Changes in direction, level, and range may be made quickly or slowly. The perceptive coach notes the controlled speed of his players and their potential for increasing speed or utilizing it more effectively. The good teacher provides the opportunity to develop the awareness of speed and its relationship to the spatial dimensions of movement, in order to enrich the movement experience and the concomi-tant concepts and awarenesses that develop the control of speed.

Force is an element of movement that exists simply because it can be created through muscular effort or through the effort to utilize or resist natural laws. The understanding of created force must come through a process of contrasting the extremes of strong and weak, which are described in some movements, such as heavy and light, hard and soft, harsh and gentle, or tense and relaxed. Force is used to maintain a posture, to move the body or its parts, and to resist either gravity or centrifugal force. Awareness that force can be controlled is important. Except for dance, most activities require strong movements and light landings. Force must be effectively employed for skillful movement. Understanding teachers pro-vide the opportunity to develop the awareness that force exists, that it can be created, that it can be utilized, that it can be absorbed.

The most obvious, most important element for movement effi-ciency—and unfortunately, the one receiving the least effective attention—is *flow*. The smooth flow of movement is felt by the performer and ap-preciated by the observer. Learning how to connect movement parts into a smooth-flowing sequence requires control of the speed and the force within the spatial dimensions of the movement pattern.

We say a movement is well coordinated or poorly coordinated, for-getting that the important element in coordination is flow—economy of movement. As one strives for excellence, whether for greater accuracy, better play, or superior technique, repetition is required to ensure the flow of movement without unnecessary interruption. We know that coaches work hard to achieve this quality of flow in the performance of their athletes. It is equally necessary for the teacher of physical education to recognize the dependence of well-coordinated movement upon flow and to provide continuous opportunity for the intelligent development of those basic body-management skills that develop the control necessary to achieve flow. Children must learn to arrest one movement and to prepare for the next. They must learn to combine two, three, four, and more parts into sequences. They must learn that skills are combinations of simpler parts. They must learn to work for excellence—the best they can do—and not be satisfied with mediocrity.

Movement is a physical experience. It takes movement to learn movement. The challenge to do it better must be presented to children as soon as they are capable of responding and feeling the satisfaction of success. Skillful guidance is required since sloppy performance should not be tolerated beyond the initial stages of exploration. Control prevents accidents and increases the confidence of the learner. The feeling of good movement is its own reward. Excellence begets excellence but mediocrity perpetuates itself. The learning environment is the responsibility of the teacher.

No teacher should attempt to think for children. They must learn how to think for themselves and to be responsible in large measure for their own learning. Only a problem-solving methodology and perceptive guidance permit the instructional flexibility that best meets the individualized needs of children. Only a learning environment that fosters the development of responsible freedom challenges the student to work toward greater self-realization. While we know that problems can be verbalized by the teacher, more opportunity must be presented to the students to develop their own problems through small group activity, and they must also have time to verbalize them.

Attention must be given to the natural challenge of the physical education environment. A bare floor, a flat field or play area inhibit creative imaginative play, yet the natural problem-solving challenges offered by gymnastic apparatus and wooded lots and hills are often neglected. Why do all play areas have to be flat?

It is unfortunate that the concern for safety often serves to delay or to minimize the imaginative use of gymnastic apparatus. The foundation for personal safety is best formed during the primary years of school. Finding many ways of moving over, under, around, and on apparatus enables children to develop an acquaintance with landing from varying heights, supporting, swinging, balancing, and traveling in all sorts of ways from the floor to the apparatus and back again. The freedom to choose gymnastics is not handicapped by inadequate experience which frustrates the learner at the later stages. During the intermediate years, girls in particular can develop in a very natural way highly efficient levels of performance in gymnastics if they have had a good movement foundation.

Movement education must be a child-centered program that is movement-oriented. The foregoing remarks about the necessity for a wide range of movement opportunities guided toward the development of control at all times helps children to develop a positive self-image: they have the feeling, "I can." Such a feeling results from countless meaningful successes. Children measure and compare themselves by what they can do, and the greater the variety, the greater the opportunity. Since young children are least affected by group pressures and performance standards, the emphasis upon a strong movement-oriented program cannot be overemphasized. Each child will emerge into the preadolescent peer-group pressure years better prepared to cope with the challenging array of group activities that require a reasonably high level of personal skill. Continual involvement in movement education enables the interested child to find a greater degree of success in sports education or physical education.

"Give me a boy who can move and I'll teach him how to play" is the often quoted remark of coaches. If this is true, then movement education will enable a larger number of children to freely choose the sports in which they would like to excel and enable them to proceed intelligently in their quest for success. Freedom to choose is enhanced by the feeling of "I can," which enables the individual to take the next step and say "I will" in his desire for self-fulfillment.

8

Movement –
A Way of Learning

GLADYS ANDREWS FLEMING

Is there anything more thrilling in the whole world than to see children *moving*, m-o-v-i-n-g, M-O-V-I-N-G, moving because they are alive, moving because they have something to say, moving because they have tasks to achieve? Movement is the universal language of boys and girls and their most natural form of expression. It is a form of expression free of vague verbalizations, a language that speaks through the whole body, communicating and responding in purposeful ways. All children move. Movement gives their lives increasing meaning. To be alive is to move! The extent to which adults prize this vital, vibrant, basic characteristic of children determines the extent of movement development for individual children. Movement is one of the most dynamic of human essentials.

How wonderful it would be if adults had as much concern about the development of children's movement skills as for a baby's crawling, standing and walking! These early stages of growth are but the beginning; subsequent development is equally significant. Adults need to understand, encourage and make it possible for children to develop movement competencies. In specific ways, movement becomes a self-motivating force for each child, helping him not only to express himself more adequately, but to live a fuller, more vital life.

There is a synonymity between children and movement. That is to say, children's movement is an inherent part of them as individuals—one of their nonverbal forms of expression; the urge for which is especially strong in children for whom large, unstructured actions are natural outlets for communicating thinking and feelings. Boys and girls solve many of their problems as well as respond to situations through movement. They react to the world about them, using movement as their form of communication either spontaneously or after considered thinking. Until we know something about their "movement quotients," it is impossible to "know" children. The inherent need of children to *move*, to express and communicate through *movement*, demands the thoughtful appreciation and understanding of all those adults working in early childhood and elementary

From Bulletin 23-A, *Physical Education for Children's Healthful Living,* Copyright 1968, pp. 37-49. Reprinted by permission.

education, not just the "specialist" or "special teacher." In the past the responsibility of understanding the development of the physical skills has been delegated to a specialist, which is predisposing that a child can be developed, looked at, understood or assessed in parts. Not so!

It is understandable that comprehensive, developmental programs concerned with *movement* have not been a vital part of our classrooms; but as teachers better understand the case for movement and are able to overcome doubts about time and lack of space, realize that movement development starts before a child comes to school and can be fostered anywhere at any time, the attitude that movement education belongs outside the classroom is no longer tenable.

MEANING OF MOVEMENT

More inclusive than what has commonly been thought of as "physical activity" or "physical education," Movement is the unique ingredient of physical education and the *basis* of Physical Education from which physical activity skills emerge. But it is much more!

Movement means activity, getting one's self into action. A child might say if asked, that movement is "going across the street and looking both ways;" managing himself on a tricycle, a bicycle, roller skates or ice skates; on apparatus, the escalator or the fire escape. But it is also the activity of propelling one's self in and through various dimensions and amounts of space; it has to do with use of spaces: going sometimes fast, other times slow; in large movements or restricted; and being able to adjust the body to space available. Movement includes walking, jumping, hopping, swinging, pushing, pulling, bending, climbing, catching, throwing and skipping. It is playing games, doing stunts, participating in creative rhythms, dancing a song, kicking a ball, running races and leaping a hurdle.

Movement involves sensing and responding. This quality is essential to human existence. It is reacting to internal and external stimuli, such as protecting one's self or getting out of the way of a moving vehicle or object; it is letting go or releasing tensions; it is following directions, participating and contributing; it is the ability to "feel" and outwardly respond to the beautiful in nature or in one's surroundings. It is working and playing.

Movement involves learning. Movement is a way of expressing ideas, feelings and concepts; it is sharing what one knows or understands. It is perceiving, conceptualizing, thinking, judging, identifying and solving problems. Movement is a way of learning: it includes discovering elements in one's surroundings and adapting energy patterns accordingly. It is a way of exploring ideas, making decisions, taking responsibility, inquiring and evaluating, making adjustments, and trying out alternatives. It implies "trying again and again." Movement manifests itself in creativity as a high form of *thinking.*

Movement involves motion. Children in movement transfer the body or body parts through space, using energy, timing and pacing, adjusting the body weights. Adapting the body or body parts to external objects requires control and coordination whether movement involves contact with a pitched ball or an elevator door; or the adaptation of the body to the abstract pattern of a polka step.

Movement denotes growth. In movement, boys and girls are continually releasing energy, using strength, applying force, developing equilibrium, gaining coordination, increasing their endurance and power, as well as gaining confidence, skill, and using "my thinking." They are also perceiving relationships and interacting to people and things. Continuous growth takes place when a child

develops confidence in managing his body and skill in manipulating the objects in his environment. He learns to negotiate the curb, to climb, to pull toys, to push the chair to a more favorable spot. He learns how to bend to pick up a ball he has been chasing. He learns how to control the ball, to catch it—at least part of the time. He experiments with turning upside down as he rides a bucking bronco, pilots the fastest jet flown, or dances to the television program. He runs to hide from his playmates only to wait breathlessly until he is caught. He enjoys wrestling with a friend and even challenges his older brother or father. When he is older, he plays games, dances, swims and becomes concerned about how he is doing. The things he does and the way he does them, what other people think about him and the ways they work and play with him shape the image that he is building of himself.[1]

Movement is purposeful. No matter how viewed—as activity, catalyst for sensing and responding, a way of learning, motion or dimensions of growth—movement is purposeful. Extensive, varied movement experiences and tasks are purposeful because they help boys and girls to cope with their world and themselves. Movement does not serve the same purposes for all. Each child reveals his purposes, thus: "Can you do this?" "Bet I can do it a hundred times!" "Look at me!" "That felt good." "Look at me

---

[1] Andrews, Saurborn and Schneider, *Physical Education for Today's Boys and Girls* (Boston, Mass.: Allyn and Bacon, 1960), p. 4.

away up here!" "Man, that was a throw!" "Watch me hop." "I can't seem to make my feet go fast enough." "Look, I can button my own coat!" "Want to see me tie my shoe?"

THE OVER-ALL STRUCTURE OF MOVEMENT

In any area of curriculum there is a basic body of content reflecting the broad understandings, principles of the field and major ideas to be studied. There is design, logic and development of these principles upon which content is based.

In physical education content grows out of the nature of human movement, which is the foundation for the structure of the discipline of physical education.

BASIC MOVEMENT SYMBOLS

What is the basis of a physical education program? We might ask the same question of other areas of the school program. What is the basis of skills in arithmetic, reading, writing, music or science? Each has a series of basic symbols with a specialized vocabulary to be mastered.

In writing, many specific skills must be developed before a story can be written. Letters, words and symbols are involved. Through experiences children are helped to expand, combine and relate symbols. From basic symbols come words; from words come sentences; from sentences paragraphs; from paragraphs come compositions or stories.

Each of the following movements (which might be listed in any arrangement, since there is no particular sequence desired) may be thought of as one of the symbols for physical education:

Walking	Swinging
Jumping	Pushing and Pulling
Hopping	Twisting and Turning
Running and Leaping	Bouncing
Bending and Stretching	Shaking

Each symbol, used by children for different purposes, has its own structure, feeling, meaning and association, with a distinct label for each. A jump is a *jump;* a hop is a *hop.* Each is different, with its own structure; each can be described and characterized and is a part of the vocabulary.

Basic movement symbols cannot be performed in isolation or be unrelated. For example, one does not walk without bending or swinging the arms. When working with young children it is important that only one movement be emphasized at a time.

AN ANALYSIS OF MOVEMENT

As there is no one accepted classification of movement, so there is no particular sequence for presenting or developing basic movements.

The analysis of movement presented below has emerged over the years from the writer's work with children and teachers. To help clarify meanings of the various movement components, children's terminology is used. Their illustrations have been taken from recordings of stenographic notes from work with many groups of children and teachers in various locations, throughout the country. This material has been constantly refined, evaluated and used in work with children.

Chart I, "An Analysis of Movement"[2] consists of basic movements (Movement Symbols) and an explanation or description of the movement. Actually this is a type of working "definition" of the basic movements. Each movement is also defined and described by boys and girls. The fourth column, which includes comments children make as to meanings and/or associations, illustrates the dynamic clarity which comes with actual words of children.

It is important to start working with children, *exploring* and *developing* some of the basic movements (basic movement symbols) before progressing to more complicated movement activities.

Exploring, developing and using basic movements enable children to discover what their bodies can do. Children are eager to find various ways of handling their bodies, as a whole or by parts, as they stay in one place or move in and through *space* with varying degrees of *force* and with different rates of *speed*. Progress in gaining control and in handling one's self is predetermined by each child in comparison to himself. No two children are alike, but when given plentiful opportunities *all* children may become skillful in Movement.

---

[2] Material adapted from original work of Gladys Andrews and recorded in:

a.   Gladys Andrews, *Creative Rhythmic Movement for Children* (Englewood Cliffs, N.J.: Prentice-Hall, 1954).

b.   Robert S. Fleming, *Curriculum for Today's Boys and Girls* (Columbus, Ohio: Merrill, 1963), pp. 224-35.

Chart I Basic Movement Symbols

	BASIC MOVEMENTS	SYMBOLS	MOVEMENT VOCABULARY
Basic movements	Explanation Description	What boys and girls say	Associations— meaning for children
Walking	Transferring weight from one foot to the other. One foot is on the floor at all times.	"Going 'some place' from one foot to the other or from one foot to the other 'right here'."	Walking like bears. Duck with a feather on his head. People walking in outer space, in mud, in leaves. Walking on stilts, balance beam, ice, tightrope. Promenading in a square dance.
Jumping	Distributing weight on two feet; elevate by pushing off the floor; landing on floor with both feet simultaneously.	"With two feet take off into space and come back to floor on two feet."	Jumping like my dog, frogs, kangaroos. Salmon going up stream. Jumping like grasshoppers, "Why aren't they called grassjumpers because they jump with their back legs?" Jumping over the brook, rope, cracks in the sidewalk.
Hopping	Putting weight on one foot; elevate by pushing one's self off the floor; landing back on floor on same foot.	"On one foot go up in the air and back to floor on same foot."	"Hopping like a flamingo, puppet on a string." "Hopping sounds like rain on porch, roof, sink faucet dripping."

Running	Transferring weight from one foot to the other while the body is momentarily suspended in air.	"Being in a hurry in the air."	Running like mice; automobile engines; fireman when the siren blows; moles underground. Running to get on the bus; make the train; to catch the elevator; or to catch the ball.
Leaping	Transferring weight from one leg to other involving elevation and suspension while in the air. Uses more space and force than in running and more coordination.	"Going away up in the air, stretch out from one leg to the other."	Leaping like a dog; a deer; dancers on TV. Leaping over puddles; sidewalks; hurdles; a pile of leaves.
Swinging	Suspended, pendular, arc-like movement executed by the arms, legs or whole body.	"Going side to side or up and down, or back and forth like swaying." "Moving part of a circle or 'whole' circle."	Swinging like clock pendulum; cow's tail; monkeys in zoo; flags in the wind. Makes me think of a rainbow; bells in churches; cranes digging; trees in bad storm; swinging bridge; swinging on parallel bars.
Stretching	Extending and expanding one or more body parts.	"Reaching." "Growing tall or wide."	Stretching like my kite string; clothes hanging on line; crepe paper; a rubber band; worms when I put them on my hook; chewing gum; my Daddy's suspenders.

Chart I Basic Movement Symbols (Continued)

	BASIC MOVEMENTS	SYMBOLS	MOVEMENT VOCABULARY
Basic movements	Explanation Description	What boys and girls say	Associations— meaning for children
and			Bending and stretching like playing the trombone; the policeman telling me to cross the road; Cherokee Indians when they dance.
Bending	Contracting and flexing one or more body parts.	"Getting little." "Pulling in real small." "Humping up."	Bending like my granddaddy. Bending up like accordion.
Pushing	Shoving and thrusting away from the body, using force (pushimg also includes a stretch and bend). Exerting force against something which pushes back.	"Getting something out of my way." "Starting the revolving door."	Pushing like animals that use their heads, like goats, elephants and buffalo; rockets going off the pad; crowds of people in subway; my little brother; doll carriage; Christmas shoppers push. Pushing at the floor when we jump—pushing the ball to make it bounce.
and			

Pulling	Drawing or attracting toward a fixed base (the body) using force.	"Bring something toward me that might not want to come."	Pulling like going up in my Grandmother's apple tree. Pulling like a tug-of-war; train pulling a red caboose; pulling up the flag.
Twisting and	Changing position using some rotation around an axis or center.	"As far as you can go around without moving feet or seat. Head toward you, rest of me away from you."	Twisting like pretzels; corkscrew; licorice sticks. Twisting when I bat a ball; when I mess up my fish line. Turning and twisting like a rope.
Turning	Revolving completely around a center or base.	"All the way around." "All the way over."	Turning over and under, upside down. Over—forward roll. Turning a screw with a screwdriver; turning like airplane propellers; bicycle wheels; twisters or hurricanes.
Shaking*	Short, rapid, successive vibrating motion.	"Wiggly," "Quivering," "Shivering movement."	Shaking like Jello—when I come out of the water; stuff in my pocket; subway; my loose tooth. I shake when I'm scared like when it thunders or when there is a scarey TV program. Makes me think of milkshakes; harp strings; birds fluffing feathers; my mom shakes the can before she squirts the bugs.

* Footnote on p. 54.

Chart I Basic Movement Symbols (Continued)

	BASIC MOVEMENTS	SYMBOLS	MOVEMENT VOCABULARY
Basic movements	Explanation Description	What boys and girls say	Associations— meaning for children
Bouncing*	Back and forth or up and down motion in quick rhythmic sequences. Rebounding.	"Jiggling." "Going up and down in a hurry." "Bumpy."	Bouncing like a ball; clown in circus, or giggly bubbles in Seven-Up. Bouncing on bedsprings; trampoline; the bus; trucks. Makes me think of flowers on my Aunt's hat when she walks; story of "The Red Balloon."

* Bouncing and shaking are really qualities of pushing and pulling and other basic movements. However, small children have identified these as specific movements. Therefore, they are included here as individual basic movements.

CHART II MOVEMENT CONTINUUM*

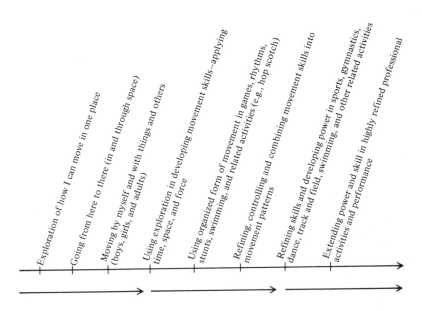

*Developed and demonstrated by Gladys Andrews and Robert S. Fleming, 1967.

As children have meaningful opportunities to use basic movement in a developmental, progressive, sequential way, combinations of basic movement or complicated movement skills emerge (Illustrative: *skip*, combination of two basic movements, the *walk* and the *hop*). Until a child can *hop* (can maintain balance, handle himself adequately with either foot with a hop), he cannot hope to skip. Other movement skills are: sliding, galloping, kicking, throwing, catching, climbing, tagging and making the ball bounce. As children gain skill in handling themselves, they become more secure and successful with objects and equipment such as tricycles, bicycles, scooters, balls, bats and ropes. Since some children are fearful of these external objects, serious difficulties may arise when they are put into situations before they are ready.

From the combinations of movement skills movement patterns develop as in catching and throwing, batting and running to a base, polkaing with a partner by combining a skip and a slide, skating or swimming.

Combinations of movement skills and patterns are intensified with other concepts as children comprehend such factors as hard and soft, small and large, here to there, fast and slow, velocity and gravity. With opportunity and practice, realizations also come concerning the relationship of time, force and space to *all movement*. This may be another principle of human movement. Such factors become meaningful as children make themselves go faster or slower, forward, backward or around, try to stay in the air, turn over in the air and make themselves light or heavy with or without equipment or with another person.

In Chart II, entitled "Movement Continuum," the progression of movement skills is shown in terms of a continuum, which illustrates the necessity for an individual to progress through a series of stages in an orderly manner. It is impossible for one to acquire perfection or power in a physical skill unless he has developed proficiency in factors which underlie the proficiency.

MOVEMENT CONTINUUM

So often teachers and parents are in a hurry to put children into complex, structured forms of Movement (games, dances or stunts) before they can adequately handle themselves in relation to time, force, or space; external objects; other boys and girls; or before they have had appropriate movement opportunities to express themselves. However, when time is provided for movement exploration and when experiences are planned sequentially, all children when given help and encouragement will have the necessary movement background to participate in organized forms of movement including games, sports, dance, gymnastics and other activities.

In summary, movement is the basis for physical education. An analysis of the various factors related to the discipline are illustrated in Chart III, "The Structure of Physical Education." Note the relationship of basic symbols, exploration, skills and skill patterns to games, rhythms, stunts and related activities.

If sound, continuous programs are to develop in the elementary schools, it is imperative that Movement and the knowledge of the basic factors therein be brought to the attention and understanding of both classroom and physical education teachers. Concentration on skills or sports for adolescents will fail to achieve goals of competence, since emphasis on learning basic movement skills must begin with very young children, the earlier the better. Every child has a right to this unique form of communication. To move, and to gain in movement, enhances the quality of being alive, of being a child!

CHART III THE STRUCTURE OF PHYSICAL EDUCATION*

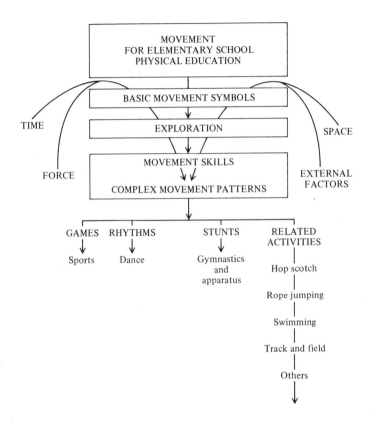

9

Movement Patterns and
Their Basic Elements – Types of Activities

MARGARET M. THOMPSON

Educators in the field of physical education have for a long time taught various types of motor activities, giving attention to the contributions of these activities to general health status, physical fitness, the social adjustment of the individual, release of mental and emotional tensions, the provision of leisure time activities, to name a few. However, little attention has been placed on the importance of these motor activities in the development of the learning process itself.

Coghill (1929), Jersild (1954), Piaget (1952), and Strauss and Kephart (1955) have indicated that the earliest learnings of the child are motor, and subsequent learnings are based on the motor learnings. Kephart has stated that to the extent the motor pattern is deficient, the subsequent learnings based on the pattern, such as perception, symbolic manipulation, and concept formation, will be deficient. The more complex activities are the result of an elaboration and an integration and organization of earlier learning activities.

It is the motor pattern that permits the child to explore: gross motor patterns permit exploration of space; fine motor patterns permit exploration of objects.

The motor activities which contribute to the child's exploration of his environment are of the greatest significance for education since the young child gains his initial information about his environment through exploration. This exploration involves movement through space and the manipulation of objects. These are dependent upon motor activities and the ability to control motor responses.

There has been research, and some programs have been initiated which deal with the relationship of motor-pattern development to other learnings. However, they have been largely restricted to children with reading problems, emotionally disturbed children, the mentally retarded, and slow learners.

Presented at the IAHPER Workshop on Movement Education and Athletics, Purdue University, West Lafayette, Indiana, December 5, 1964. The concept of movement patterns and, to some extent, the description of these patterns are based on theoretical concepts espoused by B. B. Godfrey. Reprinted by permission of the author.

A case study by Godfrey (1964) showed improvement in scholastic achievement for slow learners who participated in a program of motor therapy. The program emphasis was one of exploration of movement activities to elicit the basic motor or movement patterns. Ismail, Cowell, and Kephart (1963) studied the relationship of motor aptitude and scholastic achievement using fourth, fifth, and sixth grade children. The items showing the highest relationship with both IQ and scholastic achievement (out of 37 items) were the balance and coordination items. These balance and coordination items are of the same nature as the activities in the program in the motor therapy laboratory.

At the elementary school level in particular, more attention should be given to physical education as a process of developing basic motor patterns which can become the foundation for the more complex learnings in the classroom situation.

This task should not be difficult since the emphasis in physical education at the elementary school level has been moving in the past ten years or so toward the child-centered rather than the activity-centered point of view. This change is in keeping with the educational philosophy of the elementary school.

To say that the program is child-centered is to say that the activities—or call them movement experiences—are the avenues through which the child develops movement patterns and movement skills that are essential to coping with his environment. The activity is essentially the means to the end rather than an end in itself. Thus one considers the contribution an activity can make to the motor development of the child in selecting experiences for the physical education program.

Motor or movement patterns are the means by which the child gathers the perceptual data about his environment as the basis for learning. The movement pattern is outward observable inner motor or neurological pattern. Movement patterns are divided, according to Kephart, into four categories: (1) balance and posture; (2) locomotion; (3) contact (grasp and release or manipulation of objects); (4) receipt and propulsion of objects. In the balance and posture patterns, the center of gravity is the zero point for all spatial relations; contact patterns are concerned with exploration and manipulation of objects; locomotor patterns involve the exploration of space; and receipt and propulsion patterns are concerned with the exploration of objects in space.

These four patterns are usually discussed in physical education literature in the two categories of body handling and object handling. Thus body handling would include balance and posture and locomotion—

walking, running, sitting, standing—while object handling would include contact and receipt and propulsion—lifting, carrying, pushing, hitting, and the like.

In body handling it is the body or a body part alone that is being moved, and one needs to consider adjustments only in relation to his own weight, space, and force. Body handling patterns are thus self-focused, even though the purpose may be an external one.

In object handling an external object is being moved by the body or a body part. One now has the added consideration of the weight, space, and force of the external object. The addition of an object to the movement complex takes the focus of attention outside the body itself. The perceptual problem is thereby increased since distance receptors now assume a major role and the space surrounding the child must now be structured and stable. Unless the surrounding space is stable, the movement of the object cannot be predicted or controlled. At this stage, the adequacy of the perceptual motor match becomes significant also. The child must be able to project the perceptual data outside his own body if he is to deal with the object. Object handling can help or hinder the execution of basic body-handling patterns. For example, if one is jumping rope, this activity might enhance the locomotor pattern of jumping or skipping, adding the pleasure of rhythmic performance and satisfaction of a new way to jump— or the manipulation of the rope might cause one to trip or be unable to complete the body-handling pattern in a smooth, fluid manner.

Although I am discussing the patterns separately, body handling and object handling are, of course, combined in everyday situations and in the more complex activities, such as dribbling a ball or running to catch a football pass. After establishment, most of these patterns become reflexive in nature.

The purpose of the locomotor patterns is to change the space occupied by the body—to move the body from one place to another. A movement pattern involves the fundamental elements only and does not include the movements that may be related to the style or peculiarity of a particular individual.

The term *pattern deviation* as it is used here will refer to those differences in style existing in the absence of any element or difference which acts to interrupt the flow and continuity of the pattern or which acts to inhibit or affect the normal pattern—for example, in walking: dragging one or both feet, bouncing, shuffling or emphasis on one foot, inadequate arm swing, body rotation, etc.

Steindler has described walking as alternately losing and regaining balance. The integral responses existing within the overall pattern of walking are the extensor, or antigravity, reflex and the arm and leg opposition reflex. (The former keeps the walker erect and maintains orientation to the pull of gravity. As the body slumps forward, the antigravity muscles are put on stretch, with the result that a neurological signal is sent to them to contract, and the body then straightens up.) Though these two reflexes may show themselves earlier, by the time the child is five or six they are shown clearly in walking, and they carry over into most of his other movement patterns.

Although the time interval between phases is only a fraction of a second, the walk may be divided into a swing phase, a brief catch phase, and a supportive phase. The basic order is the swing of one leg, support of the weight on the other, alternation of one leg after the other to receive the weight, and support of the body weight on it as the other leg swings forward. During this time the body faces forward, the arms move easily in opposition to the legs and assist in a fluid transfer of weight and rhythmic alternation of sides. One may note also, in addition to the deviations suggested earlier, that body weight carried too far forward or backward can disturb the fluidity of the walking pattern. A similar disturbance may also be noted in a walk swaying from side to side. In general, we find the walking pattern well established in most of the children we get in school, and the deviations are minor and often more noticeable aesthetically than operationally.

The running pattern is essentially the same as the walking pattern in respect to the antigravity reflex and the arm and leg opposition reflex. The essential differences between run and walk are: the run has a nonsupportive phase; the ball of the foot touches first rather than the heel; there is a slightly greater body inclination forward as speed increases; and the arms are held forward and up, with the hands staying in front of the body. One can check the arm action in the run either by watching the movement of the elbows toward the back or the hands in front. The deviations one might note in the run are: unevenness, either to the side or up; body twisting (the pelvis rotates slightly, but the trunk should face forward); bending at the waist; leaning backward; a heavy or jarring landing; and flipping of the feet outward. The last is not a true run, that is, there is no unsupported phase. It is often seen in the young child who walks so fast that it may appear to be a run, but one should note carefully that one foot is always kept on the floor.

In jumping, there is a preparatory phase, during which the legs flex in preparation for the jump while the arms swing back; an action phase, in which the legs extend and produce force to propel the body while the arms swing forward to assist; and a terminal phase, in which the knees, ankles, and hips again flex to absorb the landing, and the arms swing down to assist. In the standing broad jump, as noted by Hellebradt and others, the position of the head from backward flexion to extension, to forward flexion, to backward flexion on the landing seems to be a stereotyped pattern, once jumping for horizontal distance is established. While one can check the pattern elements present, studies have shown that there is great variation in combinations of use of arms, angle of forward inclination, and the like among all children of all ages until the adult pattern of the broad jump is reached. One should expect to see some of the deviations, such as jumping off to one side, failure to maintain balance on landing, etc., and should recognize them as inhibiting the pattern. One should also provide ample opportunities for the child to gain experience in all types of jumping at the level of his capability.

Hopping evolves from jumping and requires the child to jump on one foot and land on the same foot. The arm action in the hop differs from that in the jump, in that the arms are seldom if ever brought down behind the body; they are kept in front with elbows bent, and they work together. The difference in leg action is that the knee seldom straightens fully on the hop, leaving the ankle to do most of the push and absorption. The free leg, without touching the ground, has about the same action as the hopping leg instead of swinging forward as in a jump. Some common deviations noted are: body movement in direction of nonpushing leg when arm on opposite side is kept still; peddling with the free foot; loss of balance.

Skipping combines walking with jumping or hopping. The child is required to combine a step and a hop on the same foot, then repeat the performance on the other foot. While skipping has elements of other locomotor patterns, it is generally classified as a separate pattern. The most obvious deviation is that of timing; it is a step-hop rather than a skip. Deviation may be noted also in extraneous arm movements; the arms do not move rhythmically with the legs.

In rolling, the body should be converted into the smallest package possible with respect to the circumference around which it will turn. One has a good rolling pattern if he can turn the body over in any direction, keeping it in a straight line without permitting any part of the body to protrude so that it blocks or impedes the even continuation of the roll. Deviations in forward and backward rolls are: landing on the head; failure to use hands for propulsion and/or receipt of body weight; failure to keep tucked; pushing to one side. Deviations for the side or log roll are: uneven timing of push with hips and shoulders resulting in a diagonal path; head or body part getting in the way of proper execution of the roll. Alternate movements of the hips and shoulders should be timed so that the roll takes a straight path.

The sliding pattern combines balance and locomotion through a propulsive phase and a sliding movement with a momentary supportive phase by the sliding foot. Body positioning in the form of rotation will result in a diagonal path or lack of alignment of the feet if a straight path is maintained.

OBJECT HANDLING PATTERNS

In throwing, in which a swing pattern is utilized, there is opposition of arm and leg, the body is used as a part of the total lever for distance and speed, and there is a preparatory phase, a summation of forces or propulsive phase, and a terminal phase. The adequacy of the timing for a smooth transition from one phase to the other is a crucial factor. Perhaps the most obvious deviation to physical education is the lack of arm and leg opposition. In the push type of throw one gets cross-extension rather than arm and leg opposition. Another deviation noted is the lack of adequate arm swing in either the preparatory phase or the terminal phase. Accuracy, force, etc., are signs of increased competence in the pattern rather than pattern elements.

In catching, body pose is in opposite direction from that in throwing or striking. The essential element, of course, is the ability to grasp the object. The sequence is reach, grasp, absorb, or "give," with body parts and body in accordance with weight and/or force of oncoming object.

One of the major problems in both catching and striking is that of seeing and judging the oncoming object.

The striking pattern of hitting is similar to the throwing pattern, in that it emphasizes overarm, underarm, and sidearm swings as well as a push. Arm and leg opposition, etc., occur in the same relationship. The major difference lies not in the pattern elements but in the judgment necessary to contact and propel an oncoming object—or a stationary one for that matter. If the pattern is established, the focus of the individual can be placed on this very difference.

In object handling, the individual should be able to perform most of the patterns with one hand alone and with both together.

The striking patterns of kicking, perhaps more than any other of the object-handling patterns, has balance as a crucial factor since one must contact and propel the object while supported on only one limb. This activity involves a good sense of one's own center of gravity in relation to the position change and the effect on the oncoming object.

BALANCE OR POSTURE PATTERNS

Balance control is effected by the semicircular canal, visual, tactical, and auditory senses. Kinesthetic awareness is the sense relation of the body and its parts in changing positions. The stability of the surroundings in relation to the changes is an important consideration in maintenance of balance.

In standing, as in walking and running, the antigravity reflexes allow us to remain erect or stand or sit. The elements of standing posture include having the total body aligned over center of gravity over base of support. I will do no more than mention that a sense of awareness of this relationship is crucial for an individual to have adequate control in balance positions other than on the floor.

Whether it is balance or kinesthesis, there is a difference in performance when vision is taken away from the performer—though the blind person accommodates through the other senses.

Balance, or equilibrium, when the body is in a moving situation, such as changing direction, stopping, and object handling, calls for further adjustments than to the pull of gravity and one's own weight.

It is important to note that the presence or absence of the pattern elements or components for all body handling and object handling is the essential concern. With experience through explorative use of the pattern in a variety of situations, with change of pace, with different media, etc., a pattern develops further in refinement and can then be counted on to hold up if sudden obstacles or complex situations are thrown in the individual's path.

The use of movement-pattern check lists can assist one more than casual observation in making an accurate assessment of an individual's pattern development.

Presenting a variation that is similar but not identical will assist in securing the total pattern. Thus the use of a walking board, rhythmic activities involving walking, or a game situation involving walking will help.

Where arm and leg opposition is giving difficulty in several patterns, all can be tackled by setting up a variety of problems to elicit the solution, for example, arm and leg swings, throwing for distance, etc. For development, try to set up a problem that will elicit the movement pattern rather than have the child practice specifically on the motor pattern. This procedure prevents his becoming so involved with the pattern that he is blocked in going further.

One must recognize the necessity for a child to be allowed to experiment or practice on his own (self-direction), since the level of development varies not only from child to child but from pattern to pattern for an individual child.

Object Handling

Different-sized and -shaped objects:

Throwing
Catching
Bouncing
Hitting with hand
Hitting with paddle
Hitting with bat, etc.

Variations in speed:

Force
Timing
Length of backswing
Point of release
Follow through

Variations in stance

Use of body:

One side
Other side
Both sides simultaneously

Variations in Kinds of Movement Within Given Space, Level, Direction, etc.

Range of movement
Speed of movement
Force of movement

REFERENCES

Coghill, G. E. *Anatomy and the Problem of Behavior.* Cambridge: Cambridge University Press, 1929.

Godfrey, Barbara B. "Development of a motor therapy laboratory." Paper read at summer conference, Graduate Dept. of Physical Education, University of Michigan, Ann Arbor, July 13, 1964.

Ismail, A. H., N. C. Kephart, and C. C. Cowell. "Utilization of motor aptitude tests in predicting academic achievement." *Tech. Rep. No. 1,* Indianapolis: Indiana State Board of Health, 1963.

Jersild, A. T. *Child Psychology.* Englewood Cliffs, N.J.: Prentice-Hall, 1954.

Piaget, J. *The Origins of Intelligence in Children.* New York: International Universities Press, 1952.

Steindler, A. *Kinesiology of the Human Body.* Springfield, Ill.: C. C. Thomas, 1955.

Strauss, A. A., and N. C. Kephart. *Psychopathology and Education of the Brain-injured Child.* Vol. II, *Progress in Theory and Clinic.* New York: Grune and Stratton, 1955.

10

Movement Education

EVELYN SCHURR

In recent years the physical education program in American elementary schools has been greatly influenced by programs of English physical educators. These people place a great deal of stress on studying basic movement at an early age through a developmental and an exploratory approach.

This influence reflects several factors operative in American education. There has been a trend in all subject areas in the elementary school toward a developmental approach and use of exploration and experimentation as a method of teaching. More information on the growth and development of children is available. More state legislation calling for physical education in the elementary school curriculum has been enacted in the last few years. Due to these and other changes, physical educators became increasingly interested in elementary school methods and curriculum.

As a result of several years of study, conferences, exchange teachers, and publications dealing with movement education, or movement exploration as it is called by some, there has been a definite pattern of acceptance of the English method and content in American elementary school physical education programs. There have been many modifications, and there is much diversity in use of terminology, but there appears to be wide agreement that the movement education approach is more agreeable to the developmental concept of education in America. Movement education or movement exploration is not physical education in the elementary school but it is one approach to teaching basic skills or new skills and related aspects of movement.

The work of Rudolph Laban[1] is the basis for the modern concept of the structure and development of the importance of basic movement education. The concept of a structure for studying movement as presented in the following pages is an oversimplification of Laban's analysis of movement; however, his basic theories are utilized. This structure is a result of practical application and experience with many elementary school children.

As exploration is an approach or a method of teaching, only the content and factors affecting movement are discussed in this chapter.

FACTORS OF MOVEMENT STUDY

All basic movement is studied in terms of four factors: Qualities of Movement, Space, Body Actions, Relationships.

Qualities of Movement

In the performance of all movement skills the body must make adjustments to the factors of time, force, pattern, and flow—all of these being dependent upon the purpose of the movement.

---

[1] Rudolph Laban, *Modern Educational Dance* (London, MacDonald and Evans, 1948).

Table 1 Factors of Movement Study

QUALITIES OF MOVEMENT		SPACE	BODY ACTIONS		RELATIONSHIPS
Time		*Direction*	*Nonlocomotor skills*		*Partner*
Sudden	Acceleration	Forward	Twist	Turn	Small group
Fast	Deceleration	Backward	Stretch	Bend	
Slow		*General* Sideward	Swing	Lift	Large group
Sustained		Diagonal	Push	Pull	
		Upward	Fall		Team or side
Force		*Personal* Downward	Various combinations		
					Objects
		Level	*Locomotor skills*		
Light		High	Walk	Run	Small equipment
Heavy		Medium	Jump	Hop	apparatus
		Low	Leap	Skip	
Body shape			Slide		
			Various combinations		
Direct					
Twisted			*Weight bearing*		
Flow			*Initiating movement*		
Free			*Receiving weight*		
Bound					
			Transferring weight		

Time

Time refers to the speed at which a movement t
degrees of time are sudden and sustained. There a
games and sports when a sudden explosive movement n
between beating an opponent on the take-off, reaching
wise would have been just out-of-reach, or a quick dodge in
Sustained movement allows a person to continue moving   . in
control of the body, yet capable of changing speed if necessary.   ere are
many variations of time between these two extremes. The ability to
accelerate with ease comes with an awareness of how to control the body.

Force

Force refers to the tension of the muscles of the body and the degree of
strength needed for a certain movement. Experiences in moving lightly, or
heavily, will help a child to control the tension of muscles only to the
extent that is needed to fulfill the purpose of a task. For example, contrast
the force needed to push an empty box as opposed to that needed to push
a box of sand; or the amount of force needed to get up on a high bench as
opposed to that needed to jump from it. In the latter the tension of the
muscles has to be little, yet not completely absent in order to make the
landing light but controlled.

Body shape

Body shape refers to the way in which the body moves through space,
with a straight or direct path, or with a twisted or flexible path. There are
many variations between direct and twisted. The direct manner is the most
economical and fastest. Contrast the movement of jumping up to reach a
basketball as it rebounds off the backboard with that of a fish flop
where the feet must lead, and all parts of the body must snap into action
in sequence to gain force and balance to get up on the feet.

Flow

Flow refers to the sequence of actions and the transition from one position to another. There can be a smooth, controlled series of movements
joined together which give continuity to the pattern. *Free flow* describes a
movement which must continue to a controlled conclusion, while a *bound
flow* is movement which can be stopped and balance maintained at any
time. For example, a routine on a piece of apparatus, no matter how
simple or complex, calls for both free and bound flow. Each exercise on
the equipment must flow together in a continuous pattern; however, each

...se may involve a movement that calls for building momentum to a point where momentum must be checked and a certain position sustained for a period of time before the movement is completed. Many experiences of work with skills and flow lead to efficient, graceful movement.

Space

All movement takes place in space which in itself may be quite varied. The amount of space available demands many adjustments in the performance of specific skills. There are two kinds of space. *Personal* space is the space about or around an individual which can be utilized when he is in a stationary position. The skills pertinent to use in this situation are non-locomotor or axial. *General* space is that area into which a person or all people in the room can move.

Movement into space can be in different *directions:* forward, backward, sideward, diagonally, upward, downward, and any combinations of these. It can be in different *levels* of space: high, low, or medium. Becoming aware of spatial elements will help a child learn to judge heights from which balls are approaching, opportunities to evade opponents, distances and levels at which to lead passes to opponents, distances to clear apparatus, to mention but a few practical applications.

Body Actions

This factor actually involves learning what movements or skills the body is capable of doing. There are movements that can be done in a stationary position. The body may move as a whole, or various parts may move independently or together. These are the nonlocomotor skills of twisting, turning, stretching, swinging, bending, shaking, bouncing, pushing, pulling, and combinations of these. The body can move in space utilizing the locomotor skills of walking, running, jumping, hopping, leaping, and various combinations of these.

Children should realize that any part of the body may initiate the movement into space. The weight of the body may be borne by different parts of the body and locomotor movements developed from many positions such as walking on the hands, and turning over a bar with the head leading down.

The body or parts of the body can receive weight in the form of outside objects or weight of other body parts; for example, in receiving the weight of the body as in landing from a jump or fall; in catching balls.

The body can transfer weight of the body itself or that of an outside object; for example, in dodging (the body weight must be transferred from one part of the body to another part as a base), in propelling the body in the air as in many gymnastic events, in throwing and/or striking objects.

Relationships

In most game, dance, and apparatus activities children do not move alone in space. They must move with someone, oppose someone, overcome obstacles, or use implements of some type. In early skill learnings children must have experiences where they adapt skills to performance with or in opposition to a partner, then in a small group and with a variety of obstacles and objects. When working with a partner one may imitate the other's movement pattern, do the movement together, oppose the other's pattern, or each may do his own pattern, but relate it to that of the other. When working in a group one may move following a leader, move with four or five other people, move in response or opposition to another group, work with a group in solving a problem or creating a pattern together, work in the group where each does his own movement but relates it to every other group member's pattern.

Skills in all the activity areas may be studied utilizing the four major factors just discussed whether the skill requires manipulation of the body in relation to other objects (balls, boxes, bars, bats, paddles, water) or in the expressive forms.

11

Movement Exploration
ELIZABETH HALSEY and LORENA PORTER

INTRODUCTION

Human movement has been studied from many angles. Industrial engineers have worked to eliminate unnecessary movement by time-motion analyses. Specialists in salesmanship have tried to teach the carriage that gives the best image of confidence and enthusiasm. Psychologists have studied movement as a projection of human personality. Orthopedists have recorded deviations from the normal in posture and gait as possible symp-

---

toms of pathological conditions in bone, joint, or muscle. Producers of drama on the stage or screen know that movement as well as spoken words tell the audience of tragedy, conflict, or joy; hesitation or decision; and give depth to the portrayal of character.

In physical education, skills of movement have been taught with success. In fact, physical education has been the only part of the school program that specifically has had this responsibility. Teachers and coaches taught the skills of each sport separately: blocking and tackling in football; batting and bunting in baseball; trapping and passing in soccer; and special patterns in swimming, diving, and figure skating. We have studied the human mechanism in courses such as anatomy, kinesiology, physiology and correctives, believing (quite rightly) that we should know the scientific basis of its structure and function. However, putting together the information about bones, joints, and muscles, leverage and other mechanical principles, into a useful, teachable understanding of movement at various age levels has yet to be accomplished, although promising beginnings have been made. There has also been a search for core learnings in performance that might be applied to many different specific skills and so short-cut the development of all of them. Among the many interesting approaches toward synthesis of our knowledge and experience is the elementary school program that we have called movement exploration.

MOVEMENT EXPLORATION: DEFINITION AND ORIGIN

Of course, children have always explored movement in their own way whenever they were free to do so. Here, however, we use the term to mean part of the physical education program. In brief, movement exploration may be defined as planned problem-solving experiences, progressing in difficulty, through which the child learns to understand and control the many ways in which his body may move and thus to improve many skills. Years of practical experiment and study have evolved a framework of what might be called fundamentals of movement. Within this framework the problems are organized into a sequence of progressive learnings.

Much of the pioneer experimenting in movement was done by Rudolph Laban.[1] English experts in physical education began working with Laban's basic theories of weight, time, and space, adapting them to

---

[1] Rudolph Laban, artist, choreographer, author, and teacher of contemporary dance widely known for many years in Central Europe, escaped from Nazi Germany to England where he established and directed a center for the Art of Movement until his death in 1958.

children's understanding and activities. They found children readily responsive and capable of original and creative work in developing their own action patterns built on various qualities of movement. As it progressed, the work became very generally accepted as a means of developing skill and agility in other activities.

In some English schools older children have gone on to expressive movement in silent drama, or pantomime. Using stories from the language arts or social studies the children plan and perform group drama, which becomes for them an absorbing art form. Their skilled movement and freedom from self-consciousness often give these "mimes" movements of compelling expressiveness and beauty.

In this country, also, movement exploration has a long history. As far back as the summer of 1926, Margaret H'Doubler conducted a workshop in Fundamentals of Movement relating to dance, sports, and other activities. Ruth Glassow[2] published a text on fundamentals as applied to college classes, and many others have added to literature and practice at the college level. Much work has been done at the elementary school level, and movement exploration is widely accepted as an important part of the curriculum.

Not only does it develop useful skill, but it is vigorous, it is fun, it calls for invention, imagination, and problem solving—all shown as each child finds his own solution in movement to problems set by the teacher, the class, or himself. A very important part of movement exploration is the teacher's part in guiding children so that they will use the skills and understandings they are acquiring in this form of physical education to improve their performance in other forms such as games, sports, self-testing, and dance. Thus movement exploration becomes a useful method of learning as well as valuable content in the program.

CONTENT

The content of movement exploration is found in problems based on the fundamentals of movement that are common to all forms of physical education. Those identified in this text are described below.[3] The components listed under each of the fundamentals serve as the themes for lessons

---

[2] Ruth Glassow, *Fundamentals in Physical Education.* Philadelphia: Lea & Febiger, 1932.
[3] Adapted from Rudolph Laban's principles of movement as presented at the workshop on movement exploration held at the State University of Iowa, Summer 1961. Director: Lorena Porter.

organized by the teacher around one or more problems. Progression through a series of lessons or from one grade to another is achieved by leading children from the exploration of simple patterns to those involving variations and combinations so that complex patterns and greater skills are evolved. In all lessons knowledge and understanding of principles of movement are fostered through guided observations and evaluation; also the children's capacity for working with partners or in small groups is improved.

FUNDAMENTALS OF MOVEMENT

1. Focus on purpose: Why do we move?

Best learning occurs when the child is working toward a purpose (goal) he has adopted. The effectiveness of his movement depends, in part, on how well he focuses on that purpose. The teacher helps each child to accept increasingly complex goals:

To learn new ways of moving, new skills.
To find out, explore use of equipment and apparatus.
To solve problems, invent movement patterns.
To express feelings, tell a story in movement.
To use movement better in a game or dance.
To grow stronger, more fit.

2. Perception of space: Where do we move?

Very early the child may learn the difference between his own space in the playroom and the common space, where everyone moves freely without interfering with anyone else. He then goes on to other learnings:

Direction: floor patterns in circles, in straight lines, forward, backward, sideways, diagonally; space patterns.

Level: moving high, low, or in between.

Range: making large or small movements, variations.

Game patterns: anticipating movement of opponents and of teammates; throwing ahead of a moving target and intercepting a moving object; picking openings on offense and covering openings on defense.

3. Control of quality of movement: How do we move?

If the child learns to feel and control different elements of movement singly in the beginning and in combinations of increasing complexity later, he will eventually learn and control a variety of skills, and use movement to express ideas. The elements taught are:

Speed: fast or slow, with variations.

Force: strong or light.

Configuration: straight or twisting, curved, devious; out from the center of the body, or in toward the center.

Continuity: smoothly sustained or with sudden breaks and holds.

4. Use of body: With what do we move?

The body's capabilities for movement, joint action, interdependence of parts, elementary application of mechanical principles—this knowledge is of great interest to the child, and may well be taught at different grade levels; in the intermediate grades it may be integrated with appropriate learnings in science.

Parts of the body and how they move: joint action of flexion, extension, and rotation in neck, spine, shoulder girdle, arms, elbows, wrists, hands, trunk, hips, legs, ankles, feet; interdependence of moving parts.

Locomotor movement: walk, run, hop, jump, gallop, skip, slide, leap; combinations and variations.

Nonlocomotor movement: bend, stretch, twist, push, pull, swing, fall; combinations and variations.

Balance: on what parts of the body can balance be maintained; moving from one balanced position to another; moving through space with body weight carried on different parts of body; keeping balance when changing direction at full speed; when playing a ball that is hard to reach.

Posture: balance of effort and relaxation in walking, sitting, standing.

5. Relationship: With whom do we move?

Basic consideration for others is taught in every lesson.

In exploring space: using common space without interfering with others; moving with a partner or group to make a floor pattern; moving with others at different levels.

In controlling quality of movement: moving with partner in matching or contrasting actions; moving with a group in telling a story or expressing an idea.

In self-testing: working together in taking out, putting away and using equipment; doing double or group stunts.

In games: being a useful part of a group, a side, a team; helping to evaluate class progress.

In dance: working well with a partner or a group.

Movement fundamentals and their component parts will be made more specific and more inclusive later in the chapter, when problems are described in detail.

METHOD

As the child applies these fundamentals of movement in other forms of physical education he is using moving exploration as a method of improving a variety of skills. Whether he is successful in this application depends on how his learning is being guided and on what methods of teaching are followed in his class.

First of all, movement exploration should use the problem-solving method. It should follow such basic procedures as: (1) setting the problem; (2) experimentation by the children; (3) observation and evaluation; (4) additional practice using points gained from evaluation. Answers to the problems, of course, are in movements rather than words. The movements will differ as individual children find the answer valid for each. The teacher does not demonstrate, encourage imitation, nor require any one best answer. Thus the children are not afraid to be different, and the teacher feels free to let them progress in their own way, each at his own rate. The result is a class atmosphere in which imagination has free play; invention becomes active and varied.[4] Improvement occurs through observation and evaluation, practiced when rest periods are needed. Evaluation is positive and encouraging rather than negative. If one group is watching another in action, the observers are asked what they liked about what they saw. With guided experience in observation they will watch for quality of movement, body leads, level and direction, or whatever fundamentals are involved in the problem. Of course improvement is helped by the teacher's suggestions: "Can you make a straighter line with your legs and feet?" "Can your arms help your feet to make your skipping light?" Sometimes these suggestions are made to individuals, sometimes to the whole class. Evaluations and suggestions must be brief and to the point, leaving most of the time for vigorous movement.

---

[4]Robert Scofield, "A Creative Climate," *Educational Leadership,* Oct. 1960, p. 5.

Obviously, self-direction is an important characteristic of method in movement exploration, as in other forms of physical education. Even first graders, given to understand that they may practice stunts they like (always using the common space well) as soon as they come into the gymnasium, will start right out with bunny hops, high skipping, cartwheels, and other lively action. Fortunately they *want* to be active, and when they understand that responsible self-direction is the quickest way to get into the things they want to do, they will be motivated to take this responsibility. In many second and third grades, children will sometimes start their individual "work sessions" with only a reminder that they may work at their own problems. These problems are the child's own selection to meet his particular needs for improvement in the skills to be used in the rest of the lesson, be it games, self-testing, movement exploration, or dance. Habits and skills of self-direction should persist as he grows older, and help the individual to watch, analyze, and plan his own learning, both in school and in out-of-school recreation.

12

The Movement Education Approach to Teaching in English Elementary Schools

SHIRLEY HOWARD COOPER

Movement education is a dynamic aspect of the total education program in England. Since its inception some twenty-five years ago, when movement education was first introduced to physical education in the elementary schools, the concept has developed in breadth and depth. The approach is now typical in elementary schools throughout the country. In secondary schools also, applications of the movement concepts have developed in both gymnastics and dance. Professional education programs in colleges are using movement education concepts in developing the personal skills of

A report based on observations of participants in the Second Anglo-American Workshop on Movement Education. From *JOHPER*, January 1967. Reprinted by permission of the author.

prospective teachers. The approach is widely advocated as a basis for instruction in physical education at both the elementary and secondary school levels.

The widespread adoption of the concepts of movement education by British educators is easy to understand when the approach is examined in terms of current educational philosophy. First, the individual development of each student is paramount. Every student has many opportunities to experience satisfaction from successful use of his body. Thus, success contributes to the improved self-confidence of the student, enhances his self-image, and provides the basis for his seeking more challenging tasks. The problem-solving type of approach popular today in curriculum planning for many teaching fields is the basic method used in the English approach to movement education. It requires total involvement of students in their own learning situation. In this approach students structure their own movements, within the restrictions of the problem, in ways which are meaningful to them, which enables each student to develop understanding and appreciation of movement as well as to improve his movement skills. Creativity is encouraged, because there is no single response to the problems.

The English movement education approach is centered around concepts in three areas: the use of the body (what moves), the use of space (where you move), and the quality of the movement (how you move). Themes to develop concepts of body awareness include transfer of weight, reception of weight, and shaping movements by such means as curling, stretching, and twisting. In addition to individual work, body use is developed through partner and group work in problems involving matching movements, contrasting movements, meeting and parting, and passing around, over, and under. Ability to use a variety of directions and levels serves as the core for spatial concepts. The quality of movement is described in terms of three factors: the "strength" of the movement as characterized by strong or light; the "time," characterized by quick, slow, acceleration or deceleration; and "flow," characterized by continuous, broken, successive, or simultaneous movement.

The teacher using the movement approach to physical education presents a problem emphasizing a single concept or, with older students, a combination of concepts. Each student then responds with movements that enable him to improve control of his body while also expanding his understanding of how this concept affects his ability to move. The problem-solving situation enables each student to gain satisfaction from moving within his own capacities.

In elementary schools, as well as in secondary schools and professional preparation programs at the college level, these movement experiences are further developed in relation to apparatus or what the British call modern educational gymnastics. Initially, students are given free choice of how they use the apparatus, both Olympic type and a variety of other interesting pieces. They are encouraged to move continuously, still with free choice of movement. Gradually the students are directed toward supporting and suspending their bodies on different parts of the apparatus and toward developing a variety of ways for mounting, dismounting, and moving on the apparatus. The teacher then further structures problems by specifying the path of the movement, the types of movement, or the quality of movement. This progression is designed to improve body management, confidence, and initiative in movement.

A feature of the excellent gymnastic programs in England is the abundance of apparatus available in even the smallest, most remote schools. In elementary schools apparatus is generally found both indoors and outdoors. Frequently it has been constructed so that it is portable and can easily be moved by smaller children. In harmony with the emphasis of the movement approach on student initiative and problem solving, British gymnasium equipment is highly flexible in arrangement. Students of all ages are able and encouraged to arrange and rearrange the equipment to suit their particular needs. Many pieces of apparatus are installed in the gymnasium on ceiling tracks; climbing ropes and vertical poles are quickly and efficiently moved into use. Other heavy pieces, such as horizontal beams and bar arrangements, are on a pivotal axis with anchor plates on the floor. Portable connecting bars and beams further extend the variety of possible arrangements.

Parallel to modern educational gymnastics, modern educational dance has developed from movement education in the elementary schools and in the girls' programs at the secondary and college levels. As in gymnastics, the emphasis is on freedom of movement as well as on creative and expressive movement response to dance stimuli. Dance themes are developed from music, rhythm instruments, and dramatic content. Variety in movement responses by children appears to be related to the variety of movement experiences which have preceded the introduction of dance. In the elementary schools, classroom activities of art, music, and creative writing are frequently integrated with the dance activities.

The applications of movement education to ball handling and game skills are not as widespread as are the applications to dance and gymnastics. In many elementary schools, educational gymnastics occupies the physical education session two of the five periods a week, while one period is devoted to games, including ball skills; one period is devoted to rhythms; and one is spent on athletics (track and field). Some of the teachers are able to apply the problem-solving approach to the entire curriculum; others use the movement education approach for educational gymnastics but return to traditional teaching methods for the other areas of the curriculum.

In general, the physical education program is enhanced by the large variety and quantity of equipment available for instructional use. Balls of varied size and type, paddles, jump ropes, bean bags, hoops, stilts, and wands provided each student maximal activity during each class period.

In the ball handling lessons observed, the children showed amazing ability both in dodging and in ball control. A representative lesson began with individual practice in tossing and catching, each child with his own ball. The children then threw to moving partners; children and balls were going in all directions, but the children seldom dropped the ball, touched one another, or hit anyone with a ball. The boys then demonstrated many football (soccer) skills which had been developed from such problem-solving tasks as stopping the ball with different parts of the body, putting the ball into the air from the floor without using the hands, passing the ball with the feet, and keeping the ball in the air with different parts of the body. Many of the boys could keep the ball in the air for a great length of time with their heads and showed amazing skill with their feet in all the techniques one would see in a professional game. The girls then demonstrated their skills with the ball. They first worked individually, keeping the ball in the air with their hands without catching and throwing, demonstrating beautiful over-head volleys with very little movement of the feet and excellent extension. They then worked in groups of three volleying the ball back and forth and while moving about the room.

The skill with which the boys and the girls handled the balls was an outgrowth of carefully structured problem-solving experiences and was accomplished without specific instruction as to how to do it. The skills gained are only later put to use in game situations.

Swimming skills are also developed from general movement experiences. Children learn to relax in the water and propel themselves through the water prior to any specific stroke analysis. Shallow, portable swimming pools are a recent addition to many elementary school facilities. Sometimes these pools are small enough to be placed in an empty classroom. In some cases, children change clothes in their classroom and go outdoors to a pool. A classroom teacher, who is interested and skilled in swimming, conducts the teaching for the school. Parent associations often raise the money for construction of the pools; the school systems support the maintenance of the facilities.

Another exciting application of the movement approach was observed in a film of a special school for severely physically handicapped children. The program utilized a positive approach, emphasizing the development of physical skills in spite of the varying restrictions of each student's physical capacities. A teen-age boy, with limited use of his legs, moved with ease when walking on his hands. Generally, the students used apparatus and executed skills far beyond our expectations.

In considering the values of movement education in England, there was much agreement among the participants in the workshop. Generally, a high proficiency in body management skills was observed along with a freedom of movement. Students exhibited considerable interest and involvement in their movement experiences. Each student had many opportunities to experience success in movement because of the individualized nature of the instructional process. Physical fitness was highly developed and a natural outcome of the continuous movement and vigorous action inherent in this approach to teaching. The extent to which potential values were realized, of course, varied with individual teachers. Discipline problems were not seen; because children were so interested and so deeply involved and because they had the opportunity to perform at their own level, there was no question of maintaining discipline.

The movement education approach in England is fully supported by the school systems through the provision of a daily instructional program and an abundance of apparatus and small equipment. Supervisory assistance is available on request, and in-service workshop opportunities are provided by the school systems.

Selected reactions of the participants summarize the observations made in England and reveal their stimulating effect on the American delegation.

"The student learns to respect his own abilities as well as the abilities of others."

"The movement approach seemed to draw out the shy, self-conscious child and lead him to other experiences."

"Children are not afraid to express their emotions."

"Continuous activity was emphasized throughout the lessons."

"All the children felt success in what they were doing."

"The major contribution to learning is that movement education tends to develop a positive self-concept."

"The sense of adventure, daring, creativity, and ability to handle themselves on large apparatus impressed me as I watched the five- to seven-year-olds."

13

Toward an Understanding of Basic Movement Education in the Elementary Schools

ELIZABETH A. LUDWIG

Many early efforts to stimulate and support a "foundations" approach to content in physical education are only now taking a firm hold in the elementary school programs. Confusion still exists at this time in this country as to the meaning and status of "basic movement education," "movement fundamentals in physical education," "movement exploration," and other terms used to designate a specific program or content in physical education. In historical perspective neither the confusion nor the experimentation with the program content is new.

A review of changes related to philosophy and programs in physical education in the United States since the first quarter of the century reflects shifting emphases from rigidly structured programs of gymnastics, calisthenics, folk dance, and simple games stressing physical fitness to carry-over activities that develop recreational and social values through participation. With the changes in general educational philosophy that occurred since the era of Dewey, a number of forward-looking leaders in physical education were re-thinking the philosophy of physical education slowly but surely as early as the 1920's. Pioneers such as Thomas D. Wood, Jesse F. Williams, Rosalind Cassidy, and Dorothy LaSalle were pointing to "new directions in physical education." Clue words such as "child-centered," "the whole child," "opportunities for creative expression," and "skill learning" appeared in the professional literature in physical education in the 1920's and 1930's.

From *JOHPER*, March 1968. Reprinted by permission of the author.

From the early 1930's on a number of movements or changing directions were taking form although their relevance to contemporary changes are only now becoming evident. Margaret H'Doubler proposed new concepts in educational dance and applied her theories to basic movement education as the foundation for all physical education. Women's physical education staffs in a number of universities and colleges introduced courses in "movement fundamentals." More functional approaches to the study of kinesiology and biomechanics and research in motor learning were begun at the universities of Wisconsin, California, Iowa, Illinois, Nebraska, and others. The fields of physical therapy, mental health, and recreation contributed to an understanding of the importance of motor skill development in the healthy and well-adjusted individual. Research findings from many areas of the child growth and development field affirmed the developmental needs of the child and the wholeness or integrity of the individual; studies in learning, motivation, and other aspects of educational psychology suggested more effective teaching procedures. The growing responsibility of the school in meeting the child's basic needs in the area of motor skill development as well as in the more academically-oriented areas was recognized.

During this time the leaders in physical education who were vitally concerned with the content of the elementary school physical education program as well as the improvement of teaching on this level included Gladys Andrews, Delia Hussey, Edwina Jones, Dorothy LaSalle, Ruth Murray, Elsa Schneider, and others.[1] It is important to mention this vanguard of leaders because the present effort to improve the elementary school physical education program has, in turn, been stimulated by individuals who were influenced by the efforts of these early leaders.

After World War II there was a great deal of travel between this country and England, Germany, Scandinavia, and other European countries. Ideas were exchanged, and a fresh look was taken at developments at home and abroad. Changes were occurring all over the world, and in England there developed a different approach to basic movement education in elementary schools. English teachers were seeking answers to the same problems that had interested teachers in the United States for many years. Leadership in England was centered in the Ministry of Education under the influence of such persons as Ruth Foster, Peter Stone, and Diana Jordan. They found support in Rudolph Laban, an Austrian dancer

---

[1] The writer recognizes that our indebtedness extends to many other men and women who have exerted leadership both on the local and national levels. This list is not meant to be inclusive.

who came to England during the war and introduced his theory of movement principles. Two Anglo-American workshops and a number of visits helped develop a strong rapport and unity of spirit among English educators and their American counterparts. Some of the materials and procedures developed in England were instituted in this country by those who participated in the workshops and study trips.

Certain periods in history seem right for the flowering of ideas which may have been generating for a long time. During the past ten years there has been a concerted rush for better programs of physical education in the elementary schools—better teaching procedures, better facilities, and better prepared teachers. During this decade there has also been a renewed effort to include in the elementary school program a greater emphasis on basic movement experiences as the foundation for all physical education, particularly in the primary grades.

SUPPORT FROM OTHER AREAS OF RESEARCH

A related emphasis in American education that has given support and impetus to these efforts is the interest in creativity in teaching and the recognition of the importance of developing and encouraging the creative learner. A great deal of research has been undertaken in this area in an effort to identify the factors that are important in producing both the creative teacher and the creative learner. Providing the opportunity for the learner to solve his own problems or to discover unique solutions to problems in which he is given certain basic conditions and factors to work with is considered necessary in "best learning." This ability is one of the characteristics of the creative thinker and performer. Experimentation with approaches to teaching consistent with the newer theories of education that stress problem solving and discovery on the part of the child has been a part of the attempt to develop the total basic movement education approach. The importance of discovering common elements in fundamental motor skills and of analyzing activities for their use in basic movement patterns also has been recognized as essential. Accelerated research in kinesiology, motor learning, teaching theory, and other related fields has given support to interest in developing programs that include more than the traditionally structured games, dances, and gymnastics of the typical elementary school program.

The following brief summary of "where we are" at this time in the development of basic movement education programs is made with full recognition of the fact that there are no two programs exactly alike, nor should there be, if the tradition of the American educational philosophy is to be maintained. Generally speaking, however, certain elements of philosophy are recognized and certain common content and teaching procedures are used.

It is generally agreed that basic movement education is the foundation upon which all the activity areas of physical education are built. It is also agreed that the aim of basic movement education is to help children become aware of their own potentials for moving effectively in all aspects of living, including motor tasks involved in daily activities for work or recreation. Fundamentals of movement are explored and built upon so that a child develops an awareness of each part of the body as it moves through space, with variations in time and force. A child learns to use his body with power and economy of movement; he experiences in a wide variety of ways the degree of effort required for easy, fluent, and efficient performance of the particular movement task he has undertaken. He solves problems dealing with gravity, direction, and controlling objects such as balls as conscious experiences. Efficient and effective movement results within the innate capacity of each child.

Some children will learn to perform better than others because they have inherited this kind of facility. Some individuals will become more highly skilled than others because they work harder and/or have the desire to perform well. Each individual is limited, however, only by his inherited potential.

EXPERIENCES IN BOTH BREADTH AND DEPTH

The *content* of the program consists of all those experiences that will assist the child to develop skill in using his body—stretching, twisting, rolling, jumping, hanging, running, walking, hopping, sliding, pushing, pulling, throwing, catching, striking, and the many combinations of these movements that are within the capability of the human structure. It is not possible here to categorize these movements or to discuss those which are basic and which are combined movements. Movement patterns are developed in anticipation of later use in games, skills, dance, gymnastics, and other activities. The content is not chosen randomly; it has a purpose and is planned but it is not necessarily specific to a particular game or other structured activity. The child experiments with many variations of movement or skill so that his experiences are in breadth as well as depth.

The content of a particular lesson may deal with problems that emphasize the concept of space and the body's relationship to space or may place emphasis on the factors of time and force. Because these are interrelated, all are always considered, but one may be stressed for a particular reason. Obstacles or restricting equipment may be used to give the child experience in handling his body within certain limitations. The use of restricting equipment is fundamental to providing for the many experiences needed as a basis for developing games and gymnastics skills. Balls, paddles, ropes, hoops, bean bags, and stilts and climbing, hanging, jumping, and vaulting equipment may be used. When emphasis is placed on developing an understanding of the quality of movement, the effect of rhythm and timing, tone and design, a foundation for the more structured aspects of dance, is fostered. Emphasis on timing and rhythm also aids in the highly developed skills of the expert gymnast and diver.

The *process* or the teaching procedure used is a direct outcome of the content in that the movement experiences are those of the child and he must learn for himself what his body can do. Problem solving is involved, the problem of learning to handle the body. Sometimes the problem proposed by the teacher involves pure exploration by the child. Then the solution will be largely discovery. Some problems may be restricted in order to elicit specific responses. The teacher uses the particular technique suited to the needs of the child and the task. Basically, problem solving and the move toward discovery are intimately related to the content.

An aspect of both content and method that is stressed is teaching the "why" and "how." Principles of movement mechanics, rhythm, and timing plus other knowledges and understandings are taught. This procedure is not unique to basic movement education but the fundamental purposes of this method are consistent with and require the total involvement of the child—both intellectually and physically. The challenge of this kind of involvement gives the physical education experience an exciting dimension that tests children of every range of ability and gives purpose and meaning to the program.

The values that are evident to those who have been working with children using basic movement education as a medium of instruction may be summarized as a conclusion to understanding basic movement education in the elementary schools.

1. Success is within the reach of every child because the goals are personal. Quality performance (at different levels) is stressed, expected, and usually obtained from the children.

2. Self-discipline and self-direction are expected results. The child must make decisions constantly and he is held reponsible for them.

3. The situation provides a laboratory for freedom to create, to express, and to try out one's own solutions without fear of being a loser or a "dub."

4. When game elements are added, an "it" or a "goal," the child is ready for the challenge because he has attained a comfortable degree of skill.

5. Although children are quite serious and totally involved in the teaching-learning situation, satisfaction and fun result. This is movement with a purpose and is so recognized by the child; it is exciting to him, as skills develop and success is experienced.

14

Learning about Movement
NAOMI ALLENBAUGH

Through the decades, elementary physical education has progressed through three major stages, the major emphasis of these stages being participation, socialization, and physical fitness. A rapidly developing fourth stage, one of greater sophistication, combines these three earlier stages and adds an emphasis on understanding the environment, movement, and man. It focuses on education for efficiency of movement and for self-discovery, self-direction, and self-realization while incorporating from the earlier emphases such specifics as understanding of and improvement in fundamental and specialized motor skills.

The great increase in knowledge has brought sharply into focus the need for each child to have a broad understanding of many areas and how they relate to each other. Physical education, like every other discipline, can be organized so each child can gradually develop the main ideas of the discipline through the accumulation, comprehension, and synthesis of the related subject matter. Let us examine three of many broad concepts around which it can be organized: Man moves to survive; man moves to discover and understand his environment; man moves to control and adjust to his environment.

The first concept, *man moves to survive,* recognizes the anatomical and physiological nature of man and his need to acquire physiological understanding and readiness for efficient movement. The individual must develop, maintain, and value muscular strength, endurance, flexibility,

From *The NEA Journal,* March 1967. Reprinted by permission.

agility, and balance if he is to survive without unusual dependency on others.

Young children force parents and nursery school teachers to recognize the second concept—*man moves to discover and understand his environment.* Yet when the elementary school child enters the gymnasium to participate in physical education, his drive to examine and explore is frequently destroyed or destructively limited rather than released, encouraged, and guided. As a child comes to understand his environment and use it successfully in movement, he acquires a more realistic body image and a more wholesome self-concept. With the resulting sense of power, he can then accept the task of developing his individual potential rather than wastefully trying to imitate other people.

As the understanding of self and environment evolves, the third concept—*man moves to control and adjust to his environment*—takes on deeper meaning for the individual. He begins to recognize that control of and adjustment to the environment are dependent upon efficiency of movement. Thus he begins to work for the advantageous use of the elements of movement—space, time, force, and flow.

For example, he works to develop the ability to apply appropriate force in his movements in relation to the space and time available to him. He works to develop a smoothness, a flow, a unity of all parts of the body involved in movement. He acquires the ability to understand his movement and he learns ways of improving it.

This ability involves the development of a comprehension of the mechanics of motion. His movement leads him to ask:

What is the center of gravity in my body? How does it influence equilibrium? How do I use my body to maintain balance?

How can my arms, my legs, my whole body serve as levers to increase the force and speed with which I move?

To gain an understanding of the principles of movement, he begins to ask: How can I distribute my weight to gain accuracy, force, and speed, yet maintain my balance? Why does continuing movement in the direction of projected or received force increase my efficiency? Why is my whole body involved in effective movement?

In seeking and finding the answers to these questions, he increases the vocabulary from which he can select the movements most effective in meeting specific demands of the moment. In order to choose which movements are appropriate for various activities, he must develop an understanding of efficient performance of locomotor skills (how to walk, run, hop, leap, slide, skip, and perform combinations of these), nonlocomotor skills (turn, twist, stretch, bend, and swing), and manipulative skills (throw, hit, and catch).

Finally he becomes proficient in the *instant organization* of any combination of these skills demanded for an efficient response to a given situation. He uses his movement vocabulary purposefully.

What experiences can the teacher provide to help the child grasp the meaning of the movement concepts just discussed, to develop movement proficiency, and to become a self-accepting, productive individual?

One answer is to have all children working independently but simultaneously to discover the many different ways in which each child can move *within, through,* and *with* his environment and to establish the requisites for effective movement. The teacher can base problems on the elements of movement (space, time, force, and flow) and their various dimensions so the child moves alone or with others or he moves upon, through, around, and with moving or stationary objects.

In solving these problems, the child uses many fundamental motor skills. Sometimes, at a very young age, he will discover and use combinations of movements which in reality are specialized motor skills normally used in the complex organization of a dance, a sport, or a game. The important factor in the use of problems is the emphasis on body movement as it relates to space, time, force, and flow.

Elements and Dimensions of Movement

Space	*Levels:* high, medium, low.
	Ranges: wide-narrow, far-near.
	Directions: forward-backward, upward-downward, sideward, circle, diagonal.
	Shapes: round, straight, angular, twisted.
Force	Heavy-light, strong-weak, tight-loose.
Time	Slow, medium, fast.
Flow	Free, bound, sequential.

Body Focus

Body relationships	Head or feet above, level with, or below torso, and combinations.
Body leads	Shoulder, hip, head, knee, foot, etc., combinations.
Body supports	Feet, knees, hands, back, shoulders, head etc., combinations.
Body control	Starts-stops.

The direct teaching of an exact skill may follow these earlier experiences or the problems may be deliberately designed so the exact skill will gradually emerge. Such movement experience allows each child to progress at his own rate and to feel comfortable with the way he moves rather than to be blocked in his initial learning by the necessity to move exactly as the teacher says he must.

Some specific examples of problems developed around the elements and dimensions of space will serve to illustrate the above ideas:

In what different directions can you move (forward, backward, and the like)?

At how many different levels (high, low, medium) can you move: through space, in your own space, in space with an object, through space with an object, with a partner through space, with a partner in your own small space, sending an object through space to a partner, moving yourself through space as you send an object through space to a partner?

How many different ways can you change the width and length of your body (wide to narrow, long to short, and the like)?

What different shapes can you make with your body (round, straight, angular, curled, twisted)?

Problems using the elements of force and time can be developed in a similar manner. Following these experiences, the children can deal with increasingly complex problems, such as combinations of dimensions within an element (high, backward, wide), combinations of dimensions selected from the different elements (high, forward, fast; high, forward, slow; high, backward, fast; high, backward, slow).

In experimenting with such problems, the child experiences contrasts in dimensions and discovers the ease or difficulty of movement inherent in certain combinations. Throughout these experiences the teacher can raise questions to direct pupils' attention to *what* they are doing, *why* some combinations of movements are more difficult than others, *what* is valuable in the movements, and *how* pupils can become more proficient.

Such movement experiences, which lead into fundamental motor skills and then into specialized motor skills, should lead the student to value the concepts of survival, of discovery and control of the environment, and of self.

15

Concepts and Issues Within the Theories

ROBERT T. SWEENEY

A theory established by consensus rather than developed as an individual or small-group project has, if nothing else, more advocates. The various theories of movement education presented in this section consider similar if not the same concepts within their framework, but, depending on the theory discussed, the consideration given to the concepts may range from maximum to minimum. Some theories are indeed built upon concepts that others find completely irrelevant.

The purpose of this article is to emphasize the main concepts found in the theories set forth in the preceding articles. Fully realizing that this article is unlike all the others—having been written after rather than before compilation—I would like to state that it represents my viewpoint concerning the concepts that *should* be included in a movement theory.

As a starting point I propose that we place each concept by itself on a continuum from maximum to minimum. Each separate concept does or does not function according to the theorist's view of its degree of importance within his theory. This can be represented as

Play concept

Maximum importance ⸻⸻⸻⸻⸻⸻⸻⸻⸻⸻ Minimum importance

The importance of any concept may also vary with other variables within any theory, such as student characteristics, subject matter covered, time allotted, etc.

Controversial issues can and do exist between the theories. Where they exist, the reader should seek his own answers by investigation.

The concepts to be investigated fall into three areas: the learner, the content, and the learning process. While separation is necessary for descriptive purposes in writing, we must consider the interrelatedness of the three areas in practice.

In the study of the learner, concepts of growth and development are most prevalent. They are integrated development, the interaction theory, individual differences, critical stages of development, and the physical attributes of the various behavioral abilities of perceptual-motor skills, physical fitness, motor fitness, motor ability, movement patterns, and motor skills.

The interaction theorists [6] in the study of growth and development—the middle-of-the-road group between the extremes, environmentalists and hereditarians—believe that growth (heredity) and development (environment) serve and complement each other through their interaction. Each affects the other, depending on the circumstances. The idea of complementation is also prevalent in the integrated-development concept, [4] which concerns the integration of physical, emotional, social, and intellectual characteristics within the individual. Each serves and complements the other rather than being a totally separate side of the same person. The individual-differences concept [1, 3] incorporates and itemizes the specifics of the integrated-development concept. Each individual is integrated with more or less of each existing variable than are other individuals. The concept of critical stages, or periods, of development [5] is caught up somewhere in the maturation-readiness concept that we all discuss with tongue in cheek. The interaction theorists are somewhat responsible for the current ambivalence about the concept that there is a best time for learning certain behaviors and that not learning them at the appropriate time prevents the learner from ever achieving their optimum potential. These four concepts of growth and development are very broad and diverse. Readers should investigate them to gain more complete understanding.

The remaining concepts relevant to growth and development—perceptual-motor skills, physical fitness, motor fitness, motor ability, movement patterns, and motor skills—may be better understood in the form of a diagramed, hierarchical model (Fig. 1), which should be read from bottom to top to stress the foundational aspect of the concepts. Each grouping of abilities may possibly reach a higher level of development if the underlying abilities are more fully developed. A reversal of the developmental process may suffice to guide necessary remedial work. The exact cause-effect relationship has not been established between the components as such. (Figure 1 is an extension of Clarke's Chart of Physical Elements. [2] Additions include the perceptual-motor abilities, eye-body coordination, and rhythm. Additional research is recommended to the reader who wishes to document the chart more fully.)

The constructs of perceptual-motor skills, physical fitness, motor fitness, and motor ability are developed in and interpreted through movement, as indicated on the chart. Movement patterns and motor skills, the two remaining areas of growth-and-development concepts, are the basic

CHART I

Opportunities to use movement in society

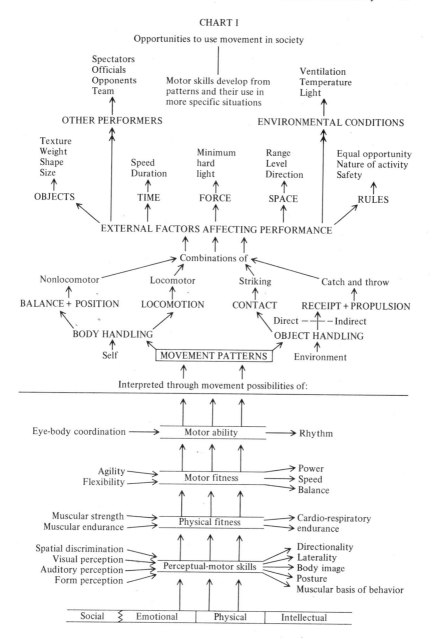

Fig. 1 Concepts of movement education. (Read from bottom up.)

groupings of movement. Not to be confused with dance terminology, *pattern* as used in the growth-and-development concept refers to a general type of movement, with or without continuous repetition. It is unlike pattern in dance, which refers to a floor plan or path of movement execution. Patterns may be accumulated into *sequences.* Motor skills differ from patterns in that they are more specific to a purpose, e.g., throwing a horseshoe versus just throwing underhanded.

The content organization within movement education can be termed the curriculum, and the concepts to be considered are the subject matter, its arrangement, its purposes, and the relationship of the student to it.

It is sometimes suggested that the process or method involved in learning content should itself be considered the content. This approach is supported by the "learning to learn" or "learning to move, moving to learn" slogan attached to movement education. Such a slogan emphasizes the child-centered, cognitive involvement of movement education. The analysis of movement, in which the student utilizes the effective factors of movement, constitutes a major portion of the subject matter. The concept is that of student conceptualization and verbalization, and it ranges from complete analysis combined with physical performance to just one or the other. The issue of cognitive processes and their development surrounds the use of the effective factors as content. Is teaching for thinking possible?

The developmental-movement concept supports the position that content can be separated from the process involved in teaching, that there is something intrinsic within content that makes it separate. Content is the activity in a continuous arrangement from simple to complex, based on a degree-of-difficulty continuum. While developmental movement deals specifically with fitness components, the ratings of degree of difficulty can be applied to any movement. A systematic analysis of movement can be achieved by utilizing the factors that affect movement: space, time, force, and the external variables. Those factors can establish a degree-of-difficulty ranking for all activities. The student-centered approach in movement education applies also in developmental movement; each student is placed on the degree-of-difficulty continuum where his abilities dictate. Thus the student is working on his movement needs in that particular activity.

The arrangement of subject matter can be structured or unstructured, teacher-directed or student-directed. A continuum for each is possible, with the teacher on one end and the student on the other. The main criterion for the use of each depends on the purpose for its use, such as the ability to control body movements, physical fitness, or sport. With sport comes another intrinsic concept, competition. Do we use sports activities as the media through which we accomplish our purposes, or is sport itself a major purpose for having body control? It seems illogical that we might want to eliminate sport and competition from our program. It seems less so that we might attempt to control them as a major influence in our society.

The concept of play, which can be placed on the student-teacher continuum, requires a great deal of consideration within our thinking about movement education.

It would be inappropriate not to mention the content factors of equipment, safety, and facilities. When we consistently ask for cognitive involvement on the part of the student, we must not overlook the fact that the limitations of facilities and equipment, the expectations with regard to their use, and the safety involved become necessary segments of student content.

The learning process constitutes the third area of concept groupings. The concepts of philosophy, goals, teaching behaviors, and learning behaviors belong in this category, which need not be discussed because a full section is devoted to that purpose. The main concepts are those of creativity, exploration, problem solving, discovery, and the behaviors of the teacher.

Involvement, or participation, which is a major concept within movement education, is the result of the organization of the learning process. The maximum-participation concept has ramifications for content also. We may actually have maximum involvement in vicarious activities, but we may nonetheless not be providing the best possible learning climate. Ball-handling activities in which every student has his own ball allow for direct contact or practice for all in the activity being taught. A ball-bouncing relay in which four or more persons share a ball not only provides less direct practice but has additional elements that may not result in the most efficient learning. Compare such a relay with a writing exercise in which four or more students use one pencil and one sheet of paper to learn to write. It is inefficient. If we plan the learning experience to allow for maximum direct contact of the student with the activity, we have greater possibilities of attaining our student goals.

Evaluation as a concept is important in any educational venture, but it is especially important in a child-centered program. It is the thread of consistency that enables us to maintain, correct, or change our program. We hope that through constant evaluation movement education will mesh into a functioning program that will enable us to meet our movement objectives.

BIBLIOGRAPHY

1. H. Harrison Clark. *Nature and Extent of Individual Differences and Their Significance for Physical Education and Athletics.* Eugene, Ore.: Oregon School Study Council, University of Oregon, 1967.

2. H. Harrison Clarke. *Application of Measurement to Health and Physical Education.* Englewood Cliffs, N.J.: Prentice-Hall, 1967, p. 202.

3. Robert M. Gagné. *Learning and Individual Differences.* Columbus, O.: Merrill, 1967.

4. Indiana AAHPER, *et al. Report of a Symposium on Integrated Development.* Indiana AAHPER, 1964.

5. Henry W. Maier. *Three Theories of Child Development* New York: Harper and Row, 1965.

6. Celia Burns Stendler. *Readings in Child Behavior and Development.* New York: Harcourt, Brace and World, 1964.

Section 2

Teacher and Methods

The topics of methods and the teacher are considered jointly because of their unique relationship. The teacher and the decisions he makes concerning teaching are the main bridge between the students and their projected behaviors based on their interactions with the class content.

In the age of new terminology and advances in teaching behavior, we have to contend with change before we are secure in what we are doing. New teaching strategies, learning sets, behavioral objectives, teaching hardware, programming, and many others—all highlight the need for deep thought, concern, and action to offer direction to teachers. Physical education researchers have not been so actively involved in attempting to understand the consequences of our teaching practices as have other researchers. Physical educators have to begin asking themselves many questions regarding their teaching methods and their personal teaching behavior in the teaching-learning situation.

All the material provided here focuses on the teacher, though Hamachek's article does so most specifically. The remainder display our need to understand the conceptual structure of the intentions of the method used, as well as provide some "cookbook" examples to illustrate uses of the methods. Understanding is basic to further application, analysis, and evaluation of the teaching behavior utilized in movement education.

Although the process through which the child progresses may teach him something, we should not divorce the process of movement education from the content, the student, or the teacher. The relationship of each to the other should be of paramount concern to us. A more unified construct of student-content-method-teacher should produce the type of individual toward which that construct is directed.

1

Characteristics of Good Teachers and Implications for Teacher Education

DON HAMACHEK

It is, I think, a sad commentary about our educational system that it keeps announcing both publicly and privately that "good" and "poor" teachers cannot be distinguished one from the other. Probably no issue in education has been so voluminously researched as has teacher effectiveness and considerations which enhance or restrict this effectiveness. Nonetheless, we still read that we cannot tell the good guys from the bad guys. For example, Biddle and Ellena[2] in their book, *Contemporary Research on Teacher Effectiveness,* begin by stating that "the problem of teacher effectiveness is so complex that no one today knows what *The Competent Teacher* is." I think we *do* know what the competent—or effective, or good, or whatever you care to call him—teacher is, and in the remainder of this paper I will be as specific as possible in citing *why* I think we know along with implications for our teacher-education programs.

WHAT THE RESEARCH SAYS

By and large, most research efforts aimed at investigating teacher effectiveness have attempted to probe one or more of the following dimensions of teacher personality and behavior: 1) personal characteristics, 2) instructional procedures and interaction styles, 3) perceptions of self, 4) perceptions of others. Because of space limits this is by no means an exhaustive review of the research related to the problem, but it is, I think, representative of the kind and variety of research findings linked to questions of teacher effectiveness.

Personal Characteristics of Good Versus Poor Teachers

We would probably agree that it is quite possible to have two teachers of equal intelligence, training, and grasp of subject matter who nevertheless differ considerably in the results they achieve with students. Part of the

From *Phi Delta Kappan,* February 1969. Reprinted by permission of publisher and author.

difference can be accounted for by the effect of a teacher's personality on the learners. What kinds of personality do students respond to?

Hart[7] conducted a study based upon the opinions of 3,725 high school seniors concerning best-liked and least-liked teachers and found a total of 43 different reasons for "liking Teacher A best" and 30 different reasons for "liking Teacher Z least." Not surprisingly, over 51 percent of the students said that they liked best those teachers who were "helpful in school work, who explained lessons and assignments clearly, and who used examples in teaching." Also, better than 40 percent responded favorably to teachers with a "sense of humor." Those teachers assessed most negatively were "unable to explain clearly, were partial to brighter students, and had superior, aloof, overbearing attitudes." In addition, over 50 percent of the respondents mentioned behaviors such as "too cross, crabby, grouchy, and sarcastic" as reasons for disliking many teachers. Interestingly enough, mastery of subject matter, which is vital but badly overemphasized by specialists, ranked sixteenth on both lists. Somehow students seem willing to take more or less for granted that a teacher "knows" his material. What seems to make a difference is the teacher's personal style in *communicating* what he knows. Studies by Witty[14] and Bousfield[3] tend to support these conclusions at both the high school *and* college level.

Having desirable personal qualities is one thing, but what are the results of rigorous tests of whether the teacher's having them makes any difference in the performance of students?

Cogan[4] found that warm, considerate teachers got an unusual amount of original poetry and art from their high school students. Reed[10] found that teachers higher in a capacity for warmth favorably affected their pupils' interests in science. Using scores from achievement tests as their criterion measure, Heil, Powell, and Fiefer[8] compared various teacher-pupil personality combinations and found that the well-integrated (healthy, well-rounded, flexible) teachers were most effective with *all* types of students. Spaulding[12] found that the self-concepts of elementary school children were apt to be higher and more positive in classrooms in which the teacher was "socially integrative" and "learner supportive."

In essence, I think the evidence is quite clear when it comes to sorting out good or effective from bad or ineffective teachers on the basis of personal characteristics. Effective teachers appear to be those who are, shall we say, "human" in the fullest sense of the word. They have a sense of humor, are fair, empathetic, more democratic than autocratic, and apparently are more able to relate easily and naturally to students on either a one-to-one or group basis. Their classrooms seem to reflect miniature enterprise operations in the sense that they are more open, spontaneous, and adaptable to change. Ineffective teachers apparently lack a sense of humor, grow impatient easily, use cutting, ego-reducing comments in class, are less well-integrated, are inclined to be somewhat authoritarian, and are generally less sensitive to the needs of their students. Indeed, research related to authoritarianism suggests that the bureaucratic conduct and rigid overtones of the ineffective teacher's classroom are desperate measures to support the weak pillars of his own personality structure.

Instructional Procedures and Interaction Styles of Good Versus Poor Teachers

If there really are polar extremes such as "good" or "poor" teachers, then we can reasonably assume that these teachers differ not only in personal characteristics but in the way they conduct themselves in the classroom.

Flanders[6] found that classrooms in which achievement and attitudes were superior were likely to be conducted by teachers who did not blindly pursue a single behavioral-instructional path to the exclusion of other possibilities. In other words, the more successful teachers were better able to range along a continuum of interaction styles which varied from fairly active, dominative support on the one hand to a more reflective, discriminating support on the other. Interestingly, those teachers who were *not* successful were the very ones who were inclined to use the same interaction styles in a more or less rigid fashion.

Barr[1] discovered that not only did poor teachers make more assignments than good teachers but, almost without exception, they made some sort of textbook assignment as part of their unyielding daily procedure. The majority of good teachers used more outside books and problem-project assignments. When the text was assigned they were more likely to supplement it with topics, questions, or other references.

Research findings related to interaction styles variously called "learner-centered" or "teacher-centered" point to similar conclusions. In general, it appears that the amount of cognitive gain is largely unaffected by the autocratic or democratic tendencies of the instructor. However, when affective gains are considered, the results are somewhat different. For example, Stern[13] reviewed 34 studies comparing nondirective with directive instruction and concluded:

Regardless of whether the investigator was concerned with attitudes toward the cultural out group, toward other participants in the class, or toward the self, the results generally have indicated that nondirective instruction facilitates a shift in a more favorable, acceptant direction.

When it comes to classroom behavior, interaction patterns, and teaching styles, good or effective teachers seem to reflect more of the following behaviors:

1. Willingness to be flexible, to be direct or indirect as the situation demands

2. Ability to perceive the world from the student's point of view

3. Ability to "personalize" their teaching

4. Willingness to experiment, to try out new things

5. Skill in asking questions (as opposed to seeing self as a kind of answering service)

6. Knowledge of subject matter and related areas

7. Provision of well-established examination procedures

8. Provision of definite study helps

9. Reflection of an appreciative attitude (evidenced by nods, comments, smiles, etc.)

10. Use of conversational manner in teaching—informal, easy style

Self-Perceptions of Good Versus Poor Teachers

We probably do not have to go any further than our own personal life experiences to know that the way we see, regard, and feel about ourselves has an enormous impact on both our private and public lives. How about good and poor teachers? How do they see themselves?

Ryans[11] found that there are, indeed, differences between the self-related reports of teachers with high emotional stability and those with low emotional stability. For example, the more emotionally stable teachers 1) more frequently named self-confidence and cheerfulness as dominant traits in themselves, 2) said they liked active contact with other people, 3) expressed interests in hobbies and handicrafts, 4) reported their childhoods to be happy experiences.

On the other hand, teachers with lower emotional maturity scores 1) had unhappy memories of childhood, 2) seemed *not* to prefer contact with others, 3) were more directive and authoritarian, 4) expressed less self-confidence.

We can be even more specific. Combs,[5] in his book *The Professional Education of Teachers,* cites several studies which reached similar conclusions about the way good teachers typically see themselves, as follows:

1. Good teachers see themselves as identified with people rather than withdrawn, removed, apart from, or alienated from others.
2. Good teachers feel basically adequate rather than inadequate. They do not see themselves as generally unable to cope with problems.
3. Good teachers feel trustworthy rather than untrustworthy. They see themselves as reliable, dependable individuals with the potential for coping with events as they happen.
4. Good teachers see themselves as wanted rather than unwanted. They see themselves as likable and attractive (in a personal, not a physical sense) as opposed to feeling ignored and rejected.
5. Good teachers see themselves as worthy rather than unworthy. They see themselves as people of consequence, dignity, and integrity as opposed to feeling they matter little, can be overlooked and discounted.

In the broadest sense of the word, good teachers are more likely to see themselves as good people. Their self-perceptions are, for the most part, positive, tinged with an air of optimism and colored with tones of healthy self-acceptance. I dare say that self-perceptions of good teachers are not unlike the self-perceptions of any basically healthy person, whether he be a good bricklayer, a good manager, a good doctor, a good lawyer, a good experimental psychologist, or you name it. Clinical evidence has told us time and again that *any* person is more apt to be happier, more productive, and more effective when he is able to see himself as fundamentally and basically "enough."

Perceptions of Others by Good Versus Poor Teachers

Research is showing us that not only do good and poor teachers view themselves differently, there are also some characteristic differences in the way they perceive others. For example, Ryans[11] reported several studies which have produced findings that are in agreement when it comes to sorting out the differences between how good and poor teachers view others. He found, among other things, that outstandingly "good" teachers rated significantly higher than notably "poor" teachers in at least five different ways with respect to how they viewed others. The good teachers had 1) more favorable opinions of students, 2) more favorable opinions of democratic classroom behavior, 3) more favorable opinions of administrators and colleagues, 4) a greater expressed liking for personal contacts with other people, 5) more favorable estimates of other people generally.

That is, they expressed belief that very few students are difficult behavior problems, that very few people are influenced in their opinions and attitudes toward others by feelings of jealousy, and that most teachers are willing to assume their full share of extra duties outside of school.

Interestingly, the characteristics that distinguished the "lowly assessed" teacher group suggested that the relatively "ineffective" teacher is self-centered, anxious, and restricted. One is left with the distinct impression that poor or ineffective teachers have more than the usual number of paranoid defenses.

It comes as no surprise that how we perceive others is highly dependent on how we perceive ourselves. If a potential teacher (or anyone else for that matter) likes himself, trusts himself, and has confidence in himself, he is likely to see others in somewhat this same light. Research is beginning to tell us what common sense has always told us; namely, people grow, flourish, and develop much more easily when in relationship with someone who projects an inherent trust and belief in their capacity to become what they have the potential to become.

It seems to me that we can sketch at least five interrelated generalizations from what research is telling us about how good teachers differ from poor teachers when it comes to how they perceive others:

1. They seem to have generally more positive views of others—students, colleagues, and administrators.

2. They do not seem to be as prone to view others as critical, attacking people with ulterior motives; rather they are seen as potentially friendly and worthy in their own right.

3. They have a more favorable view of democratic classroom procedures.

4. They seem to have the ability and capacity to see things as they seem to others—i.e., the ability to see things from the other person's point of view.

5. They do not seem to see students as persons "you do things to" but rather as individuals capable of doing for themselves once they feel trusted, respected, and valued.

WHO, THEN, IS A GOOD TEACHER?

1. A good teacher is a good person. Simple and true. A good teacher rather likes life, is reasonably at peace with himself, has a sense of humor, and enjoys other people. If I interpret the research correctly, what it says

is that there is no one best better-than-all-others type of teacher. Nonetheless there are clearly distinguishable "good" and "poor" teachers. Among other things, a good teacher is good because he does not seem to be dominated by a narcissistic self which demands a spotlight, or a neurotic need for power and authority, or a host of anxieties and tremblings which reduce him from the master of his class to its mechanic.

2. The good teacher is flexible. By far the single most repeated adjective used to describe good teachers is "flexibility." Either implicitly or explicitly (most often the latter), this characteristic emerges time and again over all others when good teaching is discussed in the research. In other words, the good teacher does not seem to be overwhelmed by a single point of view or approach to the point of intellectual myopia. A good teacher knows that he cannot be just one sort of person and use just one kind of approach if he intends to meet the multiple needs of his students. Good teachers are, in a sense, "total" teachers. That is, they seem able to be what they have to be to meet the demands of the moment. They seem able to move with the shifting tides of their own needs, the student's and do what has to be done to handle the situation. A total teacher can be firm when necessary (say "no" and mean it) or permissive (say "why not try it your way?" and mean that, too) when appropriate. It depends on many things, and good teachers seem to know the difference.

THE NEED FOR "TOTAL" TEACHERS

There probably is not an educational psychology course taught which does not, in some way, deal with the highly complex area of individual differences. Even the most unsophisticated undergraduate is aware that people differ in readiness and capacity to handle academic learning. For the most part, our educational technology (audio-visual aids, programmed texts, teaching machines, etc.) is making significant advances designed to assist teachers in coping with intellectual differences among students. We have been making strides in the direction of offering flexible programs and curricula, but we are somewhat remiss when it comes to preparing flexible, "total" teachers. Just as there are intellectual differences among students, there are also personality and self-concept differences which can have just as much impact on achievement. If this is true, then perhaps we need to do more about preparing teachers who are sensitive to the nature of these differences and who are able to take them into account as they plan for their classes.

The point here is that what is important for one student is not important to another. This is one reason why cookbook formulas for good teachers are of so little value and why teaching is inevitably something of an art. The choice of instructional methods makes a big difference for certain kinds of pupils, and a search for the "best" way to teach can succeed only when learners' intellectual *and* personality differences are taken into account. Available evidence does not support the belief that successful teaching is possible only through the use of some specific methodology. A reasonable inference from existing data is that methods which provide for adaptation to individual differences, encourage student initiative, and stimulate individual and group participation are superior to methods which do not. In order for things of this sort to happen, perhaps what we need first of all are flexible, "total" teachers who are as capable of planning around people as they are around ideas.

IMPLICATIONS FOR TEACHER EDUCATION

Research is teaching us many things about the differences between good and poor teachers, and I see at least four related implications for teacher education programs.

1. If it is true that good teachers are good because they view teaching as primarily a human process involving human relationships and human meanings, then this may imply that we should spend at least as much time exposing and sensitizing teacher candidates to the subtle complexities of personality structure as we do to introducing them to the structure of knowledge itself. Does this mean personality development, group dynamics, basic counseling processes, sensitivity training, and techniques such as life-space interviewing and encounter grouping?

2. If it is true that good teachers have a positive view of themselves and others, then this may suggest that we provide more opportunities for teacher candidates to acquire more positive self-other perceptions. Self-concept research tells us that how one feels about himself is learned. If it is learned, it is teachable. Too often, those of us in teacher education are dominated by a concern for long-term goals, while the student is fundamentally motivated by short-term goals. Forecasting what a student will need to know six months or two years from now, we operate on the assumption that he, too, perceives such goals as meaningful. It seems logical enough, but unfortunately it doesn't work out too well in practice. Hence much of what we may do with our teacher candidates is non-self-re-

lated—that is, to the student it doesn't seem connected with his own life, time, and needs. Rather than talk about group processes in the abstract, why can't we first assist students to a deeper understanding of their own roles in groups in which they already participate? Rather than simply theorize and cite research evidence related to individual differences, why not also encourage students to analyze the individual differences which exist in *this* class at *this* time and then allow them to express and discuss what these differences mean at a more personal level? If one values the self-concept idea at all, then there are literally endless ways to encourage more positive self-other perceptions through teaching strategies aimed at personalizing what goes on in a classroom. Indeed, Jersild[9] has demonstrated that when "teachers face themselves," they feel more adequate as individuals and function more effectively as teachers.

3. If it is true that good teachers are well-informed, then it is clear that we must neither negate nor relax our efforts to provide them with as rich an intellectual background as is possible. Teachers are usually knowledgeable people, and knowledge inculcation is the aspect of preparation with which teacher education has traditionally been most successful. Nonetheless, teachers rarely fail because of lack of knowledge. They fail more often because they are unable to communicate what they know so that it makes a difference to their students. Which brings us to our final implication for teacher-education programs.

4. If it is true that good teachers are able to communicate what they know in a manner that makes sense to their students, then we must assist our teacher candidates both through example and appropriate experiences to the most effective ways of doing this. Communication is not just a process of presenting information. It is also a function of discovery and the development of personal meanings. I wonder what would happen to our expectations of the teacher's role if we viewed him less as dispenser, answerer, coercer, and provoker and more as stimulator, questioner, challenger, and puzzler. With the former, the emphasis is on "giving to," while with the latter the focus is on "guiding to." In developing ability to hold and keep attention, not to mention techniques of encouraging people to adopt the reflective, thoughtful mood, I wonder what the departments of speech, theater, and drama on our college and university campuses could teach us? We expose our students to theories of learning and personality; perhaps what we need to do now is develop some "theories of presentation" with the help of those who know this field best.

This paper has attempted to point out that even though there is no single best or worst kind of teacher, there are clearly distinguishable characteristics associated with "good" and "bad" teachers. There is no one *best* kind of teaching because there is no *one kind* of student. Nonetheless, there seems to be enough evidence to suggest that whether the criteria for good teaching is on the basis of student and/or peer evaluations or in terms of student achievement gains, there are characteristics between both which consistently overlap. That is, the good teacher is able to influence both student feeling and achievement in positive ways.

Research is teaching us many things about the differences between good and bad teachers and there are many ways we can put these research findings into our teacher-education programs.

Good teachers do exist and can be identified. Perhaps the next most fruitful vineyard for research is in the classrooms of good teachers so we can determine, by whatever tools we have, just what makes them good in the first place.

REFERENCES

1   A. S. Barr, *Characteristic Differences in the Teaching Performance of Good and Poor Teachers of the Social Studies.* Bloomington, Ill.: The Public School Publishing Co., 1929.

2   B. J. Biddle and W. J. Ellena, *Contemporary Research on Teacher Effectiveness.* New York: Holt, Rinehart, and Winston, 1964, p. 2.

3   W. A. Bousfield, "Student's Rating on Qualities Considered Desirable in College Professors," *School and Society,* February 24, 1940, pp. 253-56.

4   M. L. Cogan, "The Behavior of Teachers and the Productive Behavior of Their Pupils," *Journal of Experimental Education,* December, 1958, pp. 89-124.

5   A. W. Combs, *The Professional Education of Teachers.* Boston: Allyn and Bacon, 1965, pp. 70-71.

6   N. A. Flanders, *Teacher Influence, Pupil Attitudes and Achievement: Studies in Interaction Analysis.* University of Minnesota, U. S. Office of Education Cooperative Research Project No. 397, 1960.

7   W. F. Hart, *Teachers and Teaching.* New York: Macmillan, 1934, pp. 131-32.

8   L. M. Heil, M. Powell, and I. Feifer, *Characteristics of Teacher Behavior Related to the Achievement of Children in Several Elementary Grades.* Washington D.C.: Office of Education, Cooperative Research Branch, 1960.

9   A. T. Jersild, *When Teachers Face Themselves.* New York: Bureau of Publications, Teachers College, Columbia University, 1955.

10 H. B. Reed, "Implications for Science Education of a Teacher Competence Research," *Science Education,* December, 1962, pp. 473-86.

11 D. G. Ryans, "Prediction of Teacher Effectiveness," *Encyclopedia of Educational Research,* 3rd Edition. New York: Macmillan, 1960, pp. 1, 486-90.

12 R. Spaulding, "Achievement, Creativity, and Self-Concept Correlates of Teacher-Pupil Transactions in Elementary Schools." University of Illinois, U. S. Office of Education Cooperative Research Project No. 1352, 1963.

13 G. C. Stern, "Measuring Non-Cognitive Variables in Research on Teaching," in *Handbook of Research on Teaching,* N. L. Gage (ed.). Chicago: Rand McNally, 1963, p. 427.

14 P. Witty, "An Analysis of the Personality Traits of the Effective Teacher," *Journal of Educational Research,* May, 1947, pp. 662-71.

2

The Act of Discovery

JEROME S. BRUNER

Maimonides, in his *Guide for the Perplexed,*[1] speaks of four forms of perfection that men might seek. The first and lowest form is perfection in the acquisition of worldly goods. The great philosopher dismisses such perfection on the ground that the possessions one acquires bear no meaningful relation to the possessor: "A great king may one morning find that there is no difference between him and the lowest person." A second

Jerome S. Bruner, "The Act of Discovery," *Harvard Educational Review,* **31,** Winter 1961, 21-32. Copyright © 1961 President and Fellows of Harvard College.

[1] Maimonides, *Guide for the Perplexed* (New York: Dover Publications, 1956).

perfection is of the body, its conformation and skills. Its failing is that it does not reflect on what is uniquely human about man: "he could [in any case] not be as strong as a mule." Moral perfection is the third, "the highest degree of excellency in man's character." Of this perfection Maimonides says: "Imagine a person being alone, and having no connection whatever with any other person; all his good moral principles are at rest, they are not required and give man no perfection whatever. These principles are only necessary and useful when man comes in contact with others." "The fourth kind of perfection is the true perfection of man; the possession of the highest intellectual faculties. . . ." In justification of his assertion, this extraordinary Spanish-Judaic philosopher urges: "Examine the first three kinds of perfection; you will find that if you possess them, they are not your property but the property of others. . . . But the last kind of perfection is exclusively yours; no one else owns any part of it."

It is a conjecture much like that of Maimonides that leads me to examine the act of discovery in man's intellectual life. For if man's intellectual excellence is the most his own among his perfections, it is also the case that the most uniquely personal of all that he knows is that which he has discovered for himself. What difference does it make, then, that we encourage discovery in the learning of the young? Does it, as Maimonides would say, create a special and unique relation between knowledge possessed and the possessor? And what may such a unique relation do for a man—or for a child, if you will, for our concern is with the education of the young?

The immediate occasion for my concern with discovery—and I do not restrict discovery to the act of finding out something that before was unknown to mankind, but rather include all forms of obtaining knowledge for oneself by the use of one's own mind—the immediate occasion is the work of the various new curriculum projects that have grown up in America during the last six or seven years. For whether one speaks to mathematicians or physicists or historians, one encounters repeatedly an expression of faith in the powerful effects that come from permitting the student to put things together for himself, to be his own discoverer.

First, let it be clear what the act of discovery entails. It is rarely, on the frontier of knowledge or elsewhere, that new facts are "discovered" in the sense of being encountered as Newton suggested in the form of islands of truth in an uncharted sea of ignorance. Or if they appear to be discovered in this way, it is almost always thanks to some happy hypotheses about where to navigate. Discovery, like surprise, favors the well prepared mind. In playing bridge, one is surprised by a hand with no honors in it at all and also by hands that are all in one suit. Yet all hands in bridge are equiprobable: one must know to be surprised. So too in discovery. The history of science is studded with examples of men "finding out" something and not knowing it. I shall operate on the assumption that discovery, whether by a schoolboy going it on his own or by a scientist cultivating the growing edge of his field, is in its essence a matter of rearranging or transforming evidence in such a way that one is enabled to go beyond the evidence so reassembled to additional new insights. It may well be that an additional fact or shred of evidence makes this larger transformation of evidence possible. But it is often not even dependent on new information.

It goes without saying that, left to himself, the child will go about discovering things for himself within limits. It also goes without saying that there are certain forms of child rearing, certain home atmospheres that lead some children to be their own discoverers more than other children. These are both topics of great interest, but I shall not be discussing them. Rather, I should like to confine myself to the consideration of discovery and "finding-out-for-onself" within an educational setting—specifically the school. Our aim as teachers is to give our student as firm a grasp of a subject as we can, and to make him as autonomous and self-propelled a thinker as we can—one who will go along on his own after formal schooling has ended. I shall return in the end to the question of the kind of classroom and the style of teaching that encourages an attitude of wanting to discover. For purposes of orienting the discussion, however, I would like to make an overly simplified distinction between teaching that takes place in the *expository mode* and teaching that utilizes the *hypothetical mode*. In the former, the decisions concerning the mode and pace and style of exposition are principally determined by the teacher as expositor; the student is the listener. If I can put the matter in terms of structural linguistics, the speaker has a quite different set of decisions to make than the listener: the former has a wide choice of alternatives for structuring, he is anticipating paragraph content while the listener is still intent on the words, he is manipulating the content of the material by various transformations, while the listener is quite unaware of these internal manipulations. In the hypothetical mode, the teacher and the student are in a more cooperative position with respect to what in linguistics would be called "speaker's decisions." The student is not a bench-bound listener, but is taking a part in the formulation and at times may play the principal role in it. He will be aware of alternatives and may even have an "as if" attitude toward these and, as he receives information, he may evaluate it as it comes. One cannot describe the process in either mode with great precision as to detail, but I think the foregoing may serve to illustrate what is meant.

Consider now what benefit might be derived from the experience of learning through discoveries that one makes for oneself. I should like to discuss these under four headings: (1) The increase in intellectual potency, (2) the shift from extrinsic to intrinsic rewards, (3) learning the heuristics of discovering, and (4) the aid to memory processing.

1. Intellectual Potency

If you will permit me, I would like to consider the difference between subjects in a highly constrained psychological experiment involving a two-choice apparatus. In order to win chips, they must depress a key either on the right or the left side of the machine. A pattern of payoff is designed such that, say, they will be paid off on the right side 70 per cent of the time, on the left 30 per cent, although this detail is not important. What is important is that the payoff sequence is arranged at random, and there is no pattern. I should like to contrast the behavior of subjects who think that there *is* some pattern to be found in the sequence—who think that regularities are discoverable—in contrast to subjects who think that things are happening quite by *chance*. The former group adopts what is called an "event-matching" strategy in which the number of responses given to each side is roughly equal to the proportion of times it pays off: in the present case R70:L30. The group that believes there is no pattern very soon reverts to a much more primitive strategy wherein *all* responses are allocated to the side that has the greater payoff. A little arithmetic will show you that the lazy all-and-none strategy pays off more if indeed the environment is random: namely, they win seventy per cent of the time. The event-matching subjects win about 70% on the 70% payoff side (or 49% of the time there) and 30% of the time on the side that pays off 30% of the time (another 9% for a total take-home wage of 58% in return for their labors of decision). But the world is not always or not even frequently random, and if one analyzes carefully what the event-matchers are doing, it turns out that they are trying out hypotheses one after the other, all of them containing a term such that they distribute bets on the two sides with a frequency to match the actual occurrence of events. If it should turn out that there is a pattern to be discovered, their payoff would become 100%. The other group would go on at the middling rate of 70%.

What has this to do with the subject at hand? For the person to search out and find regularities and relationships in his environment, he must be armed with an expectancy that there will be something to find and, once aroused by expectancy, he must devise ways of searching and finding. One of the chief enemies of such expectancy is the assumption that there is nothing one can find in the environment by way of regularity or relationship. In the experiment just cited, subjects often fall into a habitual attitude that there is either nothing to be found or that they can find a pattern by looking. There is an important sequel in behavior to the two attitudes, and to this I should like to turn now.

We have been conducting a series of experimental studies on a group of some seventy school children over the last four years. The studies have led us to distinguish an interesting dimension of cognitive activity that can be described as ranging from *episodic empiricism* at one end to *cumulative constructionism* at the other. The two attitudes in the choice experiments just cited are illustrative of the extremes of the dimension. I might mention some other illustrations. One of the experiments employs the game of Twenty Questions. A child—in this case he is between 10 and 12—is told that a car has gone off the road and hit a tree. He is to ask questions that can be answered by "yes" or "no" to discover the cause of the accident. After completing the problem, the same task is given him again, though he is told that the accident had a different cause this time. In all, the procedure is repeated four times. Children enjoy playing the game. They also differ quite markedly in the approach or strategy they bring to the task. There are various elements in the strategies employed. In the first place, one may distinguish clearly between two types of questions asked: the one is designed for locating constraints in the problem, constraints that will eventually give shape to an hypothesis; the other is the hypothesis as question. It is the difference between, "Was there anything wrong with the driver?" and "Was the driver rushing to the doctor's office for an appointment and the car got out of control?" There are children who precede hypotheses with efforts to locate constraints and there are those who, to use our local slang, are "pot-shotters," who string out hypotheses noncumulatively one after the other. A second element of strategy is its connectivity of information gathering: the extent to which questions asked utilize or ignore or violate information previously obtained. The questions asked by children tend to be organized in cycles, each cycle of questions usually being given over to the pursuit of some particular notion. Both within cycles and between cycles one can discern a marked difference in the connectivity of the child's performance. Needless to say, children who employ constraint location as a technique preliminary to the formulation of hypotheses tend to be far more connected in their harvesting of information. Persistence is another feature of strategy, a characteristic compounded of what appear to be two components: a sheer doggedness component, and a persistence that stems from the sequential organization that a child brings to the task. Doggedness is probably just animal spirits or the need for achievement—what has come to be called *n-ach*. Organized persistence is a maneuver for protecting our fragile cognitive apparatus from overload. The child who has flooded himself with disorganized information from unconnected hypotheses will become discouraged and confused sooner than the child who has shown a certain cunning in his strategy of getting information—a cunning whose principal component is the recognition that the value of information is not simply in getting it but in being able to carry it. The persistence of the organized child stems from his knowledge of how to organize questions in cycles, how to summarize things to himself, and the like.

Episodic empiricism is illustrated by information gathering that is unbound by prior constraints, that lacks connectivity, and that is deficient in organizational persistence. The opposite extreme is illustrated by an approach that is characterized by constraint sensitivity, by connective maneuvers, and by organized persistence. Brute persistence seems to be one of those gifts from the gods that make people more exaggeratedly what they are.[2]

Before returning to the issue of discovery and its role in the development of thinking, let me say a word more about the ways in which information may get transformed when the problem solver has actively processed it. There is first of all a pragmatic question: what does it take to get information processed into a form best designed to fit some future use? Take an experiment by Zajonc[3] as a case in point. He gives groups of subjects information of a controlled kind, some groups being told that their task is to transmit the information to others, others that it is merely to be kept in mind. In general, he finds more differentiation and organization of the information received with the intention of being transmitted

---

[2] I should also remark in passing that the two extremes also characterize concept attainment strategies as reported in *A Study of Thinking* by J. S. Bruner *et al.* (New York: J. Wiley, 1956). Successive scanning illustrates well what is meant here by episodic empiricism; conservative focusing is an example of cumulative constructionism.

[3] R. B. Zajonc (Personal communication, 1957).

than there is for information received passively. An active set leads to a transformation related to a task to be performed. The risk, to be sure, is in possible overspecialization of information processing that may lead to such a high degree of specific organization that information is lost for general use.

I would urge now in the spirit of an hypothesis that emphasis upon discovery in learning has precisely the effect upon the learner of leading him to be a constructionist, to organize what he is encountering in a manner not only designed to discover regularity and relatedness, but also to avoid the kind of information drift that fails to keep account of the uses to which information might have to be put. It is, if you will, a necessary condition for learning the variety of techniques of problem solving, of transforming information for better use, indeed for learning how to go about the very task of learning. Practice in discovering for oneself teaches one to acquire information in a way that makes that information more readily viable in problem solving. So goes the hypothesis. It is still in need of testing. But it is an hypothesis of such important human implications that we cannot afford not to test it—and testing will have to be in the schools.

2. Intrinsic and Extrinsic Motives

Much of the problem in leading a child to effective cognitive activity is to free him from the immediate control of environmental rewards and punishments. That is to say, learning that starts in response to the rewards of parental or teacher approval or the avoidance of failure can too readily develop a pattern in which the child is seeking cues as to how to conform to what is expected of him. We know from studies of children who tend to be early over-achievers in school that they are likely to be seekers after the "right way to do it" and that their capacity for transforming their learning into viable thought structures tends to be lower than children merely achieving at levels predicted by intelligence tests. Our tests on such children show them to be lower in analytic ability than those who are not conspicuous in overachievement.[4] As we shall see later, they develop rote abilities and depend upon being able to "give back" what is expected rather than to make it into something that relates to the rest of their cognitive life. As Maimonides would say, their learning is not their own.

---

[4] J. S. Bruner and A. J. Caron, "Cognition, Anxiety, and Achievement in the Pre-adolescent," *Journal of Educational Psychology* (in press).

The hypothesis that I would propose here is that to the degree that one is able to approach learning as a task of discovering something rather than "learning about" it, to that degree will there be a tendency for the child to carry out his learning activities with the autonomy of self-reward or, more properly by reward that is discovery itself.

To those of you familiar with the battles of the last half-century in the field of motivation, the above hypothesis will be recognized as controversial. For the classic view of motivation in learning has been, until very recently, couched in terms of a theory of drives and reinforcement: that learning occurred by virtue of the fact that a response produced by a stimulus was followed by the reduction in a primary drive state. The doctrine is greatly extended by the idea of secondary reinforcement: any state associated even remotely with the reduction of a primary drive could also have the effect of producing learning. There has recently appeared a most searching and important criticism of this position, written by Professor Robert White,[5] reviewing the evidence of recently published animal studies, of work in the field of psychoanalysis, and of research on the development of cognitive processes in children. Professor White comes to the conclusion, quite rightly I think, that the drive-reduction model of learning runs counter to too many important phenomena of learning and development to be either regarded as general in its applicability or even correct in its general approach. Let me summarize some of his principal conclusions and explore their applicability to the hypothesis stated above.

I now propose that we gather the various kinds of behavior just mentioned, all of which have to do with effective interaction with the environment, under the general heading of competence. According to Webster, competence means fitness or ability, and the suggested synonyms include capability, capacity, efficiency, proficiency, and skill. It is therefore a suitable word to describe such things as grasping and exploring, crawling and walking, attention and perception, language and thinking, manipulating and changing the surroundings, all of which promote an effective—a competent—interaction with the environment. It is true of course, that maturation plays a part in all these developments, but this part is heavily overshadowed by learning in all the more complex accomplishments like speech or skilled manipulation. I shall argue that it is necessary to make competence a motivational concept; there is *competence motivation* as well as competence in its more familiar sense of achieved capacity. The

---

[5] R. W. White, "Motivation Reconsidered: The Concept of Competence," *Psychological Review*, LXVI (1959), 297-333.

behavior that leads to the building up of effective grasping, handling, and letting go of objects, to take one example, is not random behavior that is produced by an overflow of energy. It is directed, selective, and persistent, and it continues not because it serves primary drives, which indeed it cannot serve until it is almost perfected, but because it satisfies an intrinsic need to deal with the environment.[6]

I am suggesting that there are forms of activity that serve to enlist and develop the competence motive, that serve to make it the driving force behind behavior. I should like to add to White's general premise that the *exercise* of competence motives has the effect of strengthening the degree to which they gain control over behavior and thereby reduce the effects of extrinsic rewards or drive gratification.

The brilliant Russian psychologist Vigotsky[7] characterizes the growth of thought processes as starting with a dialogue of speech and gesture between child and parent; autonomous thinking begins at the stage when the child is first able to internalize these conversations and "run them off" himself. This is a typical sequence in the development of competence. So too in instruction. The narrative of teaching is of the order of the conversation. The next move in the development of competence is the internalization of the narrative and its "rules of generation" so that the child is now capable of running off the narrative on his own. The hypothetical mode in teaching by encouraging the child to participate in "speaker's decisions" speeds this process along. Once internalization has occurred, the child is in a vastly improved position from several obvious points of view—notably that he is able to go beyond the information he has been given to generate additional ideas that can either be checked immediately from experience or can, at least, be used as a basis for formulating reasonable hypotheses. But over and beyond that, the child is now in a position to experience success and failure not as reward and punishment, but as information. For when the task is his own rather than a matter of matching environmental demands, he becomes his own paymaster in a certain measure. Seeking to gain control over his environment, he can now treat success as indicating that he is on the right track, failure as indicating he is on the wrong one.

In the end, this development has the effect of freeing learning from immediate stimulus control. When learning in the short run leads only to

---

[6] *Ibid.,* pp. 317-18.

[7] L. S. Vigotsky, *Thinking and Speech* (Moscow, 1934).

pellets of this or that rather than to mastery in the long run, then behavior can be readily "shaped" by extrinsic rewards. When behavior becomes more long-range and competence-oriented, it comes under the control of more complex cognitive structures, plans and the like, and operates more from the inside out. It is interesting that even Pavlov, whose early account of the learning process was based entirely on a notion of stimulus control of behavior through the conditioning mechanism in which, through contiguity a new conditioned stimulus was substituted for an old unconditioned stimulus by the mechanism of stimulus substitution, that even Pavlov recognized his account as insufficient to deal with higher forms of learning. To supplement the account, he introduced the idea of the "second signalling system," with central importance placed on symbolic systems such as language in mediating and giving shape to mental life. Or as Luria[8] has put it, "the first signal system [is] concerned with directly perceived stimuli, the second with systems of verbal elaboration." Luria, commenting on the importance of the transition from first to second signal system, says: "It would be mistaken to suppose that verbal intercourse with adults merely changes the contents of the child's conscious activity without changing its form. . . . The word has a basic function not only because it indicates a corresponding object in the external world, but also because it abstracts, isolates the necessary signal, generalizes perceived signals and relates them to certain categories; it is this systematization of direct experience that makes the role of the word in the formation of mental processes so exceptionally important."[9, 10]

It is interesting that the final rejection of the universality of the doctrine of reinforcement in direct conditioning came from some of Pavlov's own students. Ivanov-Smolensky[11] and Krasnogorsky[12] published papers showing the manner in which symbolized linguistic messages could

---

[8] A. L. Luria, "The Directive Function of Speech in Development and Dissolution," *Word*, XV (1959), 341-464.

[9] *Ibid.*, p. 12.

[10] For an elaboration of the view expressed by Luria, the reader is referred to the forthcoming translation of L. S. Vigotsky's 1934 book being published by John Wiley and Sons and the Technology Press.

[11] A. G. Ivanov-Smolensky, "Concerning the Study of the Joint Activity of the First and Second Signal Systems," *Journal of Higher Nervous Activity*, I (1951), 1.

[12] N. D. Krasnogorsky, *Studies of Higher Nervous Activity in Animals and in Man*, Vol. I (Moscow, 1954).

take over the place of the unconditioned stimulus and of the unconditioned response (gratification of hunger) in children. In all instances, they speak of these as *replacements* of lower, first-system mental or neural processes by higher order or second-system controls. A strange irony, then, that Russian psychology that gave us the notion of the conditioned response and the assumption that higher order activities are built up out of colligations or structurings of such primitive units, rejected this notion while much of American learning psychology has stayed until quite recently within the early Pavlovian fold (see, for example, a recent article by Spence[13] in the *Harvard Educational Review* or Skinner's treatment of language[14] and the attacks that have been made upon it by linguists such as Chomsky[15] who have become concerned with the relation of language and cognitive activity). What is the more interesting is that Russian pedagogical theory has become deeply influenced by this new trend and is now placing much stress upon the importance of building up a more active symbolical approach to problem solving among children.

To sum up the matter of the control of learning, then, I am proposing that the degree to which competence or mastery motives come to control behavior, to that degree the role of reinforcement or "extrinsic pleasure" wanes in shaping behavior. The child comes to manipulate his environment more actively and achieves his gratification from coping with problems. Symbolic modes of representing and transforming the environment arise and the importance of stimulus-response-reward sequences declines. To use the metaphor that David Riesman developed in a quite different context, mental life moves from a state of outer-directedness in which the fortuity of stimuli and reinforcement are crucial to a state of inner-directedness in which the growth and maintenance of mastery become central and dominant.

3. Learning the Heuristics of Discovery

Lincoln Steffens,[16] reflecting in his *Autobiography* on his undergraduate education at Berkeley, comments that his schooling was overly

---

[13] K. W. Spence, "The Relation of Learning Theory to the Technique of Education," *Harvard Educational Review,* XXIX (1959), 84-95.

[14] B. F. Skinner, *Verbal Behavior* (New York: Appleton-Century-Crofts, 1957).

[15] N. Chomsky, *Syntactic Structure* (The Hague, The Netherlands: Mouton & Co., 1957).

[16] L. Steffens. *Autobiography of Lincoln Steffens* (New York: Harcourt, Brace, 1931).

specialized on learning about the known and that too little attention was given to the task of finding out about what was not known. But how does one train a student in the techniques of discovery? Again I would like to offer some hypotheses. There are many ways of coming to the arts of inquiry. One of them is by careful study of its formalization in logic, statistics, mathematics, and the like. If a person is going to pursue inquiry as a way of life, particularly in the sciences, certainly such study is essential. Yet, whoever has taught kindergarten and the early primary grades or has had graduate students working with him on their theses—I choose the two extremes for they are both periods of intense inquiry—knows that an understanding of the formal aspect of inquiry is not sufficient. There appear to be, rather, a series of activities and attitudes, some directly related to a particular subject and some of them fairly generalized, that go with inquiry and research. These have to do with the *process* of trying to find out something and while they provide no guarantee that the *product* will be any *great* discovery, their absence is likely to lead to awkwardness or aridity or confusion. How difficult it is to describe these matters—the heuristics of inquiry. There is one set of attitudes or ways of doing that has to do with sensing the relevance of variables—how to avoid getting stuck with edge effects and getting instead to the big sources of variance. Partly this gift comes from intuitive familiarity with a range of phenomena, sheer "knowing the stuff." But it also comes out of a sense of what things among an ensemble of things "smell right" in the sense of being of the right order of magnitude or scope or severity.

The English philosopher Weldon describes problem solving in an interesting and picturesque way. He distinguishes between difficulties, puzzles, and problems. We solve a problem or make a discovery when we impose a puzzle form on to a difficulty that converts it into a problem that can be solved in such a way that it gets us where we want to be. That is to say, we recast the difficulty into a form that we know how to work with, then work it. Much of what we speak of as discovery consists of knowing how to impose what kind of form on various kinds of difficulties. A small part but a crucial part of discovery of the highest order is to invent and develop models or "puzzle forms" that can be imposed on difficulties with good effect. It is in this area that the truly powerful mind shines. But it is interesting to what degree perfectly ordinary people can, given the benefit of instruction, construct quite interesting and what, a century ago, would have been considered greatly original models.

Now to the hypothesis. It is my hunch that it is only through the exercise of problem solving and the effort of discovery that one learns the working heuristic of discovery, and the more one has practice, the more likely is one to generalize what one has learned into a style of problem solving or inquiry that serves for any kind of task one may encounter—or almost any kind of task. I think the matter is self-evident, but what is unclear is what kinds of training and teaching produce the best effects. How do we teach a child to, say, cut his losses but at the same time be persistent in trying out an idea; to risk forming an early hunch without at the same time formulating one *so* early and with so little evidence as to be stuck with it waiting for appropriate evidence to materialize; to pose good testable guesses that are neither too brittle nor too sinuously incorrigible; etc., etc. Practice in inquiry, in trying to figure out things for oneself is indeed what is needed, but in what form? Of only one thing I am convinced. I have never seen anybody improve in the art and technique of inquiry by any means other than engaging in inquiry.

4. Conservation of Memory

I should like to take what some psychologists might consider a rather drastic view of the memory process. It is a view that in large measure derives from the work of my colleague, Professor George Miller.[17] Its first premise is that the principal problem of human memory is not storage, but retrieval. In spite of the biological unlikeliness of it, we seem to be able to store a huge quantity of information—perhaps not a full tape recording, though at times it seems we even do that, but a great sufficiency of impressions. We may infer this from the fact that recognition (i.e., recall with the aid of maximum prompts) is so extraordinarily good in human beings—particularly in comparison with spontaneous recall where, so to speak, we must get out stored information without external aids or prompts. The key to retrieval is organization or, in even simpler terms, knowing where to find information and how to get there.

Let me illustrate the point with a simple experiment. We present pairs of words to twelve-year-old children. One group is simply told to remember the pairs, that they will be asked to repeat them later. Another is told to remember them by producing a word or idea that will tie the pair together in a way that will make sense to them. A third group is given the mediators used by the second group when presented with the pairs to aid them in tying the pairs into working units. The word pairs include such juxtapositions as "chair-forest," "sidewalk-square," and the like. One can distinguish three styles of mediators and children can be scaled in terms of

---

[17] G. A. Miller, "The Magical Number Seven, Plus or Minus Two," *Psychological Review*, LXIII (1956), 81-97.

their relative preference for each: *generic mediation* in which a pair is tied together by a superordinate idea: "chair and forest are both made of wood"; *thematic mediation* in which the two terms are imbedded in a theme or little story: "the lost child sat on a chair in the middle of the forest"; and *part-whole mediation* where "chairs are made from trees in the forest" is typical. Now, the chief result, as you would all predict, is that children who provide their own mediators do best—indeed, one time through a set of thirty pairs, they recover up to 95% of the second words when presented with the first ones of the pairs, whereas the uninstructed children reach a maximum of less than 50% recovered. Interestingly enough, children do best in recovering materials tied together by the form of mediator they most often use.

One can cite a myriad of findings to indicate that any organization of information that reduces the aggregate complexity of material by imbedding it into a cognitive structure a person has constructed will make that material more accessible for retrieval. In short, we may say that the process of memory, looked at from the retrieval side, is also a process of problem solving: how can material be "placed" in memory so that it can be got on demand?

We can take as a point of departure the example of the children who developed their own technique for relating the members of each word pair. You will recall that they did better than the children who were given by exposition the mediators they had developed. Let me suggest that in general, material that is organized in terms of a person's own interests and cognitive structures is material that has the best chance of being accessible in memory. That is to say, it is more likely to be placed along routes that are connected to one's own ways of intellectual travel.

In sum, the very attitudes and activities that characterize "figuring out" or "discovering" things for oneself also seems to have the effect of making material more readily accessible in memory.

3

Teaching Skills
for Creative Ways of Learning:
Introduction

E. PAUL TORRANCE

There has always been a fairly general recognition that man prefers to learn creatively—by exploring, questioning, experimenting, manipulating, rearranging things, testing, and modifying ideas or solutions. Generally, however, education has insisted that man learn by authority—by being told. Teachers have maintained that it is more economical to teach by authority than to foster the more natural ways of learning.

I have taken the rather controversial position that many things can be learned more economically and effectively if they are learned in creative ways rather than by authority. I have also maintained that some individuals have a strong preference for learning creatively, learn a great deal if allowed to use their creative thinking abilities in acquiring knowledge and educational skills, and make little progress when teachers insist that they learn by authority. Such ideas open up exciting possibilities for doing a more effective job of individualizing instruction and for educating some individuals who do not respond favorably to present educational programs.

Furthermore, creative ways of learning have a built-in motivation for educational achievements that makes unnecessary the application and reapplication of rewards and punishment. Even when rewards and punishments succeed temporarily in motivating learning, they may not supply the inner stimulation necessary for continued effort and achievement. Such motivation is usually short-lived and requires continuous reapplication to sustain effort on the part of the learner. The inner stimulation from creative ways of learning makes this unnecessary.

To learn creatively, a person must first become aware of gaps in knowledge, disharmonies, or problems calling for new solutions. He must then search for information concerning the missing elements or difficulties, trying to identify the difficulty or gap in knowledge. Next he must search for solutions, making guesses or approximations, formulating hypotheses, thinking of possibilities, and predicting. Then come the testing, modifying, retesting, and perfecting of the hypotheses or other

From E. Paul Torrance, *Improving Teaching Skills.* ©1969, Science Research Associates, Inc. Reprinted by permission of the publisher.

creative products. Finally, there is the communication of the results. The process is a natural one. Strong motivations are at work at each stage. Once the process is set in motion, it is difficult to stop it.

Man is an inquisitive, exploring, searching kind of being. He is self-acting and cannot keep his restless mind inactive even when there are no problems pressing for solution. He continues to find problems and cannot keep from digging into things, turning ideas over in his mind, trying out new combinations, searching for new relationships, and struggling for new insights. This comes from man's cognitive needs—his needs to know and to dig deeper into things. Man's esthetic needs—his needs for beauty, the balanced relationship, the graceful and certain movement—are almost as relentless. Cognitive and esthetic needs are served by creative ways of learning which develop the motivations and skills for learning throughout life.

Both casual and systematic observations of classroom behavior indicate that creative ways of learning in classrooms at all levels of education are rare. Numerous experiments have demonstrated that by deliberate efforts teachers can modify their behavior in such ways as to increase significantly the creative functioning and development of their pupils. In fully as many experiments teachers who were assigned some creative way of teaching failed to modify their behavior, and no significant change occurred in the creative functioning or development of their pupils. They lacked the teaching skills necessary to carry out successfully the creative ways of teaching to which they were assigned.

Any skill must be practiced to be developed and perfected, and teaching skills are no exception. The skills that most teachers have practiced so well are not those that are important in encouraging and facilitating creative growth among their pupils. Thus they must acquire, practice, and perfect those skills by deliberate effort.

4

Seven Guides to Creativity

E. PAUL TORRANCE

I have a tremendous respect for the potential contribution of health education, physical education, and recreation programs to the development of creative thinking abilities and the use of these abilities to acquire knowledge. Educators generally have limited the definition of "knowledge" and "intellectual development" to narrowly linguistic aspects. Because of this and other misconceptions, fields such as health education, physical education, and recreation have been handicapped in coming into their own, insofar as the development of the ability to think creatively is concerned.

For the past seven years, I have been engaged in a program of research in schools and colleges relative to the development of the creative thinking abilities, creative ways of learning, and the conditions that make possible healthy creative growth. These studies have involved children, young people, and adults at all educational levels from kindergarten through graduate school in a variety of localities in the United States and in several countries outside of the United States. The incidents, although few, in which I have specifically studied the development of the creative thinking abilities through health education, physical education, and recreation have convinced me that these fields can make important contributions to the general freeing and development of the creative thinking abilities in schools. I also believe that this program of research has given me some valid insights about the things that can be done to make this contribution.

AN EXPERIENCE IN CREATIVE MOVEMENT

A key experience that has made me aware of the potential of these fields was my excursion to observe the work in creative movement conducted by Gertrude Baker, former head of the Department of Physical Education for Women at the University of Minnesota, in the primary grades of a local school. As I observed her first and second grade groups, it seemed obvious that they were engaged in a great deal of very sound creative thinking and that development was occurring. I was particularly impressed with their

---

From *JOHPER,* April 1965. Reprinted by permission of Commonwealth of Pennsylvania.

use of the warm-up experience, the fluency of the ideas expressed in movement, the flexibility and originality of thinking manifested, and the way in which they elaborated their ideas. I was immediately curious to know what effect this was having on the development of their creative thinking abilities. Arrangements were then made in February 1964 to administer a battery of the Minnesota Tests of Creative Thinking (Non-Verbal Form B) to the first and second grade classes that had been working with Dr. Baker for about five months and to the third grade class with which she had just started working. The battery included the Picture Construction, Incomplete Figures, and Closed Figures Tests.

Much to our surprise, we found that almost one-half of the first and second graders achieved scores that exceeded the **mean** for the fifth grade on measures such as fluency, flexibility, originality, and elaboration. Not one of the 42 third graders just beginning the creative movement class achieved a score that reached this level.

The third graders were retested, with an alternate form of the creative thinking test, however, in May after about four months of work in creative movement. As shown in the following table, the growth in fluency, flexibility, and originality were dramatic. Only the ability to elaborate failed to show a statistically significant gain.

Perhaps more dramatic than these statistics were some of the changes that occurred in the development of individual children. For example, one third grade boy had created problems in the classroom for some time. His participation in classroom learning activities was minimal and he manifested hostility in many ways. At first he also manifested hostility in the creative movement class. As he found acceptable ways of expressing hostility through movement, his hostility began to diminish and he began

Means and Standard Deviations of Pre- and Post-Test Scores on Fluency, Flexibility, Originality, and Elaboration on the Minnesota Tests of Creative Thinking (Non-Verbal Forms A and B) by Third Grade Pupils in Creative Movement Class

Variable	Pre-Test		Post-Test		t ratio
	Mean	Stand. Dev.	Mean	Stand. Dev.	
Fluency	15.57	4.79	21.55	5.64	8.318[a]
Flexibility	12.29	3.89	16.12	3.66	6.937[a]
Originality	13.81	5.19	27.19	8.94	10.750[a]
Elaboration	36.24	16.02	38.48	14.11	1.169

[a]Gain is significant at better than the .001 level.

to participate in the creative movement class with absorption. Similarly, his general classroom attitude was transformed. His parents also noted a difference.

SUGGESTED GUIDELINES FOR CREATIVE TEACHING

Drawing now from a variety of studies (Torrance, 1962, 1963, 1965), I shall suggest a few guidelines that will be productive in developing creative thinking abilities through health education, physical education, and recreational programs in schools.

1. Do Not Leave Creative Development to Chance

Only a few years ago, it was commonly thought that all kinds of creativity had to be left to chance. Similarly, it was believed that gifted performances in physical education and recreational activities had to be left to chance, after practice, drill, and rigorous training regimes had been observed. High level performances have been regarded as artistry and have been clothed with an air of the mysterious. Deliberate methods of creative problem solving were rarely used.

With the demonstrated successes of deliberate methods of problem solving in recent years, it is difficult to understand how a well-informed person can still hold these views. The record of inventions, scientific discoveries, and other creative achievements and evidences of creative growth is impressive.

2. Encourage Curiosity and Other Creative Characteristics

Beginning quite early, natural curiosity has been discouraged in children as though it were something unnatural and evil. Whole areas of experiencing and investigation are placed off limits for children because of their sex, social class, race, or religion. This is particularly true in the areas of experience of interest to workers in the fields of health education, physical education, and recreation.

Curiosity about one's own body is especially discouraged; children fail to learn some of the simplest and most fundamental things about their bodily functioning. As a result, they are extremely ineffective in using experiences from their bodies and in developing healthy attitudes concerning the enjoyment of their bodies. Restrictions on this kind of curiosity are more severe on girls than on boys. Numerous studies, for example, indicate that men are more effective than women in using experiences from their bodies and are more aware of and attentive to their bodies.

Using a list of 66 characteristics that have been found to differentiate highly creative people from less creative people, a panel of serious students of the creative personality rated the following ten characteristics as most important in creative functioning (Torrence, 1965):

1. Courage (intellectual courage, courage in convictions)
2. Curiosity
3. Independence in thinking
4. Independence in judgment
5. Willingness to take risks
6. Intuitiveness
7. Absorption in tasks
8. Persistence
9. Unwillingness to accept things on mere say-so
10. Visionary

It should be challenging to design guided, planned learning experiences in health education, physical education, and recreational programs to encourage the development of these and other creative characteristics.

3. Be Respectful of Questions and Unusual Ideas

Early in our research, we became convinced that one of the simplest and most powerful ways of encouraging creative growth was to respect the questions that children ask, respect the ideas that they present for consideration, show them that their ideas have value, encourage opportunities for practice and experimentation without evaluation and grading, and encourage and give credit for self-initiated learning and thinking. We made these principles the basis for some of our early teachers' manuals and in-service education programs.

These principles have elicited a wide range of reactions. While some have attacked them as unvalidated hypotheses, others have attacked them as "self-evident truisms and annoyingly pat exhortations." Nevertheless, our observations showed that teachers are generally not very skillful in applying these principles. Even when they try deliberately to do so, some teachers are unable to apply them with any degree of fidelity. Teachers who were able to apply them with fidelity, however, found that their teaching was virtually transformed as a result. Measured changes at a statistically significant level were found in creative growth not found in control groups.

4. Recognize Original, Creative Behavior

Original, creative behavior is rarely recognized by teachers. One of the things that teachers should work at is to be on the lookout for original, creative solutions among their own students, whether in the classroom, on gymnastic apparatus, or in a basketball game. Most teachers are surprised at the quantity and quality of the sound, original work their students will do.

Almost everyone has been amazed and impressed by the creative achievements of high school students in the summer institutes of the National Science Foundation. New groups of high achievers also emerge when students are taught in such a way that they are permitted to do original thinking and go beyond the mastery of existing knowledge. Jablonski (1964) reports some amazing successes in one of these programs. He believed that if high school students could do such outstanding work in the summer they should continue throughout the school year. Through some of the public schools, he arranged for a continuous program with results that amaze seasoned professional research scientists. He estimates that 25 percent of these high school students are producing publishable research in competition with mature researchers. He then extended this work into the elementary grades and found a readiness for research beyond his expectations. His elementary school group has made some excellent contributions to cancer research projects. One of Jablonski's high school students with an IQ of 86 produced some ideas of his own that some of the "brighter" students are now researching—and that some of the university people are picking up and trying (Jablonski, 1964).

5. Ask Questions That Require Thinking

Another obvious but not easily achieved thing that almost every teacher could do to improve the quality of the learning of their students is to ask more questions that call for thinking. In one of our tests of creative thinking ability, we ask subjects to ask divergent questions, questions that are thought-provoking rather than questions that call only for facts. Most teachers find difficulty in doing this. Although they know that they are not supposed to ask factual questions, most of their questions still call only for reproduction of textbook facts. Analysis of questions asked in the classroom and on examinations indicate that about 90 percent of such questions deal only with the recognition or reproduction of textbook information.

6. Build onto the Learning Skills That Your Pupils Have

There are many discontinuities in our educational system, but the most glaring and upsetting ones occur when the child enters school for the first time, between the third and fourth grades, and between the sixth and seventh grades. It shows up in many of our tests of creative thinking when we find drops rather than gains or even plateaus in the developmental curves. The most disturbing element in this problem is the apparent rise in personality disturbance, behavior problems, and inability to learn and achieve in school.

Even when children first enter school, they have already developed a variety of skills for learning. They already know how to learn by experimenting, manipulating objects, rearranging them in different ways, singing, drawing, dancing, fantasy, story-telling, playmaking, and the like. It is quite likely that there would be fewer difficulties in learning and development if teachers made use of these learning skills and grafted education onto them, gradually building up the repertoire of learning skills rather than suddenly demanding that things be learned in ways strange to the child. This technique should be used all the way up the educational ladder.

7. Give Opportunities for Learning in Creative Ways

Man seems to prefer to learn creatively, by exploring, questioning, experimenting, testing, and modifying ideas or solutions. Generally, however, the schools operate on the principle that it is cheaper to teach by authority. Our studies suggest, however, that many things now taught by authority can actually be learned more effectively and economically if they are learned creatively. Some individuals have strong preferences for learning in creative ways, learn a great deal if permitted to learn in these ways, and make little progress when we insist that they learn by authority. This means that we may be able to educate to a higher degree many people whom we have not been very successful in educating—our dropouts and school failures.

A variety of experts show that as teachers vary the way in which children are encouraged to learn, different types of children in terms of mental abilities become the star learners or nonlearners. Traditional measures of mental age or intelligency correlate more highly with measures of achievement when knowledge is acquired by authority than when acquired creatively. Measures of originality and the like correlate more highly with measures of achievement when knowledge is acquired creatively than when acquired by authority.

REFERENCES

Jablonski, J. R. "Developing Creative Research Performance in Public School Children." In C. W. Taylor (ed.), *Widening Horizons in Creativity.* New York: John Wiley & Son, Inc., 1964.

Torrance, E. P. *Guilding Creative Talent.* Englewood Cliffs, N.J.: Prentice-Hall, Inc., 1962.

Torrance, E. P. *Education and the Creative Potential.* Minneapolis: University of Minnesota Press, 1963.

Torrance, E. P. *Rewarding Creative Behavior: Experiments in Classroom Creativity.* Englewood Cliffs, N.J.: Prentice-Hall, Inc., 1965.

5

Problem-Solving

JOAN TILLOTSON

Far be it from anyone to dictate the types of problems which might be presented to specific classes for movement solutions. However, guides can be suggested and steps presented to assist in understanding the methodology of problem-solving as it applies to basketball skills. Thus this article is designed to recommend steps through which students may be led toward

Reprinted by permission of the author.

the successful completion of a skills problem. Further, these steps are illustrated with an example of a fairly complex skills problem for an elementary school child.

STEPS IN PROBLEM-SOLVING

Five steps are suggested for the development of a movement or skills problem. Each teacher is encouraged to use these steps with her own interpretation and for her own purposes.

1. Identification of the problem. The teacher of basketball recognizes the progression of skills needed for playing the game. Identifying these skills and translating them into problem questions is the first step.

2. Presentation of the problem. Verbal presentation of the problem is suggested rather than the explanation-demonstration approach often used. The purpose of problem-solving is to enable the students to develop their own movement responses without a specific picture of what the end product should be.

3. Guided exploration of the problem. Individualized guidance cues from the teacher are important here. The students are busy working toward a variety of solutions to the problem while the instructor gives words of encouragement, hints for well-defined, quality responses, and cues specifically designed for the varied skill levels of the students.

4. Identifying and refining the final solution. The important points here are:

a. Verbal reinforcement of the original problem.
b. Verbal cues to the total class which will encourage control of the movement skill being developed.
c. Verbal reinforcement of the need for concentrated, serious work on the part of each individual, if this seems to be necessary.
d. Individual assistance for those having difficulty identifying their best solution to the problem.

5. Demonstration for analysis, evaluation, and discussion. Suggestions for selecting demonstrators follow:

a. Allow as many students to present their finished product as is feasible and worthwhile.
   i) One student may show her pattern to another for analysis and comment.

> ii) One half of the class may present their solutions to the other half, followed by teacher-directed discussion.
>
> iii) A small group of students may present their solutions, followed by teacher-directed discussion of the major points under consideration.

b. All students should have the opportunity to demonstrate their solutions at some time during problem-solving lessons.

c. The teacher should direct the discussion session carefully, pointing out quality of response as well as simple completion of the problem, so that the students will gain experience in observing movement patterns.

It should be noted that following the completion of one problem, final solutions should be transferred to game situations as quickly as possible. In this way, the students will gain purpose from exploring and developing skills patterns.

THE DEVELOPMENT OF A BASKETBALL PROBLEM

The Problem

While moving around the floor, bounce the ball continuously, changing speed as you move, and throw the ball against the wall three times, using a different method each time. Catch the ball on the fly. (*Note:* Step 1 in the problem-solving technique has already been accomplished. The teacher has identified specific skills which need careful attention by the class. She has established the purposes of the problem: to develop controlled bouncing of the ball, to learn to change speed while bouncing the ball, and to develop three different kinds of throws.)

Progressive Development of the Problem

Instructions	Steps involved
1. Practice a controlled bounce in one spot.	2, 3
2. Keeping this bounce controlled, move around the spaces on the floor quite slowly.	2, 3
3. Move faster, still with control.	2, 3
4. Now change speed anytime you wish: fast to slow, slow to medium, slow to fast, and so on.	2, 3
5. Standing as close to the wall as you need to be, throw and catch with the wall.	2, 3
6. Throw in three different ways. Be able to repeat these three throws as accurately as possible. We will show some of them to the class.	2, 3, 5
7. Now combine the bouncing and the throwing. Think about the change of speed as you move from one wall to the other. Also, concentrate on the use of the three different throws you have just developed.	2, 3
8. What important points should we be concerned about in this problem?	4 (verbal)
9. Finish up your pattern as well as you can in the next few minutes.	3, 4
10. Rest. Sit near a partner. One stands and shows the pattern to the other. Do your pattern three or four times and return to your partner. The observer should be able to tell the mover what kinds of throws and what changes of speed were used. When partners have discussed this, the observer becomes the mover.	5
11. Who felt that her partner solved the problem of change of speed, controlled bouncing, and three different throws very capably? (*Hint:* Choose two students to show their patterns; follow with discussion.)	5
12. Let's choose one of those two solutions and see if all of us might be able to perform it successfully. (*Hint:* All should help in deciding upon the one solution to perform. All analyze speed used and types of throws used.)	5
13. How many had difficulty with the pattern? Why? (*Hint:* Importance of individual differences should be brought out through this discussion.)	5

Soccer via Problem-Solving

Spacial awareness	*Ball handling*
Spread out on field far away from others:	*Note:* A ball can be added in spacial awareness games at any time. Emphasis is therefore split between ball handling and space awareness.
touch line and go back to home, touch another, etc.;	
go to straight line nearest you, farthest from you;	*Experiment* with ball in small space: What can you do with ball close to your body?
go to curved line nearest you, farthest from you;	What can you do with ball and different parts of your feet?
move in a straight line to nearest line, farthest line;	What parts other than hands and feet can you use?
move in a zigzag (curved) way to nearest/farthest line.	How can you kick the ball hard; soft; in this direction; in any direction; on the ground; in the air?
Change speed and direction in above.	
Start with large (or small) space and close (or open) door.	*Note:* Partner work can be started with some of these same problems.
Move close together without bumping.	What unusual way can you get the ball to a partner? Is this an efficient way? Is it fast and smooth?
Use jumpers to create obstacles.	Can you share the ball with your partner?
Use balls to create obstacles.	
Use various boundary markers to change size and area of space and/or as obstacles.	Can you keep it away from your partner?
Partners: work behind one another, alongside one another during space games, trying to maintain same distance; vary distances between partners.	How can you stop the ball without hands? a high ball? low? fast? slow?
	Partner work
Use length of field in line awareness.	Passing: spacial awareness passing to front, back, side, running down and back keeping space while passing to partner.
Use more than 2's, 3's, etc.	
Work with small group getting as close to each other as possible without collisions; add ball for Keep-a-way and space awareness.	Limit formation: 2 vs. 3 within certain area.
	How many different ways can you get the ball to your partner while letting it bounce off different parts of your body?

Spacial awareness	*Ball handling*
Team work	Awareness of looking where you are going rather than at the ball.
Many people passing to others; one ball.	
Scrimmage: passing and shooting around opponents who are stationary.	*Goal work* (Use traffic markers, ropes, etc.)
	Shooting toward the goal:
Opponents moving: passing around to teammates. (form of Keep-a-way).	How many places can you kick from and get the ball into the goal?
Explore within own limits as to where one can move with others on the field.	How many different ways can you get the ball into the goal from one spot?
	With what parts of your feet can you kick the ball to the side?
Motivation—set up many ways to score: if ball gets into certain area of the field, a point is scored; if a certain number of completed passes is made, a point is scored, etc.	Kick to partner; kicks so that partner cannot get the ball easily.
	Goalie: Two people stand apart the width of the goal; kick to each other. How big can you spread out to get the ball? small? stretch? fall, roll and get up? When do you think you would use these practices?
Lead-up games	
Develop games as child's ability and interest dictate: alley soccer, line soccer, soccer tag, others?	
	Skills & drills (oriented by rules)
	Overhead throw: in or kick-in
	Present problems for solving this skill requirement as the need arises.
	Same with: corner kick; penalty kick; goal kick.
	Skills drills (if needed)
	Refer to specific soccer text for specifics: heading, dribbling, goal tending, tackling, etc.

6

Drill Versus the Problem-Solving Approach
ROBERT N. SINGER

Different educational teaching philosophies have been emphasized at various periods in this century. The revolt against the traditional method of learning (concerned with course content) inspired learning not by mere repetition but through questioning and probing. Deweyism brought about consideration for individual differences in interests, rates of learning, and, in general, a problem-solving approach to learning. Lately, many experts on educational curriculums have spoken out against so-called student-oriented courses in favor of teacher-oriented courses. The plea is for a return to traditional teaching methods, i.e., "the command performance." Whether material can be learned more effectively through drill and memorization or problem solving and probing is the current argument. Perhaps different material can be learned better under either condition.

What about a comparison of the application of these methodologies to motor-skill learning? Drill has always been the basic means of teaching motor skills, primarily because it does provide results and possibly because it does not require much creativeness and ingenuity on the part of the instructor. Arranging a situation which encourages the students to think, reason, and then act toward a goal is a methodology rarely practiced by physical educators and coaches; hence, its merits are difficult to ascertain. However, it should be of interest to speculate on the effectiveness of drill and problem solving with motor learners.

There has been considerable attention given lately to exploration skills, especially by women physical educators interested in educating elementary school children. Instead of perpetuating traditional teaching methods, these people have attempted to guide youngsters to a greater awareness of factors associated with any activity, namely time, force, and space. The approach is such as to initiate individual creativity in mastering basic movement skills, those which underlie simple and complex sport activities in varying degrees. This rationale appears to be justifiable and the approach is refreshing. How effective the immediate and long-term results are in comparison with those of traditional teaching methods is a question unanswerable at the present time.

As to the athletic skills of older children, the drill method has the advantage of facilitating the execution of an act until it is habit-like. This method is fine for the high jumper, broad jumper, and diver, to name a few, who basically demonstrate a skill under the same static environmental conditions with each performance. Comparing this situation to the one faced by the tennis player, basketball player, and soccer player, we can observe that in the former case the environment is relatively stable; fixed responses are not only allowable, they are encouraged.

In the latter circumstance, environmental conditions are dynamic. Unpredictable stimuli require the performer to have a flexible repertoire of responses. If the player (say, the basketball player) becomes routinized in his movements, an alert opponent will take advantage of him. The player who can drive to the right side and invariably stops short to take a jump shot is easier to defend against than the player who is a threat to move in any direction and who varies his shots. A team which is overcoached may reflect this practice in the following manner. The offensive pattern calls for the guard to dribble the ball toward the side-line and pass it to the forward and then cut through the middle on the opposite side. From there perhaps a few team patterns may be executed. A smart defensive team expects the guard's initial pass to the forward and intercepts one or two passes. The guard has been so trained to perform the same routine that he does not adjust properly and perhaps his and the team's play may disintegrate totally.

Players who have been exposed to diverse game circumstances, who are not overdrilled, will react more favorably to the unexpected. Drill has its function. It encourages a consistency in performance and a skillfully executed act. Obviously, certain skills must be developed before complex movement patterns may be elicited. But if coaches or physical educators merely *train* instead of *educate,* if they make robots of their pupils, they have done them a great disservice. Active youngsters must be able to reason quickly in challenging situations and have the abilities to express their thoughts. Therefore, both drill and problem-solving approaches serve in meeting teaching and student goals.

Even in sports that demand a skill to be performed in a relatively predictable environment, the problem-solving method might promote the learning of more complex skills. When the student is introspective and does not only repeat an act continually without understanding what he is really doing, he probably will gain quicker insight into other relevant skills. Perhaps overall swimming objectives are taught more effectively when the student, with teacher guidance and supervision, is encouraged to think of means of propulsion through the water on the side, back, and front, and then to react in a supervised trial-and-error method. The drilled individual learns the skill but maybe nothing more; the individual who has to reason and learn in a loosely structured situation may learn the skill as well as water principles, confidence, safety, and ways of transferring elements to other strokes and water conditions.

Traditional and innovated methods of teaching physical education skills are in existence throughout the world. Supporters of the teacher-completely-dominating drill approach, however, appear to be diminishing. Perhaps because the value of drills has been questioned, Wickstrom (1967) has seen fit to present a strong argument on behalf of the utilization of this teaching methodology. His emphasis is on skill development, however, and the importance of strengthening S-R bonds for the play that will follow later. Drills, like other teaching techniques, must be administered in an effective manner if their true value is to be realized. Wickstrom offers the following suggestions for successful results from the usage of drills:

1. Concentrate on drills until basically correct form starts to become automatic and thereby habitual. Drills need not be the only form of skill practice employed but they should be emphasized.

2. Encourage students to concentrate on the correct execution of the skill or skills used in the drills. Drills which are performed sloppily are useless and probably far more harmful than beneficial. If students do not improve in performance the situation must be analyzed to determine the cause.

3. Constantly make corrections during drills to keep attention on the proper techniques of performance. Early corrections of a general nature made with enthusiasm and to the entire group are stimulating and effective. Along with the corrections, general comments on the correct fundamentals are positive in nature and of particular value. The students should be kept aware of the purpose and objectives of the drill while they are doing it. It should be remembered that the drill is an opportunity to concentrate on certain aspects of correct performance and develop a consistency in the performance.

4. Make drills game-like as often as possible. Drills of this sort are more interesting and challenging because they are a movement in the direction of regular play.

5. Advance to the use of multiple-skill drills to emphasize the proper use of combined skills. The transition from drills to the game is easier if drills have been devised to reflect the choices and problems possible in the actual game.

6. Make extensive use of modified games to create the much desired competitive atmosphere. Most games can be modified to emphasize

one or two skills and still offer controlled practice. The modified game is one of the easiest ways to maintain a high level of interest and still retain the essential spirit of the drill.

7. Keep drills moving at a brisk pace and involve as many participants as possible. This procedure will increase the amount of individual participation and practice. Since motor learning involves the factor of trial-and-error, the student needs many opportunities to participate, evaluate and change. One or two chances per individual in a drill would not have much impact on learning.

Other physical educators are looking beyond the teaching approach that treats all individuals alike and in which the teacher dominates the activity. A stimulating new book by Mosston (1966) offers modern ways of teaching physical education students. After discussing the weaknesses of the traditional teaching method, which he calls the "command style," he delves into more desirable techniques, culminating in the *guided discovery style,* of which the problem-solving approach is an extension.

The individualized learning process, according to Mosston, brings the learner to a high level of development in four dimensions: the physical, the social, the emotional, and the intellectual. The teacher induces discoveries to problems in all activities, the solutions of which are not predetermined. That is to say, there are a number of ways of approaching a situation, and each student may cope with the problem in his own individualized manner. After all, there are many means by which one can express himself whether they be oral or physical. Examine the following example found in Mosston's book[1] of a problem to solve in movements on the parallel bars:

The first area of problem design is the initial relationship between the body and the parallel bars. How do we get on? In relating the body to the given equipment (Level 1 in the structure of subject matter), one can observe that several possibilities exist in terms of *where* to mount the parallel bars. Thus, there is a need to develop problems, the solution of which will establish the possible relationships between the position of the body, the movement, and the position on the equipment.

Mounts onto the parallel bars are possible at the following locations:

1. At the end of both bars, outside the bars.
2. At the end of both bars inside the bars.
3. In the middle of both bars, inside the bars.
4. At *any* point of both bars, inside the bars.

---

[1] Muska Mosston, *Teaching Physical Education,* Charles E. Merrill Publishing Company, Columbus, Ohio, 1966. Reprinted by permission of the publisher.

5. At the above proposals, entry can be performed above, below, and between the bars.

6. 1–4 can be done from under or over the bars.

7. Some of the above can be done using only *one* bar. Which one?

8. Some of the above can be done alternating one and two bars. Which ones?

9. Are there other locations?

10. Are there other possible bar combinations (excluding for a moment various slope arrangements)?

Let us examine some problems to solve in mounting *at the end of both bars (from the outside), facing the bars:*

1. Design two mounts from a standing position which will land you in support position.

2. Using each one of the solutions of the previous problems, *end* in three different support positions.

3. Design four different mounts from four starting positions *other than* standing, ending in each of the suggested supporting positions of 2.

4. Are there still other alternative starting positions from which you can execute four discovered mounts? How many? Are they all good? How do you determine that?

5. Using the new alternative starting positions, can you still find another mount to a support position?

6. Is it possible to end the previously discovered mounts in positions other than the front support position?

7. Can you end *any* of the previously discovered mounts with a turn? What kind of a turn?

8. Can you end any of the mounts on top of both bars?

9. Can you find three different end-mount positions on top of both bars?

10. On top of one bar?

11. Could you end the mount on no bars? Would this constitute a mount?

Although there are more steps on the parallel bars offered by Mosston, the quoted material should be adequate to reflect some possible procedures to follow in the problem-solving approach. The approach could be utilized with all sports, and Mosston does present some sports examples such as soccer, tumbling, and football. However, the approach need not be consistent from teacher to teacher, and there is plenty of room for individual creativity in the formulation of problems.

There is no firm evidence to support a stand for the drill or problem-solving approach to all types of motor-skill learning. One may assume the prerogative of conjecture, as the writer has just done, to determine the values of each method. From an educational point of view, a problem-solving approach certainly is consistent with the philosophy of our leading physical educators. From a skill-learning point of view, arguments can be justified for either method. Perhaps, to be considered at the onset, is the nature of the skill, its relation to other material to be taught, and the objectives of the teacher.

Whilden (1956), although not comparing the drill to the problem-solving approach, did investigate the effects of pupil-dominated and teacher-dominated groups. Two classes of junior high school girls learned beginning basketball skills. At the end of the unit, the teacher-dominated group (traditional instructional methods) was judged to display better basic skills, but the pupil-dominated group demonstrated a greater knowledge of the rules, a better attempt at improving the social status of near-isolated girls, and played together better as a team. Each learning method had unique value, and certainly an approach other than the conventional one apparently can fulfill particular objectives more nearly.

7

Exploration – A Method for Teaching Movement: Discussion and Summary
KATE ROSS BARRETT

Throughout this manual the examples of possible movement experiences used were developed in reference to the principles of movement as outlined by Rudolf Laban. The reason for this was that Educational Gymnastics, from which the American interest developed, was based on these principles. In this form of gymnastics the movement goals differ slightly from the movement goals in some of the movement education programs

Reprinted by permission of the author.

found in this country. The fact that this difference exists should not affect the choice of exploration as a method for teaching movement; however, its final application must be developed in relation to the type of movement goals sought.

In the development and application of any method to the teaching of movement, it is imperative that the teacher choose and understand a set of principles upon which movement is based. Students of human movements may vary in their interpretation of what these basic principles may be, or in the development of terminology relating to movement, or in their emphasis on factors considered essential in the teaching of movement. The important point is that without the concept of common movement principles, teaching will be fragmentary and goals randomly determined. The final choice of material is based upon this understanding of movement, of the child in movement, and of the group with which the teacher is working.

In deciding which approach to use, the teacher must realize the potential benefits that each method can contribute to the total experience of the group, and upon that, base her selection. The pronounced benefit highlighted in the exploration approach, in comparison to the direct approach (more teacher-directed, less child-directed), is the increased amount of child involvement in obtaining the final outcome. Other benefits of this approach are as follows:

1. Through carefully constructed movement experiences the child's creative potential and capabilities are encouraged by allowing more self-discovery.

2. By the development of these movement experiences to allow for more child-direction and less teacher-direction, intrinsic motivation and self-direction are encouraged.

3. Because of the increased individual participation in such a method, opportunities for the child to work at his own rate are more pronounced, thus allowing for individual differences.

Exploration as a method can be used in far more teaching situations than those involving free movement or free movement with small apparatus. It was not within the scope of this material, however, to apply exploration to the teaching of more specific skills.

In relation to the actual accomplishment of movement skills and knowledges, no statement as to depth of understanding or standard of performance can be made. In all methods the development of motor skill and knowledge is an objective. It is possible that one could teach a child to perform a specific skill more quickly through a teacher-directed approach than with an exploratory approach. However, there is no evidence that this is necessarily true. It is possible that some children may be inhibited by the teacher-directed approach, whereas if they were allowed more self-direction, they might accomplish the goals faster. It is also possible that some children in a teacher-directed situation would be ready for more advanced work and, consequently, be held back, while in a less teacher-directed situation, they would be able to advance at their own rate. Anyone who has taught through exploration has had the experience of having children perform motor skills which the teacher could not have developed easily with direct teaching or would have considered too complex at that stage of "readiness." Even the possibility that direct teaching might accomplish the development of specific skills more rapidly than an exploration method accounts for only the end result and not the process in the learning situation.

To provide movement experiences through exploration means more time will be spent on an experience than one is accustomed to allowing. At the beginning, responses may not demonstrate breadth of scope. As the teacher becomes more adept in handling this approach and the child more adept in self-direction, the scope and future accomplishments will broaden. Final accomplishments should be thought of as results of a series of experiences, not simply of one experience on one day.

Once the movement goals have been identified, three important elements emphasized in this analysis must be considered: the way in which the teacher develops and handles the actual movement experiences (guided progression); the development of skilled observation (demonstration-observation); and finally, the assessing of the outcomes during each experience and at the end (evaluation).

Following the selection of movement experiences desired, the importance of the construction of each problem should be emphasized. A vital concept is that every problem has varying degrees of exploration inherent in its structure. Some problems will be so constructed that the child has a great deal of responsibility in relation to the final outcome, and in others the teacher will have more responsibility and the child less. In an understanding of what is meant by a less disciplined problem, it is essential that the teacher be able to construct problems that will elicit purposeful work right from the beginning.

When a problem, because of its construction, becomes more child-directed and less teacher-directed, it does not follow that the teacher is less important. Here she still works closely with the child as a guide for his emerging efforts. Guiding a child during this type of experience means being totally aware of his work, the stage of its development, and the way it has developed to that point. Often the teacher assists the child by recognizing his ideas, discussing the direction his work seems to be taking, adding to his ideas, refining his ideas, and responding to his questions. No matter how the teacher guides the child, the child must feel the teacher knows what he is doing and how he is progressing. This can be accomplished only by a complete involvement with each child and the work he is doing. At the completion of every lesson, the teacher should know how every child responded and the type of work he was developing. She should know something about the child that she did not know before. After each class experience she should know each of them better. Then, and only then, will the teacher successfully be able to guide the movement experiences to their completion.

To the inexperienced teacher it may seem at first that she is not "teaching" the child anything, since there will be times when the teacher is only observing and not actively talking. The observing is what makes possible the necessary information about each child's capabilities and limitations, however, and from it she is able to help him develop his efforts. The teacher's role is a continuous one of reacting with the child and to the child, and it is continually changing in respect to the stage of development of any movement experience or experiences.

To gain deeper insight into the finer points of developing movement experiences, six possible stages that would aid toward the final achievement of a goal were discussed:

1. statement of the problem,
2. initial exploration,
3. selection,
4. clarification or further exploration,
5. reselection,
6. perfection.

Each stage is dependent upon the preceding one. How long to continue developing each experience before varying it or moving to the next stage depends on what the teacher wants to accomplish and how the group is responding. The precise time to move from one stage to another is an individual matter contained within each child; it is related directly to his capabilities, which the teacher is trying to develop. Each teacher, being aware of these varying capabilities through understanding the child and his movement potential, will aid in this developing process.

Once this concept is understood, it is essential to realize different possibilities in developing a problem. The teacher with little experience has difficulty taking ideas further and finally applying them to a prescribed situation involving a time limit, space, and class size. In the development of the experiences within a problem, and then from one problem to another problem, three plans were discussed. Plan 3, which combines content with class and apparatus arrangement, is the most widely used as it seems to allow for more variation. To illustrate the variations, three problems, each utilizing a different piece of small apparatus, were developed. Through these examples the possible course a problem might take was shown, and the plan by which they were developed was discussed.

In an attempt to relate these elements of exploration to a concrete and familiar situation, three lessons were developed. Their sole purpose was to show a possible way in which movement through exploration might emerge and to give the reader some idea as to how much one might expect to cover. This is often very misleading because children's reactions to situations are so different. At various times during each lesson, possible departure points for further development, other than the ones followed, are indicated. The fallacy in writing down a suggested direction that a certain movement experience might take is that it is often not the one the child or group involved will take. The variety of directions available depends upon the construction of the problem and the degree of exploration involved. If a less disciplined problem were used, it would encourage a wide diversity of possible responses from the child, whereas, in a more disciplined problem there would be fewer possibilities. If one lists the outcomes, or possible outcomes, when dealing with a creative process, the very essence of the process is removed. The material in all three lessons and in the examples showing the development from problem to problem were taken from real situations and should be looked upon as results of past experiences and not as definite predictions for future ones. Through these examples it is hoped that understanding of the basic concepts needed to develop creative work will be made more clear, and that through recognition of them, application to individual situations will be easier.

The movement education programs of today offer many opportunities to use the exploration method of teaching. However, not everyone will feel qualified and some will hesitate to begin. Since most of the work to date has been done with children of elementary school age, it is sensible to begin there. Children need a sound development of basic movement skills and knowledges before becoming involved in situations more complex. As they get older and understand their bodies, both its capabilities and limitations, they will become ready for a more advanced stage. No method in the hands of an insecure teacher will produce worthwhile experiences. The key point in the application of any method is that before it can be applied to any situation the overall objectives must be defined by the teacher. In the teaching of movement through exploration, these objectives are ultimately determined by her knowledge and philosophy of teaching.

With the willingness of the teacher to personally experience exploration, bound by the same disciplines as the child, exploring movement possibilities can become a unique experience for both. There are many ways to present worthwhile and stimulating movement experiences, and it is the sensitive teacher—the one who knows the "why"—who will be able to decide the "how."

The Question:
What Is Movement Education?

There are many different approaches to the analysis of movement education, and all the authors in this section seem to have chosen paths different from one another. They ask us to consider physical education and its relationship to movement, along with the many problems in semantics that accompany it; some practical answers to some often posed questions from an operational program; critiques and analyses; the national feeling about movement education; and suggested stages of growth and development that could help us to complete the transition to movement education programs. All aspects of our present administrative and organizational establishment are questioned, as is the operational phase of our program, which includes the face-to-face contacts of teacher and student.

Before continuing, each reader should take time to think about the overall theme of this section. Do you have your answer to "The Question"?

1

Movement Education: Wherein the Disagreement?

MARION R. BROER

What is movement education? Is "movement education" a substitute for "physical education?" Are physical educators disagreeing because of semantics? For that matter, what is meant when a physical educator speaks of "a movement?"

"A movement" is used by some in the profession in a very restricted sense to refer to a *single* movement of a *single* body part, such as flexion of the forearm. Others may use the phrase "a movement" when discussing a pattern of movement from a more or less simple coordination of eye and hand required to pick up a pencil, to a complex motor skill.

Perhaps it is little wonder that most physical educators approach the term with various concepts since Webster's definition of the word movement is very broad: "1. a moving; specifically, an action of a person or group . . ." (7:963). He goes on to define "moving" as "adj. that moves, specifically a) changing or causing to change, place or position. b) causing motion. c) causing to act . . ." (7:963). Galen defined motion by stating "When . . . a body undergoes no change from its existing state, we say that it is at rest; but if it departs from this in any respect we then say that . . . it undergoes motion. Accordingly, when it departs in various ways from its pre-existing state, it will be said to undergo various kinds of motion" (3:167). Aristotle said Nature had been defined as a "principle of motion and change . . . We must therefore see that we understand the meaning of 'motion'; for if it were unknown, the meaning of 'nature' too would be unknown" (1:278).

It appears, therefore, that it is perfectly correct to use the term in a restricted sense and equally correct to consider broader meanings. However, grammatical correctness is not the problem—it is, rather, that physical educators in their speaking and writing have not communicated to others the *particular* meaning for the term "movement" that underlies each individual's experience and education. Obviously, those who define movement in a restricted sense may reason that physical education encom-

Reprinted from *Quest*, Monograph II, April 1964, pp. 19-25. Reprinted by permission.

passes more than "movement education." Certainly few would argue that teaching isolated movements is the end of physical education.

However, if movement is defined to encompass all changes in body positions from the simple, involving one segment moving in one direction, to the most complex, involving all body segments moving in such a way that the individual is able to accomplish effectively a complicated motor task or skill, then movement education should be regarded as an important facet of the education of the individual throughout the life span. This broad definition of movement is implied by Brown and Cassidy when they write, "the field of knowledge of physical education is the art and science of movement, all the way from the toddling baby to the art form" (2:8).

Perhaps one of the reasons for the discussion concerning the importance of "movement education" in the physical education program is that, to many physical educators, the term "movement education" is coupled with dance. That is understandable. Most of dance, by virtue of its communicative and expressive objectives, does not follow a stereotyped pattern of motion. The dancer, thus, has been forced to study the various movement possibilities available to the human body in order to develop an adequate movement "vocabulary." Dancers, therefore, have studied movement and talked in terms of "movement" rather than "skills" for a much longer time than have those interested in the other phases of physical education.

Recently, the National Dance Section held a "Conference on Movement." Exploration of the six theories of movement, summarized in the "Cues to Reading" section of the current issue of *Quest,* led to the observation, "Implicit in all of these theories is a recognition that man is a biological organism whose movement is governed by physical laws" (5:26). All of these authorities describe movement in terms of energy, time and space and indicate that a movement may be primarily functional or expressive.

While it is interesting that there was not agreement in terminology among these authorities, certainly each has contributed to the body of knowledge concerning movement. The value of their contributions certainly is not restricted only to those teaching dance. Many dancers have, in their search for greater understanding of movement, investigated movements in sports. For example, in 1914, Watts, a dancer, published her philosophy of movement, which was based on a thorough study of classical Greek statues and paintings of the archer, the discus thrower, the runner, etc., and her recapitulation of the movements leading to the positions depicted (8).

Often physical educators seem to shy away from the use of the terms time-force-space in discussing the execution of a sport skill. Do they consider these to be "dance terminology"? Yet none can deny that efficient movement results only when these three elements are employed in proper relationship. Certainly force is required for motion to take place, the motion takes time and motion implies by definition a change of place or position, therefore involving space. Brown and Cassidy state, "Human Movement is the change in position of man in time-space as a result of his own energy system interacting with an environment. Human Movement is expressive and communicative, and in the interactive process changes both the individual and the environment" (2:53). They emphasized that in moving, the individual may be "expressing, communicating or coping with the environment" (2:33).

It is unfortunate that "movement education" has become, to many physical educators, synonymous with the expressing and communicating objectives. For this reason they have restricted the term to "dance movement education." Have they overlooked the fact that movement is also the individual's only means of "coping with the environment"? The expressive and communicative outcomes of movement are linked primarily to movement as an art; the developmental effects on the moving individual involve movement as an art *and* a science, while the effects of movement in developing and changing the environment may be considered to involve the science of movement.

There are primarily sports-oriented persons who for some time have pursued the study of the science of movement. It is interesting that the coaches and the professional athletes were the first persons who have been required, because of the nature of their positions, to develop students who move with a very high degree of efficiency. While "kinesiology" is defined as the science of movement, it is unfortunate that, for many years, several teachers of the subject confined their instruction to a review of anatomy and the discussion of the muscles involved in the performance of certain specific sport skills.

Some physical educators have realized that the profession has a broader purpose than teaching a group of specific sport skills and have studied movement from various aspects. Some of these persons have sought greater understanding of human movement through a study of the psychological effects of movement on the individual. They are interested in the possible uses of movement—all types of movement—in the development of an individual's concept of self, of others, and of his environment; in the control and/or release of tension; in the release and expression of emotion, etc. Some have explored the possibilities of movement which actually are available to the body. Others have increased their understanding of movement through the study of human mechanics.

Although the importance of physical laws to effective movement has been emphasized by various individuals for many years, the application of these principles in most American physical education classes is relatively recent. As long ago as 1914 Watts stated that once the principles of movement are clearly understood "they may be applied, not only to definite exercises, but to all sports, as also to the unconscious everyday movements of life, with a certainty of finding a more complete order of activity, a stronger current of force, a new power of control" (8:36). In the 1930's, Cureton, Karpovich, and a few others published articles dealing with the application of mechanics to various activities and the first text which applied these principles to the teaching of physical education was published by Glassow (4). However, it was not until the 1950's that a substantial segment of the profession evidenced a wide-spread interest in understanding basic mechanics.

Unfortunately, the term "body mechanics," when introduced into the profession of physical education, was defined in narrow terms. For years the term "body mechanics" was used to refer to the study of various postures or to the groups of activities that include standing, sitting, walking, running, pushing, pulling and lifting. Even though some physical educators accepted the fact that mechanical principles should be understood in connection with various postures, some of them still taught sport activities using descriptions of stereotyped movement sequences. These, in turn, were based on the observation of successful performers with little or no regard as to whether all of the movements were mechanically sound, and therefore actually contributing to their success. Since in *any* position and in making *any* movement, the mechanical laws must be observed, a restrictive definition of the term "body mechanics" cannot be justified.

At the National Association for Physical Education of College Women Workshop in 1956, discussion of the problems arising from misunderstanding of the terms, "body mechanics," "basic movement," "basic or fundamental activities," led to agreement on the following definitions:

Body Mechanics—the application of physical laws to the human body at rest or in motion. (The term does not denote any specific set of activities or course content.)

Basic Movement—movement carried on for its own sake, for increased understanding, or for awareness of the movement possibilities available to the human body.

Basic or Fundamental Activities—motor skill patterns that form the foundation for the specialized skills required in daily life, work, sports, dance (standing, walking, running, jumping, pushing, lifting, throwing, etc.) (6:89).

General acceptance of some such definitions might go far in reducing some of the conflict concerning movement education, since physical educators could then communicate more accurately, more readily.

Obviously, movement is the *tool* by means of which physical educators seek to develop their students. Whether this tool is employed to communicate feeling or ideas through dance movement, to hit a tennis ball, or propel the body over land or through water, to strengthen a certain group of muscles, to perform a task demanded by one's livelihood, it is still movement, the efficiency of which depends upon the effective application of the physical laws of the universe and the relationship of time, force and space. Movement can bring the individual satisfaction, not only in the accomplishment of purpose, but also in the joy which comes from feeling the use of his total being in such a way that a harmonious movement results. The dancer does not have a monopoly on sheer enjoyment of movement. This same sensation can reward the golfer as the club comes through in perfect rhythm to contact the center of the ball effectively and with considerable force. It is not just the distance the ball travels that counts, but also the joy of feeling efficient movement.

Some physical educators, believing that the profession has failed more in teaching people to move effectively than in developing specific sport skills and certain attitudes, have concluded that:

1. movement is the tool with which they accomplish their broad objectives;

2. because they deal with movement which is basic to life itself, they have the greatest opportunity of any area in education;

3. the study of movement is extremely broad and there are many avenues by which it can be approached.

The possibilities open to physical educators as they increase their understanding of the many facets of movement are countless and exciting. Is it the plethora of possibilities that blinds us?

Throughout the country the profession of physical education is being challenged. How can we anticipate understanding from those outside the profession, when some within tend to build fences, indeed sometimes walls, across the roads toward physical education goals that some colleagues are attempting to hew through the forest of knowledge? How much more rapidly the profession could advance if instead of meeting these colleagues with fences and walls to divert them to our own roads and approaches, we met them with torches, not only to attempt to see more clearly the direction in which they are headed, but even to help light their way. Is it not better to increase the number of roads and develop them into well traveled highways and freeways that can lead to the achievement of our many goals, than to keep burrowing deeper ruts in the same few approaches?

Does it really matter if some physical educators wish to use the term "movement education" instead of physical education? Will we go on dissipating our efforts in disagreement over such questions until the profession comes clattering down about our heads like a deck of cards? Or will we recognize that there are many avenues leading to the mansion which is this profession, and that there are many blocks and columns which support its framework? Instead of attempting to close possible access roads, will we help to widen them? And rather than working to crumble some of the blocks and columns, can we reinforce all with the steel of cooperative study and bind them together with the mortar of shared hypotheses and conclusions to build a solid foundation from which the profession can, in the future, rise to new heights? This is our challenge.

REFERENCES

1. Aristotle. *Physics,* Book III, *Great Books of the Western World,* Vol. 8. Chicago: Encyclopedia Britannica, Inc., 1952.

2. Brown, Camille and Rosalind Cassidy. *Theory in Physical Education, A Guide to Program Change.* Philadelphia: Lea and Febiger, 1963.

3. Galen. *On the Natural Faculties,* Book One, *Great Books of the Western World,* Vol. 10. Chicago: Encyclopedia Britannica, Inc., 1952.

4. Glassow, Ruth B. *Fundamentals of Physical Education.* Philadelphia: Lea and Febiger, 1932.

5. Gray, Mariam, et al. "Theories of Movement, Summary," *Focus on Dance II.* Washington, D.C.: American Association for Health, Phys. Educ. & Rec. 1962.

6. "Movement Group Report," *Workshop Report: Purposeful Action.* Washington, D.C.: The National Assoc. for Physical Education of College Women, 1956.

7. *New World Dictionary,* College Edition. New York: The World Publishing Co., 1957.

8. Watts, Diana. *The Renaissance of the Greek Ideal.* New York: Frederick A. Stokes Co., 1914.

2

Movement Education
VICTOR DAUER

The concept of child-centered education, the emphasis on development of the whole child, has been accepted in physical education programs for some time. Even the recent emphasis on physical fitness stresses *physical* fitness as a part of *total* fitness of the child for democratic living. While it can be argued that only lip service has been given to implementing this concept, an examination of texts, manuals, and guides in elementary school physical education over the past twenty years will reveal the broad emphasis of physical education objectives.

If this premise is accepted, movement education represents not a new kind of physical education, but essentially a new approach, a new methodology, a new way of providing learning experiences with its emphasis on the individual child. Movement education may be defined as learning to move and moving to learn. It is also variously regarded as the problem-solving approach, the self-discovery process, the educational method, the exploratory method, and child-centered learning. It is learning by, of and through movement. It is regarded as more consistent with progressive education thought and a more efficient, effective, and purposeful way of child development through physical education.

Whether to give a broad or a narrow meaning to the term "Movement Education" is a matter of choice. The author agrees with those who define movement education broadly, as the sum of all the child's experiences in movement. This makes it somewhat synonymous with the term "Physical Education."

From Victor Dauer, *Dynamic Physical Education for Elementary School Children,* Burgess Publishing Company, Minneapolis, Minn. Reprinted by permission of author and publisher.

The narrow viewpoint restricts the meaning of the term "Movement Education" to the newer methodology employing the problem-solving and exploratory approach, wherein the child has opportunity to choose either freely or within limits the movement responses he wishes to make.

If one accepts the broad concept of movement education, then another term must be applied to the problem-solving approach or the indirect method, as it is sometimes called, as this can be regarded now as a part of the overall concept of movement education. While the designation "The Indirect Method" has some acceptance, probably a better and more appropriate term would be "Basic Movement."

If the foregoing is accepted, education can be divided into four areas, each of which has a unique and important part in the physical education program.

1. Basic Movement

Basic movement is movement carried on for its own sake, offering the child the opportunity to move effectively with spontaneity and creativity. The child is stimulated to make choices as he provides answers to the problems presented. Basic movement seeks to elicit creative responses from the children within the limits of the established problem. It is concerned primarily with basic or fundamental activities, stressing basic loco-motor and non-locomotor movements (walking, hopping, twisting, turning, lifting, pushing, stretching, etc.) and efficient body management. It is a method by which fundamental movement competency can be acquired. Experimentation and exploration are the keys unlocking movement possibilities.

2. The Skills Instructional Program

The basic, fundamental skills, mentioned in the previous discussion concerning basic movement, may also be taught by the direct method with more emphasis on the skills than the methodology. Whatever the method, the basic skills should become a part of the movement competencies of the child.

In addition to the basic or fundamental skills, the more specialized skills used in sports, dancing, and gymnastic activities are the goals of the skills instructional program. The emphasis is on the "how" and "why" of known techniques, with drills and repetition of specific movements as the basis of the learning process. While it is granted that experimentation and exploration can be utilized within the concept of good technique, the emphasis is mostly on direct teaching with predetermined goals in mind as a result of the teaching process.

3. Posture and Body Mechanics

While postural considerations should be a part of all movement experiences, posture and body mechanics merit consideration as a separate area of emphasis because of the importance of good body alignment and the need for specialized knowledge and measures to maintain proper alignment. Correct use of the body is called body mechanics and it has its basis in good postural practices.

4. Perceptual-Motor Competency

Proper perceptual-motor development and maturation can contribute to a child's learning readiness. These competencies refer to balance and laterality control in basic movements, spatial orientation, and hand-eye coordination. This area holds the key for solving the baffling educational problem of why some children, who are otherwise intelligent and normal, show an inability to learn to read satisfactorily. Perceptual-motor development is a basic educational need for every child.

BASIC MOVEMENT

The key to the entire approach of basic movement is the incorporation somewhere in the methodology of the factor of self-selection, the opportunity for the child to be creative. If choice is eliminated, then the process becomes direct teaching, the traditional approach to teaching. The degree of choice, the degree of opportunity for self-discovery, indicates the extent to which basic movement concepts are employed in the learning experiences for the child. True and pure basic movement would permit the child to select for himself the activity in which he would like to participate, the apparatus (hand or large) he would like to use, and the movement experiences he would like to undergo.

At times this approach of broad choice may be of value, but for more practical purposes the teacher must place certain limitation on the type of activity the child experiences. While in movement language, this is termed as "setting a limitation" for the problem to be solved, in actuality, this is a direct command (direct teaching) establishing the extent to which the child may move. Within the limitation so set, the child has the opportunity for self-discovery, self-education, exploration, and problem-solving. Within the goal of the teacher to assist each child to attain the maximum development possible for that child, the teacher may use methods ranging throughout the entire spectrum of direct to indirect teaching. The question for the teacher is not whether or not basic movement should be employed, but the degree to which learning experiences should be so organized. Whenever possible, the child should be encouraged to experiment, create, and explore. He should be directed to apply his knowledge in many different situations in movement.

Characteristics of Basic Movement

The element of self-selection is paramount in basic movement. There must be included an opportunity for experimentation, exploration, and self-discovery. This ranges from exploration within precise and narrow limitations to opportunity for children to make choices of activity and the approach they wish to follow. It is the responsibility of the teacher to set the stage and create situations which challenge the child to develop his resources of movement. The teacher no longer dominates the lesson, but stimulates the children to use their ideas to plan different ways to carry out the movement experiences. Each child is encouraged to make what contributions he can to the whole. Since children have a desire to express themselves physically, as well as in other ways, satisfaction of this desire can only be obtained if the children have a measure of choice and an opportunity to exercise individuality.

Because the child expresses himself individually in movement, he can achieve a satisfactory measure of success *for himself* as opposed to teacher-dominated or group standards. The child progresses according to his innate abilities, stimulated by the teacher and the learning situation. No child need feel awkward or self-conscious because he doesn't measure up to predetermined standards. The fact that children differ in size, shape, maturity, and motor ability does not preclude success and satisfaction. The child makes progress according to his own rate and to his satisfaction.

There is deeper aim in satisfaction in that it seeks to develop in children not *only* what they are doing, but *how* they are moving. By this it is hoped to have the children appreciate their own ability and make better interpretation of their movement patterns. The process then becomes the acquisition of movement experiences rather than an accumulation of knowledge or subject matter. Each child should be given the opportunity to succeed in his own way according to his own capacity. There is value not only in the accomplishment of the child, but also in the manner by which he reaches this accomplishment. The teacher attempts to establish a learning experience by which the child is stimulated to think.

Some Observations About Basic Movement

It should be emphasized that a great deal of the teacher must go into the process of basic movement. To make movement purposeful and guide children toward maximum growth and development takes both a knowledge of children and of the learning process so that desirable progress can be made. The teacher who labors under the misconception that he can retire into the background after the children have chosen the activity has completely missed the point of movement methodology. This practice will not bring out good variety, let alone quality of movement. It is necessary for the teacher to approach the lesson with a plan concerning the kinds of things which are to be done; the tasks, problems, or approaches to be used; and the methods of guidance together with stress factors of importance to be considered. The lesson plan should include consideration not only for providing variety of responses, but procedures for improving the quality of movement.

Another point of contention in movement methodology is the question of how much direction should precede the introduction of a movement pattern. Some hold that every child must *first* have a chance to try out the movement pattern or skill in his own way until he has gotten the feeling of it and has experienced the difficulties and the challenges. How strictly this rule might be applied probably should be governed by the type of activity or skill. A blanket rule is not educationally sound as it takes away from the teacher the privilege and right to individual approach.

Along with the latter point, there are teachers today who feel that they are out-of-date and wrong if they are not employing basic movement. So much emphasis is placed on this method as the educational method and on the benefits of choice, self-discovery, and exploration that they feel that they are derelict in duty if not employing basic movement, at least in part. Emphasis should be placed upon the right of the teacher to determine the best approach.

A question arises about the relationship of basic movement to the development of physical fitness. When a child chooses his activity and how he will carry out the problem, how can it be assured that there will be sufficient vigorous big-muscle activity so that the major elements of physical fitness (strength, power, and endurance) will receive proper attention? In addition, how can it be assured that all areas of the body, particularly the arm-shoulder girdle and the abdominal wall, will receive proper developmental activity? It is unsound to substitute movement exploration with its stress on choice, variety, and educational concepts for developmental activities pointed toward the physical development of the child. Both developmental activities and basic movement should be included in the program.

One problem in the guidance and directive process leading to quality of movement is that group instruction becomes difficult if the children are engaged in different activities or on different pieces of apparatus. With a variety of activities, instruction becomes an individual process, limiting the effectiveness of the teacher. He can hardly center his attention on one or two children when all should be considered. This becomes even more difficult when the teacher feels that he must center his efforts on the one piece of apparatus which needs attention because of potential safety hazards.

An element of basic movement which is of concern to a number of educators is the premise that children are free to choose and free to respond in the manner they wish and at their own rate. It is postulated that this is not desirable social training for children to do only those things they choose and in the manner they choose. Few real life situations are based on this premise. To counterbalance this attitude, the teacher can include certain required activities regardless of whether or not the children approve. Children from homes where they are permitted considerable freedom often meet with problems in the school situation where more conformance is required.

3

The New Look in Elementary School Physical Education

MARGIE R. HANSON

It is now realized that if we are to make real progress in our schools priority must be given to the elementary and preschool levels for securing the finest kinds of facilities and the best qualified teachers that can be found. Within this focus, there is a nationwide surge of interest in elementary school physical education today and exciting things are happening all over the country.

Interest is evidenced by the increasing demand for specialists as teachers of elementary school physical education or as resource teachers;

Adapted from a speech by Margie R. Hanson, NEA Convention, Minneapolis, Minn., Tuesday, July 4, 1967. From Bulletin 23-A, *Physical Education for Children's Healthful Living,* pp. 71-76. Reprinted by permission of the author and the Association for Childhood Education International, 3615 Wisconsin Avenue, N.W., Washington, D.C. Copyright 1968 by the Association.

by the emphasis given to motor activities as part of remedial programs for children with learning difficulties; by the increasing number of teacher preparation institutions interested in providing either a major or special area of concentration in elementary school physical education; and by a general interest of professional people in the contributions that good physical education programs can make to the total development of all children. The emergence of a special terminology to describe the new look in elementary school physical education is another indication. Today we hear such terms as movement education, movement exploration and basic movement to describe this new look.

In the past, many teachers and parents believed that the natural play of children was sufficient activity for growth and development and that by providing a few games, dances or exercises in the school day, a child's need to move and to release energy was satisfied, and that those reasons were the primary justification for a physical education program. Recess and necessary or spontaneous play activity outside of school have often been considered adequate for a child's development.

Changing Sociological Conditions Affect Need

However, changing sociological conditions make mandatory a need today, more than ever before, for more comprehensive physical education programs in the elementary school day. Automation and mechanization reduce the amount of physical activity in an individual's life. At the same time, the population explosion reduces the natural play spaces and even the availability of ground and space for man-made play areas.

Deprivation of this opportunity for natural activity now makes us realize even more the contribution of movement to a child's total development. In experimental programs with disadvantaged children, it has been observed that for the slow learner, the underachiever, the child from the inner city and the child from crowded suburbs, activity is important not only for his physiological growth and development, but also for his social development and the development of his total learning capacity.

We Can Learn from Children

Furthermore, if we really listen to, observe and study children, we soon realize the importance of physical activity in every waking moment of their lives. As we become more knowledgeable about children's needs, we realize that physical education is not a frill or an extra, not something to be done when all the other work is done, but rather something to be done to help get all the rest of the work done! It is a necessary component of the school day, leading toward the total development of children as fully functioning human beings.

Contributions of Physical Education to Total Development

It is now accepted that children need an environment of many sensory and social experiences to facilitate learning. The medium of physical activity is a wonderful way to enrich their lives and to reach them. It is a laboratory for many types of learning. Herein children blessed with good leadership in good programs develop social relationships, learn to value, interact, observe, communicate, and to express themselves through both movement and enriched vocabulary. They recreate and they re-create. They develop new skills which enhance their poise and self-confidence and they acquire concepts such as: hard, fast, slow, up, down, around. They develop skills, attitudes, and interests for a lifetime pursuit of health and happiness thus improving their self-image, thereby becoming fully functioning human beings ready to face other tasks of their daily lives.

Curriculum Trends

Current trends in elementary education indicate an increasing interest in providing a broad physical education program for all children, beginning in nursery school. Significant changes in curriculum are taking place for children where there is good leadership in elementary school physical education.

For years the curriculum has had a limited focus on games, relays, dances and exercises. Gradually, it has been enlarged to be more comprehensive and to include stunts, tumbling, apparatus, track and field, modified sports, and other appropriate activities with particular emphasis on the specialized skills involved in each of the activities.

More recently there has been an attempt to identify core content found in all movement within daily life activities of work, play and the normal routine of living. This content is commonly referred to as basic movement which, when well developed, would enable one to manage the body efficiently in a variety of movement situations, whether walking, running, doing routine chores or participating in leisure time activities.

To develop competence in these basic movements, attention is given to the time, force and flow qualities involved, as well as to helping an individual become aware of the space in which he moves. Specific attention is also given to various movement patterns common to many activities, and lessons can be structured around these specific patterns. They are often categorized into locomotor movements—running, jumping, leaping, etc.; nonlocomotor—bending, pushing, pulling, twisting, etc.; and manipulative patterns of throwing, catching, kicking and striking.

It might well be asked, how would a lesson using this approach to curriculum differ from what is usually taught? In examining the activities of a primary grade class learning to play tag or any other of their favorite running and chasing games, one would find certain components in common, such as moving in a confined space, dodging, making quick stops and changing directions (common to many adult games also). Thus the lesson might have as an objective the development of spatial awareness and the ability to control the body in various locomotor movements.

With these objectives in mind, the physical education instructor poses movement problems that allow a child to discover his ability to move using different patterns of locomotion in the entire space without colliding with others. The scene before one would be a group of children responding with their own ideas, every child moving at the same time, all moving in different directions in various ways, each learning to use his space safely and to the best advantage before playing a game with its carefully defined rules and boundaries. Concepts of space, force, direction and timing are developed from an experience that is applicable to many other activities. Thus, the game becomes the culminating experience rather than the initial experience.

It is typical at the upper level to teach a unit on bowling, another on softball and still another on volleyball with special attention directed to the skills within each game. Study of these activities reveals similar movement patterns in all three games, e.g., the underarm movement is common to the delivery in bowling, the pitch in softball and the serve in volleyball. This movement can be extracted and applied to use in the elementary school program as a generalized experience important to many activities.

In a typical physical education class with the new look there would be at least one ball for every two children. They would be experiencing movements involving swinging, stepping with opposite foot forward, trunk rotation, transferring weight, directing the ball to the partner, before getting into the formalized game itself with its restricting rules and limited opportunities to handle the ball. No longer do teachers wait until it is time to play softball or other highly organized games to teach ball-handling skills. They can be learned through a movement education approach which can be presented to the youngest children when the tasks are appropriately structured for their developmental level.

Now this does not mean that all the usual games and dances are no longer an important part of the elementary school program or that such objectives as development of social and character traits, of specialized sports and dance skills, of fitness, are forgotten, but rather it is believed that this approach to curriculum and method enhances experiences for children and provides them with a broad background for the more specialized programs at the secondary school level.

New Emphasis on Creativity

The new look includes much emphasis on creativity and problem solving. It is compatible with modern theories of learning through discovery, meeting children's needs, allowing them to work at their own rate and level of ability, of total involvement of children in their learning experience and of de-emphasis of highly competitive or threatening situations—all features which focus on the child rather than the activity.

Much of the teaching in the past has been authoritative, formal and void of any opportunity for creativity, but as learning theories became more sophisticated and as more has been learned about children, physical education teachers have responded with programs that more nearly meet the needs of today's child—for adequate growth and development, social skills and enhancement of his total learning.

New Terminology

The most-used terms for the new look in elementary school physical education are *basic movement, movement education,* and *movement exploration.* These are often used interchangeably, and even the experts do not completely agree upon their meanings. However, *basic movement* is emerging as the term to use in identifying the core content which when well-developed should enable one to handle oneself well in a variety of movement situations. *Movement exploration* refers to the method of approaching physical education through a problem-solving process with emphasis on development of a generalized ability to handle the body efficiently. *Movement education* is a broader term used to describe elementary school physical education when it includes the basic movement content and uses the movement exploration method.

Development of Perceptual-Motor Programs

Another interesting development is the tremendous growth of remedial programs known as perceptual-motor programs for underachievers in the classroom. Various groups working with children with learning difficulties are prescribing activities to increase the child's perception; a common prescriptive activity is movement. Most motor activities recommended seem to be those which improve awareness of space, sense of direction, coordination, balance and agility.

The rationale is sound in that, as children learn to move, they will move more and learn more about the world around them; that early motor learnings serve as a base upon which other learnings are built; and that concrete sensory experiences are the bases for conceptualization. However, further study, experimentation and research are needed to identify the activities needed and specific contributions that these activities make to alleviating the difficulties of children with learning problems.

Existing Problems

To provide good elementary school physical education programs, teachers and administrators have several problems to face. These include: a shortage of elementary school physical education teachers; lack of college programs to prepare teachers for this specialty; lack of emphasis in preservice programs of the classroom teachers; insufficient attention to the primary grades; lack of supplies, equipment and facilities; weak curriculum practices; poor teaching methods. Most of these deficiencies may be due to a lack of understanding regarding the contributions that good physical education programs make to children's total learning and development.

What Can Be Done to Upgrade Programs

A teacher, wanting to evaluate his own adequacy and that of his school, might put to himself the following questions:

- Do I understand the contribution that physical education makes to total development?
- Do I allow children to work at their own rate, according to their individual needs, at their level?
- Am I providing maximum activity for every child; is it vigorous?
- Is there opportunity for creativity?
- Do we meet daily, with a planned and varied program?
- Have I been to an in-service meeting lately?
- Is the equipment of appropriate size for children?
- Is there enough equipment so no one has long to wait turns?

An administrator might ask himself:

- Do I truly appreciate the contribution that physical education makes to learning?
- Have I provided a situation which allows my teachers to answer "yes" to all the foregoing situations?
- Do I encourage my teachers to do a good job in this key area?
- Do I create a favorable climate?

A teacher preparation department might ask:

- Do we understand all of the needs of children?
- What do we offer the undergraduate classroom teacher to prepare him for this responsibility?
- How do we prepare the physical education major for this opportunity?
- What do we offer in the way of extension and graduate experiences?
- Do we have a staff member who has had experience at the elementary school level?

Summary

We are on the brink of identifying and interpreting the kinds of physical education programs that are of the most value to children now and for their future. More and more physical education teachers will be called on to help develop these programs, but at the same time the cooperation and understanding of classroom teachers and administrators remain important for the promotion of sound programs meaningful to children and worthy of the time in the school day.

Elementary school physical education is far more than "Little Games and Little Dances for Little People." It is more than a free play period or a fitness program or a remedial program or a competitive program or a problem-solving program; it is a meld of all of these elements into a sound, meaningful program which makes a far reaching contribution to the total growth and development of children.

4

Questions and Answers about Movement Education

JOAN TILLOTSON AND STAFF

The purpose of this article is to answer the questions most frequently asked of the Movement Education Staff in Plattsburgh, New York.

The answers are the combined efforts of the entire staff:

Thelma Douglas, Director of Health, Physical Education and Recreation
Joan Tillotson, Project Director
Janet Edwards, Broad Street School
Jane Fuller, Monty Street School
John Nicotera, Bailey Avenue School
Charles Novak, Oak Street School
Marilyn Williams, Monty Street School

IS MOVEMENT EDUCATION PHYSICAL EDUCATION?

We consider Movement Education as the action-oriented, child-centered Physical Education of today based on the following concepts:

a. All children move in their own unique fashion yet are encouraged, through problem-solving situations, to develop efficient and expressive ways of moving, to understand how the body moves, where it moves in space, and what its capabilities are.

b. Movement experiences help children express themselves, and that, in turn, helps us understand them.

c. Children learn to move for many purposes, gaining success, satisfaction, and positive attitudes toward activity.

Many other concepts are involved in a program of Movement Education, but rather than go into them, let's look at the diagram (Fig. 1) and see just what the subject matter is in Movement Education.

The work reported in this article was performed under a grant from the U.S. Office of Education, Department of Health, Education and Welfare. Reprinted by permission of the authors.

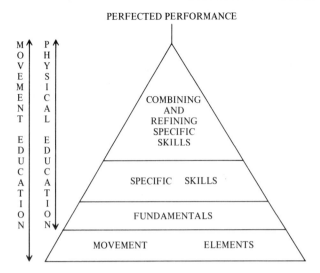

Figure 1

Physical Education programs in the elementary schools generally consist of games, rhythmic activities, and gymnastics. Usually a strong emphasis is placed on the learning of fundamental skills early in the primary grades. Children practice running, walking, skipping, hopping, jumping, throwing, catching, rolling, falling, and the like. These are the skills which, when combined, develop into specific skills for game situations. In the intermediate grades, these combined skills are refined and further combined to become the basis for our Physical Education programs in junior and senior high schools.

Movement Education purports that fundamental skills are not *the* basis for the Physical Education program. Rather, the movement elements of time, space, and force underlie the skills. These elements are inherent in every action we perform, whether we are children on a playground or adults in a work or play situation. A thorough understanding and practice of the common elements of movement are the real basis for successfully developing fundamental skills, specific skills, and refined movement patterns.

Therefore, Movement Education includes all of the games, rhythmic activities, and gymnastics of Physical Education, but initiates them through concentrated emphasis on the elements of movement. Familiarity with and analysis of these elements assists children in developing efficient ways of moving for all activities.

Then, what you are saying is that Movement Education is not just another unit to be included in a Physical Education program?

Yes, that is correct. Just learning to move for its own purpose has some value. But children need to know why they are stretching, rolling, running fast and then slowly, or working for light, controlled landings. They need to use movement experiences for practical ends: stretching for controlled head stands; rolling for a smooth, continuous sequence of stunts; running with changes of speed in order to keep away from the tagger; landing softly in order to maintain self-control.

Many of the current texts in Physical Education do discuss Movement Education but consider it as a six-week unit to be taught between other units. That is like saying we practice piano scales just so that we can become proficient at playing scales. Rather, we work with movement elements so that they can be directly applied to games and to rhythmic and gymnastic activities.

Is movement exploration synonomous with Movement Education?

No! Movement *exploration* is primarily a *method* of teaching movement experiences in Physical Education. You have brought up a common misconception that we might clarify through the use of the following brief chart.

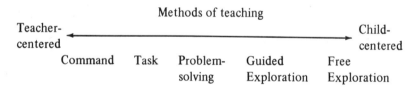

Methods of teaching

Teacher-centered				Child-centered
Command	Task	Problem-solving	Guided Exploration	Free Exploration

Here you see a continuum of teaching methods ranging from a very rigid, teacher-controlled presentation to a very free, child-controlled situation. *Free Exploration* implies that children are allowed freedom to move without restrictions or guidance from the teacher. Such opportunities *are* possible *after* safety rules and concepts are understood and practiced by the children. *Guided Exploration* implies certain restrictions and controls, established by teacher and pupils. At the same time, this guidance is open-ended enough to allow for the multitude of individual differences in classes. Presenting *Problem-solving* situations to children helps them refine movement patterns in order to gain proficiency in skills, still on an individualized basis. *Task* situations are less open-ended and require children to perform specific activities, sometimes in their own way but with more direction from the teacher. *Command* methodology allows for no individualization. Children are told what to do and how to do it.

We know that methods of teaching vary with teachers, children, objectives, purposes, equipment, facilities, administration, and a multitude of other variables. We find that in any of our classes in Movement Education there will be moments when *Command* is essential for safe, controlled movement. There are times when *Free Exploration* is encouraged for success, satisfaction, enjoyment, and a wider range of experiences. However, we find that *Guided Exploration* and *Problem-solving* situations are preferable when learning skills, developing fundamentals, and combining and refining specific skills.

We *do* use a *variety of methods* when teaching but concentrate on guiding children to explore, experiment, invent, and inquire about ways of moving for particular purposes. In this way we are not only helping children *learn to move* efficiently within their capabilities, but we are assisting them in *learning to learn.*

But if you leave it up to the children to learn efficient ways of moving, how can you be sure they learn the correct way to bat or to do a specific skill? Don't you "teach" them how to do it the right way?

The answer to this question is hard to state briefly because individual children differ in so many ways. Some of the kindergarten children we teach come to us with well-developed throwing patterns and batting swings. Our purpose with this kind of child is to further his batting and throwing skills by providing many kinds of equipment for him to use. At the same time, we find some children, even in the third and fourth grades, who have little idea of how to throw a ball. (For that matter, they have little interest and desire for this development, a fact which must be taken into consideration.) Our effort with these children is to help them understand and practice forceful actions of many varieties, as well as arm-body patterns involving flexible moves. When we help these children experiment with the elements of movement, with and without equipment, they gain insight into the complexity of the throw pattern or the batting swing, thus learning elements, mechanics, and patterns in a progressive way.

Of course, there are some children who are unable to analyze and evaluate their own patterns. They need more direct tasks to perform, such as: "Try holding the bat this way and see if you can feel the difference in the swing." Through this kind of individualized teaching, each child receives the kind of assistance he needs in order to develop movement patterns which are important to him and to the teacher as well.

We recognize that there are times when it is in the best interests of the child to be very directive. At such times, the command approach of "Do it this way!" is most beneficial and practical.

Then it appears that you are teaching all children to move well, not just the gifted or the poorly skilled. Is that correct?

Yes, that is correct. It is most important that all children receive benefit from a program of Movement Education. We have been thrilled at the progress of the gifted, who develop skills far above the rest of the class. At the same time, the "dainty doll" is encouraged to find a role for herself in all types of activity. Of course, there is the large group of children in the middle skills range who are assisted daily in enjoying, participating, and learning efficient movement skills for many purposes. Their gains are equally gratifying to us as we watch them progress.

Do you find that intermediate grade children are benefiting from exploration and problem-solving?

Our emphasis in Movement Education in Plattsburgh is just two years old. Our first-year emphasis was with the primary grade children. In the past year we have attempted to implement changes in methodology with the intermediate grade children in our four schools. Because we are at different stages in development ourselves, our answers to this question are highly individual:

"One of my fifth grade classes responds beautifully to guided exploration in apparatus activities. The other is much slower in responding favorably to open-ended questions."

"In my fifth grade class, I presented the problem: 'Using a ball and a net, develop a game which you and your chosen group of friends can play well.' One group was tossing and catching the ball, getting points for successful catches. One group was developing Newcomb as I know it. One group was serving the ball over the net and using Newcomb rules. The other group was beginning the hitting skills of volleyball."

"Individualizing skills work at the beginning of soccer is readily accepted by my sixth grade boys. However, when the game is played, they would rather play as a total class."

What we are saying is that individual classes vary in their current need for a change in methodology. However, once we have classes which have progressed through the primary grades to the intermediate level, we are confident that the process of learning to learn will be equally as important as the process of learning the game. We look forward to observing and helping develop this potential in our children.

What are the first steps in initiating a program of Movement Education?

We wish we had a blueprint for action for all teachers, but there is no such thing available. We know from experience that individual teachers differ. *We* have different years of experience and backgrounds. We have begun at different stages, with different ideas. Through weekly conferences, we have helped each other.

Some of us have found that if we look at the games, rhythmic activities, and gymnastic skills which we have been teaching, we see them in light of the *speed* of the movement, the *force* necessary, and the *pathway* which the body must take. From this analysis, we are able to assist children in analyzing how much speed, force, and space are necessary for a particular skill.

Others of us have found that the emphasis on space awareness is of prime concern. We help children experience the need for controlled movement in varying game situations by helping them concentrate on the space requirements in order to play an open game of dodgeball, soccer, basketball, and the like.

All of us have found, however, that by starting with the kindergarten children and providing situations for guided exploration with and without equipment, we are learning more about children and the ranges of their capabilities. From this controlled situation, we are able to discover the needs of children and what children consider to be important. We are constantly amazed at the individualization that takes place and the difficulty of presenting specific tasks and commands for *all* to accomplish successfully. This is reinforcement for the kind of method we use and for direction to the purposes of our classes.

5

A Way of Looking at Movement Education

RUDY MUELLER

Physical educators, like all educators, are seeking to provide educational experiences which are congruent with the philosophy and theories of American education. There is an identifiable gap between what should be and what really is happening in the gymnasium of the American public school. Teachers of physical education can no longer continue to do what they have been doing and justify what they do by making assumptions or attributions that the desirable directions are being attained. Instead, it is important to ascertain what a more congruent learning climate really looks like in physical education.

One way of attempting to establish congruency is to identify the essential components that make up the whole. In this manner, one can develop a model with its component parts or essential criteria. This method does not give one an exact or specific model, but rather a generalized model. The specific instances may be infinite in number, but they can be categorized as being in the family of (cars, houses, clothes, etc.). It can be said that such a specific instance has car(ness), house(ness), clothes-(ness), etc. It is important in education to identify the concept of educational climate(ness).

An analysis of the theories of education gives one the necessary insights as to what education climate(ness) should be. Simply stated, it should be for all, all the time, personalized to accommodate individual differences, individualized for ability and needs, and free of excessive emotional stress. If one can accept these as essential component parts of a desirable learning climate, then they have significant implications for the teaching-learning transaction.

Conceivably, they could and should act as guidelines when one is designing the specific educational climate, or they could be used to evaluate how closely one's lesson reflects the congruency between theory and implementation. Some questions—which are an extension of the essential components of a desirable learning climate—that we need to ask are: Did we include everyone? All the time? Was anyone excluded? How? Why?

Reprinted by permission of the author.

Who failed today? Who tasted defeat today? Why were they defeated? Did our environmental demands reflect single-standardness? Did we individualize for ability, needs, and thinking? Were we receptive to individual differences? Did we impose our value judgments? Did the learning climate create unnecessary pressure on students? If so, what kind of pressure? What techniques did we use to motivate? What kind of behavioral restrictions did we place on students? If we restricted them, why? If not, why not? Did we invoke our status power, the establishment? Did we use other acts of intimidation? Was there competition? If so, what kind of competition? What does it mean to be defeated by another child? What does it mean to be defeated by environmental demands? Did we promote divergent or convergent thinking and behaving? Did we manipulate subject matter? If we did, why? If not, why not? Did we correct? What did we correct? How did we correct? Did we reinforce appropriate responses? If so, how? If not, why not?

How one uses the theoretical analysis and answers the previous questions will determine the kind of learning climate. It will clearly indicate the gap between theory and practice. Unfortunately, past practices in physical education have demonstrated the glaring incongruencies which do exist. Certain practices have placed subject matter above people, group needs above individual needs, group conformity above individual expression, group control above self-control, and dependency above independence. Unfortunately, in more cases than not, it has stigmatized children and excluded them because of their abilities, limitations, personality, uniqueness, values, behaviors, and sometimes because of socio-economic standing, color of their skin, and religion.

HOW DID IT HAPPEN? WHY DID IT HAPPEN?

The answer to these questions may be very complex, but simply stated, the existing situation developed, I think, as a result of our society's preoccupation with competition—the fostering of the kind of competition that clearly demonstrates one person's superiority over another. Those who are superior and rank high are the benefactors of our system of rewards. The "less than" people reap the lesser rewards—or punishment—of the system.

Inherent in this kind of process is the need for single-standardness, for if we are to judge and rank people, we must have one set of criteria. The need to rate and rank people has implications to organizational arrangements, subject matter, equipment, and some other factors in the learning climate. It also affects the teacher's role because someone must be the judge and controller. In fact, most of the materials, activities, organizational patterns, and teaching behavior in physical education are a priori designed for identifying and isolating those *who can* from those *who cannot.* At best, physical education has made some compensations for individual differences that resulted from visible defects or handicaps. It rarely, if ever, creates a climate which focuses on the concept of *individuality.* [1, pp. 9-13, 29-40; 2, pp. 29-32; 5, pp. 1-40; 7, pp. 133-160; 11, pp. 110-111, 121-124.]

Physical educators themselves are the products of this educationally dehumanizing process. Thus their present behavior is a result of their accumulative background. This statement is not offered as an excuse but rather as a recognition of what is and as a partial explanation of why some teachers cannot change. Teachers can see the necessity for changing their professional being only if they have not been permanently desensitized and dehumanized. Change is possible only for those who are still oriented, sensitive, and committed to the demands of humanity. This idea is clearly expressed in a paper by Professor Muska Mosston entitled "Inclusion and Exclusion in Education—II." [13]

The emphasis in our professional life lies in our commitment to the public, to the community (present and future). Our commitment permeates our entire professional image and reflects our value system. Some of us are docile, some aggressive, some play the role of hidden persuaders and some are bold enough to exhort in the open. Some tacitly accept decrees and help maintain status quo; others are restless, inquiring, redesigning, experimenting and defying. Some are committed to commitment and there are those who are diligently committed to no commitment.

Regardless of the kind or degree of commitment, the Gesalt of the behavior of teachers reflects their value system. These value systems, diversified as they may be or become, can be essentially categorized in two polar groups. Those value systems committed in *Inclusion* and those committed to exclusion.

The concept of movement education has moved into the mainstream of physical education. Its development resulted from an assessment of the existing state of affairs and the recognition of the need to become more humanistically centered. The evaluators also saw the necessity for narrowing the gap between educational theory and practice. Movement education's fundamental premise is to provide an individualized experience for each child, based on all his individual differences. The concept of movement education has had some effect on physical education, and some have latched onto it because it is closer to what should be, but it too is not without its own problems and difficulties.

The concept of movement education suffers from a number of internal inconsistencies, as well as related problems of integrating theories of teaching, learning, motivation, reinforcement, internalization, self concept, and the structure of subject matter. Movement educators have not identified or integrated the essential components into a universal structure, and therefore any implementation of various movement education programs is the personalized, idiosyncratic bag of a particular person. Often it is well done but very difficult for someone else to reproduce because it failed to distinguish the common or universal elements from the idiosyncratic presentation. This situation leaves many teachers with the desire to do but without the necessary knowledge to do. Compounding its difficulty, the concept also calls for a change from what has existed. One can understand why widespread acceptance and implementation have been slow, have met with reservations, and will continue to be a problem.

In order to establish internal consistency, it is important to identify a structure's parts and its arrangement, as well as what it is and what it is not. If movement education has as its underlying essence the goal of providing inclusive, individualizing experiences for all students, then that essence must not be violated. If the experience violates the essence of the structure, it becomes something else; therefore it is undesirable and should be eliminated. In the concepts implementation, one must be cognizant of the following conditions and careful not to exclude students as a result of them.

1. Conditions under which the learner cannot satisfy the activity demands: The more specific the quantity and quality of the demands, the greater is the possibility of exclusion by failure, anxiety, fear, self assessment, etc. These inherent activity demands are the result of restrictions of equipment design, movement models or requirements, organizational patterns, rules, imposed standards, etc. The cumulative demands make up the activity's *degree of difficulty.*

2. Conditions under which teachers do not seek and accept new and alternative responses: There is a need for an accepting attitude toward different thoughts, new ideas, and/or opposing points of view. Thinkers should be encouraged, developed, and included. A new or contrary idea and its expression don't make a child disobedient, a deviant, a troublemaker, or undisciplined, but just a person with a different idea.

3. Conditions under which the group is the focus of the educational process: Group standards, group expectations, group averages, group dependency, and group control all result in the subordination of the learner's individuality.

4. Conditions under which the individual's inadequacies or a stigma becomes more apparent: As used here, *stigma* connotes a special kind of relationship between a person's limitations and his ability expectations. A stigmatized person is reduced from his total identity to the specific manifestation. We foster this labeling by analyzing and concentrating on one's inabilities rather than on his competencies.

5. Conditions under which teachers are incapable of recognizing and accepting the existence of alternative emotional behaviors: A child has the right to communicate the way he feels. Teachers are not there to impose their value judgments on his feelings or expressions but to understand what is being expressed, how it is being expressed, and what is implied by this kind of emotional message.

If these are concerns of movement education, then we must ask ourselves how the following can be instances in movement education.

1. Presentation to students of problems which are nothing more than neuro-muscular challenges, with few or no alternatives (Can you . . . ? Who can . . . ?).

2. Adherence to a single prescribed model or response (the correct way, the right way).

3. Judgments of student solutions by teachers (good, better, best).

4. Requests that everyone make the same response to the same rhythm.

5. Games of elimination, athletic-type games, close-order drill.

It becomes clear that even though we know when something violates the essential premise, we still do not know all the ingredients that make up the whole known as movement education. We need to know more about the structure of activities, movement, and teaching.

VALUE SYSTEMS OF MOVEMENT

Mr. Mosston, in his book entitled *Developmental Movement,* [12] identifies three categories of movement: *functional value, assigned value,* and *intrinsic value.*

Functional value is movement for a specific, measurable purpose in a clearly defined environment. If the purpose is accomplished, it justifies and/or excuses all previous movements. If the purpose is not accomplished, then all or part of the previous movement was either not good enough or superfluous. The functional value of human movement belongs in the domain of those who ask, "What does he do for the activity?" The answer then becomes the criterion by which we judge the worth of the individual in that environment.

Assigned value is movement to which people attribute a feeling, idea and/or mood. How one interprets the movement depends on the judging criteria, which have been predetermined; they establish a code of "good-(ness)," "beauty(ness)," and/or "form(ness)."

In assigned value the question is not "Did the performer accomplish the specific movement?" but rather, "While accomplishing the movement, how closely did he conform to the set of predetermined criteria?" In this case, one is judged by how well he adhered to a subjectively established model.

Intrinsic value is concerned with the developmental contribution that is an essential part of all movement. When one moves, he is demanding and utilizing degrees of strength, endurance, flexibility, balance, eye-body-part coordination, body-part coordination, reaction-response time, digital dexterity, kinesthetic, visual-auditory, and tactile perception, etc. These attributes and their development are void of culture or individual feelings. If one does a movement it has resultant effect on that organism and only on that one.

The intrinsic value of movement focuses on what the activity does to develop the physical attributes of people. The question is "What does subject matter do for or against people?" The person becomes the focus, and the subject-matter demands change to facilitate the learner's differences. Movement educators should concern themselves with movement from the point of view of how subject matter can facilitate the learner's growth. Both the assigned-value and functional-value systems negate total inclusion and individualization.

ACTIVITY DESIGNS

The gestalt of any specific subject-matter activity has an inherent degree of difficulty, which is not constant but relative to the learner's strengths and weaknesses, which accompany him in this relationship. If one is concerned with the concepts of inclusion and individualization, then all activity designs must be flexible enough to be moved up and down the degree-of-difficulty scale to accommodate personal development—down whenever we wish to provide success for those who have less ability and up to challenge those who have more. In order to meet the demands of individual differences, one must make an activity analysis. One must identify the variables that exist in the activity components and understand how changing the specific variables contributes to the activity's degree of difficulty.

Activities Design Sheet

Shooting Basketball

Components of activity	Variables	Specific example of a possible combination of variation
1.1 Equipment demands	1.11 Width of basket 1.12 Height of basket 1.13 Material of backboard 1.14 Stability of basket 1.15 Size of ball 1.16 Weight of ball 1.17 Special characteristics ⋮	
1.2 Performer demands	1.21 Points of contact 1.22 Relationship of body to basket 1.23 Posture 1.24 Visual cues 1.25 Distance 1.26 Angle ⋮	
1.3 Movement demands	1.31 Type of locomotion 1.32 Type of motion 1.33 Direction 1.34 Change in C. or G. 1.35 Speed or rhythm 1.36 Special demands of activity design 1.37 Subsequent action ⋮	

Components of activity	Variables	Specific example of a possible combination of variation
1.4 Organization demands	1.41 Org. pattern 1.42 Rules 1.43 Safety consideration 1.44 Quality of execution 1.45 Repetitions 1.46 Time limitations 1.47 Evaluation/reinforce- ment 1.48 Recording 1.49 Special supplies ⋮	

Balance Beam

1.0 Dynamic
    balance

Components of activity	Variables	Specific example of a possible combination of variation
1.1 Equipment demands	1.11 Width 1.12 Length 1.13 Material 1.14 Stability 1.15 Height of beam 1.16 Slant of beam 1.17 Special character- istics ⋮	
1.2 Performer demands	1.21 Points of contact 1.22 Relationship of points of contact 1.23 Posture 1.24 Visual cues ⋮	

Components of activity	Variables	Specific example of a possible combination of variation
1.3 Movement demands	1.31 Mount 1.32 Type of locomotion 1.33 Direction 1.34 Change in C. of G. 1.35 Speed of rhythm 1.36 Special demands of activity design 1.37 Dismount ⋮	
1.4 Organization demands	1.41 Org. pattern 1.42 Styles of execution 1.43 Safety consideration 1.44 Repetitions 1.45 Sets 1.46 Time limitations 1.47 Evaluation/reinforce-ment 1.48 Recording 1.49 Special supplies ⋮	

TEACHING BEHAVIOR

The teacher's behavior is a major determiner of the kind of learning climate one wishes to promote. The learner's behavior and response are greatly dependent on the teacher's behavior, and it follows that a change in teacher's behavior will have an effect on the learner. As long as the transaction is in process, there is an interplay between the sets of decisions made by teacher and learner.

The teacher's role in this interaction must change from the intuitive-idiosyncratic level, at which the teacher's background, mood, value system, personal needs, social points of view are the controlling factors, to a conscious act based on a tangible theory of instruction. Such a construct, which is based on a set of decisions that must be made for the teaching-learning process, is offered by the *spectrum of teaching styles.* [14]

The spectrum has as its theoretical backbone the concept of individualization. Each style has its own inherent degree of individualization and has uniquely different roles for teacher and student. This situation is significantly important to movement educators, for whom individualization and inclusion for all are the essentials of the learning climate. It is therefore necessary to make an analysis of each style to indicate which ones are more significant to the concept of movement education.

Command is a style in which teachers make all decisions and control the quantity and quality of all responses. The group is the focus and individualization is close to zero. This style is incompatible with movement education.

Task is a style in which students are given a specific, teacher-determined task and they may make decisions about where to stand, when to start and stop, and/or what pace or rhythm to use. The teacher may arrange the task on various levels by degree of difficulty (Range of Tasks) to begin the individualizing based on physical differences. This style would be acceptable to the "Who can?—Can you?" movement educators, who present problems that are really just neuro-muscular challenges, or to those teachers who use the functional-value system.

Reciprocal teaching is a style that allows the doer of the task the same decisions he had in the task style, but it provides him with an observer to give him immediate feedback about the quality of his performance. The teacher still decides the specific task and the criteria for the observer. This style would be acceptable to those movement educators who focus on single responses which have a correct, or right, way of being done. This style, like the task style, would be less desirable to those seeking high levels of individualization. Movement educators using this style would most likely be operating in the functional- or assigned-value systems.

Individual program (teacher-designed) is a style that provides a series of specific tasks to be executed by the learner. These tasks may be random or completely personalized, based on the students' physical differences. This style demands that the teacher manipulate the activity variables to create similar activities with varying degrees of difficulty. The execution of the program demands that students operate independently of the teacher for long periods of time and that they make self-assessments. This style would be acceptable to most movement educators, particularly if they are seeking to improve performance of a specific nature or if they need to provide a high-frequency rate of experience in a personalized program.

Individual program (student-designed) is a style in which the teacher establishes a focus and the student is asked to develop a complete program around it. For example, the student might be asked to design a developmental program for all his physical attributes, using a chair, or to design a developmental program that will focus on accuracy, using various parts of the body. This style can help those movement educators who seek high levels of physical individualization, cognitive involvement, self-evaluation, and innovative opportunities.

Problem-solving is a style of teaching in which students are asked to become cognitively involved by facing a problem and presenting alternative movement solutions. Each of the learner's solutions has a degree of difficulty, but he may base his selection of which ones to offer on his self-assessment of his involvement in each situation. The learner determines this, not the teacher. The process of Problem-solving can be symbolized as follows:

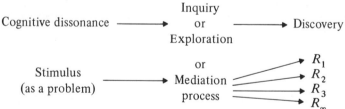

Since the student is expected to develop the specific subject-matter instance and appraise his ability to do the proposed solution, the style is more individualized than are the previous styles. All responses that fit the criteria established by the problem are correct. No one response is better than another if it is correct. Teachers who rank solutions eliminate some possibilities because students begin to make selections based on what they know the teacher is looking for. All movement educators who are seeking high levels of individualization, cognitive involvement, and creative opportunities for the students will find this style most applicable.

TEACHER VERBALIZATION

What the teacher says to the student during the teaching-learning act is also of major importance. It could enhance or destroy the entire transaction. Both teacher and student could lose as the result of an unfortunate choice of words or gestures.

Informative/descriptive verbalization. In communicating information to the student, we must be conscious of the complexity, volume, and clarity of our speech. The group should be organized to facilitate communication. There should be an awareness of the possible difficulty if we use words or concepts that the child doesn't understand. The message may be more easily understood if we use in combination more than one mode of communication, such as demonstrations, written messages, and pictures.

The rapport between the teacher and the child should be such that the child will feel it is *all right* to say, "I didn't understand you." We should not make him feel guilty about not understanding. In fact, we can help relieve all anxieties by replying, "I guess I didn't make myself clear, so let me try again," but we should avoid saying things like, "How many of you understood?" and "There! See that. Everyone understood but you," etc.

We should also endeavor to make the child secure enough to say things like "I forgot," "I don't think I can do that," "I don't like to do that," "I don't want to do that," etc. These are all important and healthy ways of communicating emotional problems, and the insights provided often prevent more difficult overt behavioral manifestations.

If necessary, we can follow up on a one-to-one basis by asking such questions as "How do you think we can get you to remember?" and "Let's see if we can find the part that makes it so hard to do," etc.

Reinforcing verbalization. Here we should address ourselves to the act itself. We should praise or make a neutral comment about the learner's performance. We should prevent projection of how we feel about the child as a result of his accomplishment, e.g., "You are a good boy; now I like you." The pitfall here is the bond that is created between accomplishment and the way in which we view the child—therefore, when he doesn't accomplish, he is a "bad boy" or "now we don't like" him.

We can promote additional personal awareness by the learner if we comment on his act and ask him for information, e.g., "That throw was very good. How did you feel about it? What did you like about it? How did you change the grip the last time you threw the ball?"

Teachers should recognize that physical gestures and physical contact are very effective reinforcing acts, and in some cases they constitute a more effective way of communicating approval.

Correcting verbalization. The danger in correcting people is that the remarks often project accusations, ridicule, threats, and excessive criticism. Such a result actually accentuates the child's inabilities and causes him to feel rejected. "Don't you ever get anything right?" "After this many times you'd think. . . ." "If you don't get it right now, I'll. . . ." "You'll do it or else!" These responses and others are examples of undesirable reactions. They often trigger defensive mechanisms in a child, and further communication is cut off.

When correcting a child, one must try to create a learning situation by providing the opportunity for the child to internalize the message. Questions cause children to think about the specific instance on which the teacher may wish to focus. Examples are: "I know it's hard to remember all the things about throwing to a target, but do you remember what was said about the eyes?" and "That jump was interesting. What did you change from your last jump, or how is this one different from the other jumps you made?"

This type of verbalization not only concentrates on the act, but it forces the child to become cognitively involved, and internalization is more likely to occur.

Deviant-behavior verbalization. Here the problem is very complex. We must be delicate but we cannot pretend that the problem doesn't exist. We cannot just identify the deviant or offensive behavior; it must be modified. Undesirable behavior that goes unchecked creates additional difficulties for teacher and children.

There are four steps we can use to modify the child's behavior. *First, we identify with the child, if possible:* "I know how hard it is when we first learn something . . ."; "You are showing signs that you are angry . . ."; etc. *Second, we verbalize what the actual behavior was:* "I could tell because you decided to stop . . ."; "When you make faces, people know you are unhappy . . ."; "Kicking things is a sign of being angry. . . ." *Third, we indicate to the child the consequence of his behavior:* "If you don't stop, some people may not like it and may call you names; some people will send you to the vice principal; they may even shout at you . . ."; "If you kick things, the owners may not like it and they may become angry and send you out of the room or make you sit down now and do it after school." *Fourth, we offer an alternative behavior:* "When you can't do something, it's O.K. to ask people for help"; "When you are angry, it's O.K. to tell people you are angry."

Behavioral changes do not occur by some strange miracle. A way to effect change is to promote consistent interaction and purposeful verbalization. Several other behavioral-modification techniques can be used in specific instances.

If the child breaks a rule, ask questions, such as: "What is the rule about running in the hall?"; "Do you remember when we can speak in class?"; etc. Reprimanding turns on defense mechanisms, promotes hostility, and cuts down on verbal interaction because statements do not demand answers.

If the child refuses to join in an activity: "When you are ready to join us you may; we will be waiting for you." If there is a need to follow up, do it on a one-to-one basis.

When a child is creating a safety problem for himself or others, step in actively: "There is a rule here that says *no one* may do that . . ."; "You could hurt _____ and no one likes to be hurt. That's why we have the rule that says . . ."; etc. I'm sure a number of other examples may be suggested, but they can be handled by utilizing the four steps of behavior modification.

SUMMARY

If movement education is to be an effective force in physical education, it must develop a structure which has more internal consistency. It must be highly individualized—physically, intellectually, and emotionally. It must be an inclusive experience for all children, and all factors in the learning climate must be manipulated to serve the learner's development. The activity (subject matter) should be viewed from the point of view of intrinsic-value system rather than from that of the functional- or assigned-value system. The teacher should use problem-solving or individual program (student-designed) when seeking cognitive involvement leading to innovative or creative alternative responses. If the purpose of the lesson is to evaluate self and to personalize subject-matter experiences, then the teacher-designed individual program is a desirable format. If one seeks individualization because of physical differences, one could use either the task or the reciprocal-teaching style.

The movement educator's role as a teacher is very important during the preclass, or preimpact phase of the lesson, but he should not be the focus during the execution phase. If the session revolves around or is dependent on the teacher during execution, it has failed in its attempt to be a fully individualized experience. The role of the teacher should be to reinforce, correct, and motivate individuals, in a manner based on their needs. He must not communicate attitudes or values that interfere or are inconsistent with the process.

The concept of movement education is not synonymous with physical education, and it may be that theoretically physical education should encompass more than movement education. Yet one might legitimately ask the question, "What is physical education in its present form doing in the American public school?" Once physical education is defined to show what it is and what it is not, one may be better able to determine its relationship to movement education. Until then, operationally, the movement education concept comes much closer to what should be happening in American education.

BIBLIOGRAPHY

1. Association for Supervision and Curriculum Development. *A Climate for Individuality*. Washington, D.C.: NEA, 1965.

2. Association for Supervision and Curriculum Development. *Humanizing Education*. Washington, D.C.: NEA, 1967.

3. W. McD. Cameron and Peggy Pleasance. *Education in Movement*. Oxford: Basil Blackwell, 1963.

4. Liselott Diem. *Corrective Gymnastics and Special Exercise Class in Schools*. Frankfurt: Limpert, 1963.

5. Liselott Diem. *Who Can*. Frankfurt: Limpert, 1965.

6. Erving Goffman. *Stigma*. Englewood Cliffs, N.J.: Prentice-Hall, 1963.

7. John Holt. *How Children Fail*. New York: Pitman, 1964.

8. Inner London Education Authority. *Educational Gymnastics*. London: 1966.

9. Inner London Education Authority. *Movement Education for Infants*. London: 1966.

10. Rudolf Laban and F. C. Lawrence. *Effort*. London: MacDonald and Evans, 1947.

11. George B. Leonard. *Education and Ecstasy*. New York: Delacorte, 1968.

12. Muska Mosston. *Developmental Movement*. Columbus, O.: Merrill, 1965.

13. Muska Mosston. "Inclusion and Exclusion in Education—II." Paper presented at University of Pittsburgh, February 1969.

14. Muska Mosston. *Teaching Physical Education*. Columbus, O.: Merrill, 1966.

15. Rudy Mueller. "A Learning Climate for Children Who Can Not." Paper presented at East Central District Conference of N.J.A.H.P.E.R., Princeton, N.J., March 1969.

16. Betty Rowen. *Learning Through Movement*. New York: Bureau of Publications, Teachers College, Columbia University, 1963.

6

A Critique of Movement Education
LAWRENCE F. LOCKE

In the field of education no widely accepted, comprehensive theory of instruction exists. Therefore, criticism of a particular instructional system must proceed from a corpus of maxims about the conditions that will optimize learning. Such standards are usually disconnected and open to considerable subjective interpretation. My criticism of movement education is no less unscientific and certainly no more free of caprice than other armchair attempts to evaluate educational methods without a full arsenal of empirical evidence.

Before discussing the strengths and weaknesses of movement education, let us first establish a basis for comparison. For the purpose of convenience, programs of physical education which are *not* movement education will be referred to here as "traditional" programs. While the creation of such a category does violence to some genuine differences among various American programs the notion of an average or modal program would probably be supported by any survey of physical education in the United States. Such a program would center upon teaching

Lawrence F. Locke, "Movement Education—A Description and Critique," from Eds. Roscoe C. Brown, Jr., and Bryant J. Cratty, *New Perspectives of Man in Action,* © 1969. Reprinted by permission of Prentice-Hall, Inc., Englewood Cliffs, N.J.

sports skills. In it the teachers would show the student how to perform and then guide his practice through correction. The elementary school program would consist largely of teaching simplified elements of the sports skills and practice in "lead-up" games. The secondary school program would consist of instruction and practice in some sequence of sports. Physical fitness activities might be added for the boys and dance instruction for the girls.

The critique will begin by noting some of the special strengths of movement education. Most of these assets can best be presented in terms of what they suggest for improving procedures in traditional physical education.

THE STRENGTHS OF MOVEMENT EDUCATION

Movement education stresses teaching method. Whether all of the behavioral rules for teachers established in movement education texts are (or ever could be) acted out by real teachers is open to some question. There can be no question, however, that the teacher's behavior in making a vast range of decisions forms the bridge between the subject matter tasks of the curriculum and the learning processes of the student. Teaching methods *are* those decisions and teaching method does matter. More to the point, movement education has provided the first stimulating, nonpedantic break with a long tradition of slighting or mistreating teaching method, both in physical education textbooks and in professional preparation programs. Exploration, problem solving, and all that these imply for the teacher's behavior are sharp breaks with an undistinguished tradition.

Movement education focuses upon children and the teachers of children. For a variety of reasons elementary physical education has not always been taken seriously by people inside or outside the profession. This is largely a matter of the sociopolitical structure of physical education as a profession and is not the result of logic. Physical educators generally acknowledge that the early elementary school years are a crucial period for developing readiness for sports skill instruction. Yet, by junior high school many members of a typical physical education class appear unable to profit from skill instruction without extensive remedial effort. It is too simple to claim that these children have poor motor ability.

Although movement education has been used with students at all age levels it is particularly well designed to fit the characteristics of young children. Movement education makes great use of the enthusiasm, creative potential, and curiosity that are the hallmarks of children. Further, movement education tries to take into account what young children cannot do, what they fear, and the importance of their own peculiar pacing for learning.

By emphasizing the crucial importance of experience in the lower grades movement educators have contributed a small nudge toward toppling the disastrous structure of contemporary physical education. In this structure, with rare exceptions, the outstanding teachers are promoted to higher grade levels in the school system. They move upward to where the rewards are found. Unfortunately, this is also where their talents often can make not a larger but a smaller contribution to the objectives of physical education.

Movement education encourages self-directed learning. Movement education stresses the attitudes and cognitive abilities necessary for the acquisition and performance of new skills beyond the school years. Few physical educators would argue that this stress is misplaced. Traditional methods of teaching sometimes make it difficult to encourage and reward the kind of analytic set that is necessary for self-tuition. Each time we demand only imitation, each time we provide a needed correction without giving the student access to how the correction was derived, we make the student more dependent upon cues emitted by the teacher. Such a process is correctly called training. Only when the student is required to add his own creative insight and skill can it be called education.

Movement education emphasizes the process of observing movement. The process of closely observing the movement of others and one's self can be a valuable aid in learning complex skills. Traditional physical education has given astoundingly little attention to instruction and practice in observing and analyzing movement. This has even been true in the preparation of physical education teachers themselves. Movement education provides much guided practice in the intelligent observation of movement.

Movement education stresses appropriate introductory experiences to movement skills. In traditional physical education programs the children are sometimes thrust forward into complex games and into demanding situations long before they have oriented themselves. In order to learn effectively a child must be familiar and comfortable with the learning situation. By providing for exploration, familiarization, and some individualization of the rate of learning, movement education has a powerful advantage over some traditional programs.

Given the great stress on appropriate introductory experiences, movement education may be regarded as *precurriculum*—as readiness training. Something of this sort is at least implicit in the movement education literature. Like the proponents of some of Bruner's theories, the movement educators do not want to teach before the child is ready. On the other hand they do not want to wait until the child is ready. They intend to teach readiness.

Movement educators recognize the importance of theory in organizing subject matter and selecting methods of instruction. Despite internecine squabbles over Laban's theories, leaders in movement education have persistently stressed the need for using some theoretical structure as a reference point in determining content and method. Traditional physical education has, too often, been governed by expediency. Methods of instruction have been selected because they could be made to work in a given situation. Such collections of pat techniques for specific situations produce a kind of educational low gear. The teacher has no guiding principles by which to make rational decisions and lacks any basis for constant self-criticism and improvement.

A good theory provides a matrix of propositions stating the way in which teaching method relates to actual changes in various kinds of learners. The propositions are anchored in carefully collected data. Movement education offers no such comprehensive theory and its supporters have largely ignored the matter of empirical data. On the other hand, movement education does provide a workable taxonomy of subject matter and at least a rough way of systematically relating content, methods, and particular kinds of learners. The importance of the theories of movement education is not so much that they are perfect or universally applicable but rather that they set a rationale for practice that is explicit and examinable.

Teachers directly involved in movement education have related to me several miscellaneous assets that seem worthy of note. Teachers have a more practical eye than authors of textbooks. Their observations thus provide a different flavor.

1. Movement education, when good teachers are available and there are small classes with adequate equipment, provides an immense amount of very genuine pleasure for children.

2. Movement education has proved to be an ideal setting in which to identify children who can profit from remedial physical education. Such children often can slip by in an ordinary physical education class.

3. Movement education has proved to be an ideal setting for identifying the quick learner and facile performer. These are the individuals destined for dance training and varsity sports.

4. Movement education has had a facilitating effect upon dance and gymnastic programs, leading to the development of suitable teaching space and the purchase of a wider range of equipment. Movement education has had a direct effect upon gymnastics in that it encourages tumbling, free exercise, and apparatus routines that are less preconceived, and which are often exciting and highly adventurous.

THE PROBLEMS PRESENTED BY MOVEMENT EDUCATION

Any system of education will present some disadvantages. Armed with an understanding of advantages and strengths let us now turn to the problems that give many physical educators serious reservations about movement education. Problems that I judge to be most important appear at the beginning of the list.

Movement education emphasizes an ultimate objective that may be impossible to attain. Movement education is a complex system which proposes to accomplish many things. Some of its objectives are immediate but most are long range. The objective that seems to me to come closest to serving the purpose of an "ultimate objective" is the intention to *teach children to move well in all activities.* More specifically, many movement educators expect to facilitate, if not accomplish, the learning of sports skills.

Movement educators either directly or by implication propose to develop a general capacity for movement that will facilitate subsequent skill learning. Whether a given educator stresses transfer to sports skills or to the more general sort of movement requirements found in adult living is an individual matter. The essence of the intention remains the same. The identification of this objective is a significant point and calls for documentation. While the following quotations are specifically selected to illustrate the point at hand, they are, I think, a reasonable representation.

Basic movement skills are designed to increase the range and effectiveness of general movement patterns fundamental to the development of highly specialized skills. (12: 1)

The purpose of these skills (educational gymnastics) is to give the individual mastery over himself in a wide variety of situations. The experience of solving problems and moving in many different ways develops kinesthetic consciousness and feeling for movement. This forms a pool of general skill which probably contributes to the learning of any physical skill. (34: 8)

As a child progresses in experiences in movement, he will be better able to achieve mastery in a variety of activities if he has been encouraged to explore his own movement from a great many different approaches and to discover for himself satisfying movement patterns. (14: 3)

It is hoped that through the training in these movement-qualities and through movement education generally, individual standards of body coordination may be raised so that a skill learner while still having to learn a new skill, does so without the clumsy, jerky, wasteful movements that characterize unskilled performances, with the result that learning occurs much more quickly and happily. (44: 30)

What, then, are the potential benefits from such an experience (movement exploration)?

1. To develop skill in and knowledge of movement through pro-gressively designed experiences which later can be applied to all phases of life. (2: 5)

One cannot learn to play tennis without playing tennis. However, the learning of tennis can be facilitated ... through the application of pre-viously learned patterns and knowledge of the way the body produces and controls force. (7: 364-65)

... the exercise of the flow of movement will enable a child to use his mobility for all practical purposes in everyday life. (27: 96)

People trained in the performance of the eight basic actions, combined with bound and fluent flow, will be more able to choose the appropriate movements for any tasks they face than those who rely entirely upon their natural gifts or intuition. (28: 18)

Movement education thus proposes to teach readiness for future movement demands. Whether it is called the pool of general movement ability, good body coordination, kinesthetic sensitivity, effective general movement patterns, a feeling for movement, or simply skill in movement, the words add up to a concept of general ability that will persistently transfer so as to facilitate learning and performance in new skills.

Can movement education accomplish what it thus proposes to do? Only two things are sure in regard to this question.

First: no reliable empirical data dealing with movement education have been published to make such a judgment possible. Movement education was initially the product of data-free theorizing. This is an acceptable and sometimes necessary process. That movement education has so far re-mained in the schools as data-free practice is less fortunate and not accept-able. The only empirical information we have that concerns the achieve-ment of objectives comes from movement education teachers. The dif-ficulty here is that the teacher's judgment can be a defective source. Long-term successes of a particular practice are not observable, and short-term results are not easily traced to the teaching methods from which they presumably arose.

Second: while the evidence presently available concerning general motor factors is not in complete agreement, it does not support the existence of unitiary faculties such as coordination, kinesthesis, or general movement ability. A movement educator must presume not only that general human faculties exist but also that he can train them so that transfer will occur in a variety of specific tasks.

The questions of transfer of training in motor tasks and general versus specific models for the organization of human motor ability have been much discussed and will not be examined in detail here. Readers interested in the substance of recent discussions in these areas should see: Battig (4), Fleishman (17, 18), Fitts (16), Cratty (9, 10), Knapp (25), and Munrow (37).

It seems likely that Cratty is correct in his observation that it is indefensible (and unhelpful) to declare perceptual-motor skills either specific or general (10). A learner can possess both kinds of ability with regard to a given task. One suspects, however, that such general factors as do exist are relatively unmodifiable. At the very least we can expect these to have been largely determined by middle childhood. Intelligence, characteristic level of arousal, persistence, and such perceptual abilities as spatial visualization are probably not open to any substantial manipulation. The remaining factors seem likely to be skills that are closely tied to the tasks in which they were acquired and between which we would expect little transfer. If these assumptions are even partly true then the movement educator may be falling between two stools.

No one, not even the most ardent supporter of movement education, would claim that a general movement lesson is a better way to learn tennis than a tennis lesson. The movement educator would argue that a child must come to the tennis lesson *ready* to learn. He must possess the necessary strength, attention span, psychological readiness for competitive sport, positive attitude towards movement activities, confidence in his own capacity to master movement skills, and some ability in the fundamental elements of running and striking. All of these are factors to which movement educators claim to make some positive contribution. It would be difficult to disagree although I am sure that normal maturation plus a traditional program of lead-up games, rhythmics, dance, and tumbling would produce the same kind of minimal readiness.

The difficulty arises when movement educators claim that movement education will provide a pool of general skill or a superior kinesthetic sense that will make the student of tennis learn faster or to a higher level of proficiency. It is much more difficult to agree with this assumption. Much in the research literature of motor learning argues against such a possibility. I grant that a skillful tennis teacher could rebuild some of the cognitive connections between tennis and what was learned in movement education. One must ask: Why bother? Why bother with movement education at all? What does it offer that a sound traditional program could not offer? No one knows the answers to these questions. We have only the raw data of limited personal observation—and our prejudices.

Understanding movement is neither as useful nor as desirable as movement educators sometimes insist. There is some risk that too much stress on problems, analysis, and intellectual content can undermine the element that makes movement such a source of pleasure. Those who truly love to move do not always insist on knowing how or why. The fresh joy of a child's running is best preserved by doing it—not by talking about it. Many physical educators would here stand with Keats.

Do not all charms fly
At the mere touch of cold philosophy?
There was an awful rainbow once in Heaven:
We know her woof, her textures; she is given
In the dull catalogue of common things.
Philosophy will clip an Angel's wings.

In focusing upon the superiority of their method when contrasted with traditional procedures movement educators have seriously misidentified and underestimated the central problems in physical education. The acceptance and enthusiasm that movement education has found in the United States are based only in part on its virtues. Many supporters are responding to the belief that traditional methods have failed to produce a sufficiently high proportion of physically educated students. The movement educator's enthusiasm, however, has led him to misidentify the source of the problem. There seems to be more reason to believe that there has been a failure of teachers and "teachers of teachers" than to believe that there has been a failure of traditional method and sports skills content. If the problem has been a failure of teachers, then administrators of movement education programs will face the same dilemma they faced in hiring traditional teachers. Where will they find good teachers? If generations of physical education teachers have abused skills teaching, nothing in movement education makes it "fail-safe" against the same teachers. Much the reverse seems to be true.

The debate between movement educators and traditional physical educators cannot become a "war of methods" because there are few facts to serve as ammunition. Both traditional methods and movement education could conceivably produce acceptable results if the teaching were in capable hands. The real problem for any instructional system remains unchanged. How to recruit, train, and retain outstanding teachers for the task of elementary school physical education?

In no sense do I mean to deny the importance of teaching method. Mosston has argued convincingly that a particular style of teaching may induce a particular style of learning (36). Some styles of learning are inextricably bound to the educational goals towards which we project our students. Nonetheless, it is unreasonable to expect superior teaching methods to produce superior teachers.

The teacher's role in movement education is deceptively simple. Some popularized accounts of movement education appearing in the United States have openly or by implication stated that:

1. it is easy to teach movement education (in terms of the teacher's time and effort).

2. little training is required—a few in-service sessions will do.

3. the teacher need not be skilled in movement.

4. any intelligent teacher can master the method required.

5. movement education makes possible, if not more reasonable, the continuing use of classroom teachers in elementary school physical education programs.

In terms of my understanding of movement education, *these are dangerously inaccurate conclusions.* Movement education presents a difficult teaching task. It requires more extensive and intimate involvement of the teacher in planning and conducting each lesson than is typically the case with traditional methods.

Munrow's observation that a movement education program truly centered upon the growth of individual children would require teachers possessing ". . . the intelligence of a genius, the insight of a poet, and the patience of a saint" (37: 262) comes close to the mark. A good movement education class is not easy to conduct, and the training necessary to teach such a class is not readily obtained or absorbed.

There is a common fallacy to the effect that what an outstanding teacher can do, an average teacher can do. It is inconceivable to think that a teacher who is not a "problem-solver" himself could teach by the problem-solving method—to say nothing of producing problem-solving students. Teachers' colleges have despaired of attempts to produce such fundamental alterations in the personal style of teacher trainees as are required by the concept of "being a problem solver."

It is important that the teacher understand what the implications of teaching method are for the process of learning. A teacher can, with practice and guidance, learn to alter his style to better meet some situations. Nonetheless, teachers are sometimes tempted or pressured into using a style not in harmony with their own personalities, with unhappy results. It seems far better to use a method of teaching that is familiar and natural than to flounder with one which is awkward and artificial. For many elementary school physical education teachers, it is my impression that the particular methods of movement education will prove unnatural.

If the goal is to be the best possible physical education for elementary school children and if, as seems to be the case, physical educators are unsure about the role to be played by the classroom teacher, then we must vigorously resist any attempt to escape the issue by recourse to the disarmingly simplistic notion that movement education can be "do-it-yourself" physical education for untrained classroom teachers. If movement education is a demanding task for the specialist it can not be other than doubly demanding for the nonspecialist.

Movement education may not be the best method of instruction for all students. For all the emphasis on individual differences little has been said about the fact that movement education provides but one alternative route among possible types of curriculum and instruction. It is sure to be a fine route for some children. Most young children will find movement education attractive. As the program is applied to progressively older groups for whom the task of physical education is better defined in terms of the acquisition of fundamental skills than in terms of the exploration of the wonders of movement, the number of students who can efficiently learn through problem-solving and discovery will grow smaller.

It seems probable that the child who learns for the sheer joy of manipulating and mastering movement would be capable of learning under any method of instruction. Those children who are not members of this select group would probably learn better under more traditional methods of instruction. Movement education seems to make no provision for *their* unique differences.

Some movement educators have made physical education seem only an accessory to academic learning. The emphasis in movement education on greater student involvement in the process of self-directed learni is laudable. Graduates with a fine array of sports skills but with no insight whatever into how they were acquired or how they can be adjusted to meet new requirements could not be counted as successes for any system of physical education. To conclude that "learning to learn" *is the objective* of physical education does *not* necessarily seem to follow from this observation. In a similar sense neither does the assumption that the disposition and ability to solve motor problems will generalize to other kinds of tasks. The dualism of physical and mental has been a haunting and troublesome problem for physical education. There seems to be a real danger in trying to meet this old problem by justifying physical education in terms of any hypothetical connection with cognitive tasks. In making this kind of claim whatever we might gain is more than offset by the fact that we have made movement a means and not an end.

Sequences of good movement problems are difficult to produce. The problems used in movement education are crucial elements in the teacher's relationship to the student. Problem-solving can easily degenerate into trial and error puzzle-solving. When this happens the teacher is placed in an "I know the answer but won't tell you" relationship to the student. This can be disastrous for the lesson. The series of problems within a lesson must be linked together in such a coherent way that both teacher and student know exactly at what problem they are working, what the task demands are, and thus, within what limits a good solution must lie. Such clarity of sequence and definition of problem elements are difficult to produce and maintain under the best of circumstances. Both extensive planning and exquisite improvisation are required.

It is sometimes difficult to know when to terminate exploration. Children cannot discover all things regarding movement with a reasonable economy of time and effort. This is especially true of complex movement patterns such as those associated with sports skills. If exploring and experimenting persist in situations where they are less than likely to produce genuine discovery, they quickly become exploring and experimenting for their own sake. This is a profitless enterprise that quickly leads to a breakdown in class morale. Furthermore, all children want to have a sense of mastering something. When the problems are diffuse and the standards of success unclear, the sense of mastery is often lost.

The kinesthetic element to which much attention is directed in movement education is not always the best focus for the learner. Focusing upon that part of feedback from movement which is available to conscious centers is of limited value in learning a complex skill. As any golfer knows, kinesthesis is inaccurate and can often mislead. The acquisition of motor skills is the gradual placement of control into automatic circuits to which consciousness is no longer adjunct. Any continuing stress on awareness defeats this process. In the final analysis, skill, from the learner's standpoint, is concerned with results in the environment and not process in the performer.

Movement education makes free use of problems in movement drawn from sports skills but usually without the implements (or velocities and forces) that are involved in the sports skills. This produces a situation in which skill is mimed. Because mime is consciously produced this leads to the sort of performance that is not at all realistic. It follows that the kinesthetic element of mime bears little relation to feedback from the real event. Recent movement education texts published in England refer to this as "danciness" and strongly caution against mimed sports movements (37, 44). In the absence of real forces and velocities the student can acquire a much distorted notion of sports movement. The missing element is what Munrow artfully calls ". . . the really shattering degree of tension evoked during impact in some striking skills, or at take-off in a long jump" (37: 195).

The range of ability and past experience to be found in a typical class often creates irritating problems for the teacher. Foremost among these is the tendency of a few quick learners to dominate the pattern of class response irrespective of the teacher's effort to provide a set for internal direction. Although imitation is in itself a skill cultivated in movement education it cannot be allowed to substitute for personal search and evaluation.

Another common difficulty is that some children tend to persevere with the first solution that produces any positive reinforcement. Failure to press on to successively superior solutions works against the basic intent of movement education. Thus, some children need *constant* encouragement to move ahead. Other children will move too fast, avoiding the necessary business of refinement and mastery.

Finally, for children whose past experience has been limited to traditional teaching methods in physical education, the initial experience with movement education is often confusing and unsatisfactory. The teacher's behavior is not consonant with their powerful expectation for direction. Teachers in schools having considerable mobility in the student population find this to be a continuing and disruptive problem.

CONCLUSIONS

Weighing the strengths of movement education in the one hand and the problems that bedevil it in the other, what sort of balance is struck? I am convinced of the special significance of movement education in the lower grades. It will probably prove especially useful with the retarded, the physically handicapped, and children with perceptual-motor impairment. Movement education might well be excellent as a remedial procedure with awkward, inhibited, and unsure adults, much as it is already used in college programs. With children and adults movement education can provide special help in the crucial problem of building confidence and a sense of command over the moving self. Certain teaching strategies closely identified with movement education such as problem-solving and the use of directed observation are techniques that can be used with profit in any kind of teaching system. *Beyond these points I am unconvinced that movement education will bring the millennium in physical education.*

It is apparent that there will be a severe temptation for some physical educators to accept movement education without critical appraisal. Movement education, as it has been defined here, requires careful matching with students, teachers, and programs, systematic planning for implementation, and thorough evaluation if the end result is to strengthen rather than weaken existing programs.

The over-all impact of movement education on American physical education could be beneficent. So long as its supporters are not driven to harden their position into a pedagogical "hang-up" we can look forward to a fruitful synthesis that blends the best parts of the old with the new.

REFERENCES

1. Andrews, Gladys, Sanborn, Jeanette, and Schneider, Elsa, *Physical Education for Today's Boys and Girls* (Boston: Allyn & Bacon, Inc., 1961).

2. Barrett, Kate Ross, *Exploration* (Madison, Wisc.: College Printing and Typing Co., Inc., 1965).

3. Bartenieff, Irmgard, and Davis, Martha Ann, *Effort-Shape Analysis of Movement* (New York: Unpublished Manuscript, 1965).

4. Battig, William F., "Facilitation and Interference," in Edward A. Bilodeau (ed.), *Acquisition of Skill* (New York: Academic Press, 1966).

5. Bilbrough, A., and Jones, P., *Physical Education in the Primary School* (London: University of London Press, Ltd., 1963).

6. Board of Education, *Syllabus of Physical Training for Schools* (London: H.M.S.O., 1933).

7. Broer, Marion, *Efficiency of Human Movement* (Philadelphia: W. B. Saunders Co., 1966).

8. Brown, Camille, and Cassidy, Rosalind, *Theory in Physical Education* (Philadelphia: Lea & Febiger, 1963).

9. Cratty, Bryant J., *Movement Behavior and Motor Learning* (Philadelphia: Lea & Febiger, 1967).

10. _____, "A Three Level Theory of Perceptual-Motor Behavior," *Quest,* Monograph VI (May, 1966), pp. 3-10.

11. _____, *A Program of Developmental Physical Education Activities for Educationally Handicapped Pupils* (Los Angeles: Los Angeles City Schools, 1966).

12. Cullen, F. Patricia, and Huelster, Laura J., *Basic Instruction in Physical Education for Women* (Urbana: Stipes Publishing Company, 1962).

13. Dance Notation Bureau—Center for Movement Research and Analysis, *The Effort-Shape Training Program* (New York: Dance Notation Bureau, 1966).

14. Detroit Public Schools, *Exploration of Basic Movements in Physical Education* (Detroit: The Board of Education of the City of Detroit, 1960).

15. Diem, Liselott, *Who Can* (Frankfort A/M., Germ.: Wilhelm Limpert, 1964).

16. Fitts, Paul M., "Perceptual-Motor Skill Learning," in Arthur W. Melton (ed.), *Categories of Human Learning* (New York: Academic Press, 1964).

17. Fleishman, Edwin A., "Human Abilities and the Acquisition of Skill," in Edward A. Bilodeau (ed.), *Acquisition of Skill* (New York: Academic Press, 1966).

18. _____, "Human Abilities and Verbal Learning," in Robert M. Gagne (ed.), *Learning and Individual Differences* (Columbus, Ohio: Charles E. Merrill, 1966).

19. Garland, Iris, *Effectiveness of Problem Solving Method in Learning Swimming.* Unpublished Master's thesis, UCLA, 1960.

20. Hackett, Layne C., and Jenson, Robert B., "Exploring Movement Experiences," *JOHPER,* XXXVI (1965), 28-29.

21. Halsey, Elizabeth, *Inquiry and Invention on Physical Education* (Philadelphia: Lea & Febiger, 1964).

22. _____, and Porter, Lorena, *Physical Education for Children* (New York: Holt, Rinehart and Winston, Inc., 1963).

23. Hunt, Valerie, "Movement Behavior: A Model for Action," *Quest*, Monograph II (April, 1964), pp. 69-91.

24. Huelster, Laura J., "A Course in Movement Fundamentals for College Women," *JOHPER*, XXXI (1960), 24-25.

25. Knapp, B., *Skill in Sport* (London: Routledge & Kegan Paul, Ltd., 1963).

26. Laban, Rudolf, *The Mastery of Movement* (London: MacDonald and Evans, Ltd., 1960).

27. _____, *Modern Educational Dance* (London: MacDonald and Evans, Ltd., 1948).

28. _____, and Lawrence, F. C., *Effort* (London: MacDonald and Evans, Ltd., 1947).

29. Locke, Lawrence F., "The Movement Movement," *JOHPER*, XXXVII (1966), 27-28, 73.

30. London County Council, *Movement Education for Infants* (London: Inner London Education Authority, 1963).

31. Ludwig, Elizabeth, *Six Lessons on Basic Movement Education.* Unpublished manuscript, University of Wisconsin at Milwaukee, Department of Physical Education for Women. n.d.

32. Ministry of Education, *Moving and Growing,* Part I of Physical Education in the Primary School (London: H.M.S.O., 1952).

33. _____, *Planning the Programme,* Part II of Physical Education in the Primary School (London: H.M.S.O., 1953).

34. Morison, Ruth, *Educational Gymnastics for Secondary Schools* (Liverpool: The Author, 1960).

35. _____, *Educational Gymnastics* (Liverpool: The Author, 1956).

36. Mosston, Muska, *Teaching Physical Education* (Columbus, Ohio: Charles E. Merrill, 1966).

37. Munrow, A. D., *Pure and Applied Gymnastics* (London: Edward Arnold, Ltd., 1963).

38. National Association for Physical Education of College Women, *Competence for Action,* 1960 Workshop Report (Washington, D.C.: AAHPER, 1960).

39. _____, *Purposeful Action,* 1956 Workshop Report (Washington, D.C.: AAHPER, 1956).

40. Pallett, G. Doreen, *Modern Educational Gymnastics* (London: Pergamon Press, 1956).

41. Plattsburgh City School District, *Program of Movement Education for the Plattsburgh Elementary Schools* (Plattsburgh, N.Y.: Board of Education City School District, Unpublished application for ESEA Title III Operational Grant, 1966).

42. Pontiac School District, *Perceptual-Motor Activities* (Pontiac, Mich.: Board of Education School District of the City of Pontiac, 1966).

43. Preston, Valerie, *A Handbook for Modern Educational Dance* (London: MacDonald and Evans Ltd., 1963).

44. Randall, Marjorie, *Basic Movement* (London: G. Bell and Sons, Ltd., 1961).

45. Russell, Joan, *Creative Dance in the Primary School* (London: MacDonald & Evans, Ltd., 1965).

46. Souder, Marjorie A., and Hill, Phyllis, J., *Basic Movement* (New York: Ronald Press, 1963).

47. Wisconsin Department of Public Instruction, *A Guide to Curriculum Building in Physical Education,* Curriculum Bulletin No. 28 (Madison, Wisc.: Department of Public Instruction, 1963).

Selected Supplementary References Concerning Movement Education

Articles

Broer, Marion, "Movement Education: Wherein the Disagreement?" *Quest,* Monograph II (April, 1964), pp. 19-24.

Brown, Margaret C., "The English Method of Education in Movement Gymnastics." *The Reporter* (New Jersey AAHPER), XXXIX (1966), 9-10, 18-19.

Crabbe, M.T., "Laban's Influence Upon Physical Education in England." *The New Era in Home and School,* XL (1959), 103-4.

Ludwig, Elizabeth, "Basic Movement Education in England." *JOHPER,* XXXII (1961), 18-19.

Meredith-Jones, Betty, "Understanding Movement." *JOHPER,* XXVI (1955), 14, 59.

Books

Lamb, Warren, *Posture and Gesture* (London: Gerald Duckworth Co., Ltd., 1965).

Mosston, Muska, *Developmental Movement* (Columbus, Ohio: Charles E. Merrill Books, Inc., 1965).

Nixon, John E., and Jewett, Ann E., *Physical Education Curriculum* (New York: Ronald Press, 1964).

Randall, Martin, *Modern Ideas on Physical Education* (London: G. Bell and Sons, Ltd., 1960).

————, and Waine, W. K., *Objectives of the Physical Education Lesson* (London: G. Bell and Sons, Ltd., 1963).

Swain, M. O. B., and LeMaistre, E. H., *Fundamentals of Physical Education* (Sydney, Australia: Ian Novak, 1964).

7

Motor Learning: Implications for Movement Education

ROBERT T. SWEENEY

Movement education is relegated to the instructional portion of the school day. It is difficult to conceive of movement education intramurals unless activities of a competitive nature are taught as movement education in the required class time. Perhaps a study of an elementary school and the ways in which movement education would change it is in order. Just what would change in the schools with which you are familiar? My visitations to schools suggest that the instructional phase of the physical education structure would be most readily affected. Consequently, I would like to offer information regarding the learning of motor skills.

Physical educators have entered the once totally private realm of the educational psychologist by concerning themselves with learning theory or, more specifically, with the learning of motor skills, which is based on learning theories. In the few prepared texts now available (Cratty [2], Singer [9], Oxendine [8], Bilodeau [1], Knapp [5], and Lawther [6]) and in many journal and periodical articles, various criteria and concepts for teaching motor skills and activities are set forth. To delineate briefly, motor learning is divided into three main areas of concern: the state of the learner, the learning process, and the conditions for learning. Content considerations permeate the total motor-learning area and are always a concern.

On learning theory, which is the foundation of motor learning, there are various schools of thought. The two main schools are the cognitivists and the behaviorists. A third, now coming into prominence, is known as the motivation-personality school. Hilgard and Bower [4] discuss these schools, each of which considers the learner, the process, and the conditions for learning.

THE STATE OF THE LEARNER

The state of the learner comprises the area of growth and development as well as sensory-motor integration throughout the child's life and the behavior resulting from the complexities that makes each child an individual. Factors that influence readiness for school and physical readiness for learning are also of major importance. Thus we highlight the vast importance of considering individual differences as they affect learning. The areas of intelligence, kinesthesis, visual capacities, reaction and movement time, lateral dominance, anthropometry, somatotype, and perception all serve to make individuals more dissimilar than similar in learning capacity.

Such physical, intellectual, and psychological characteristics combine with the social and emotional aspects of personality and the motivations of that personality to contribute to the total individuality of man. That individuality cries for consideration in the teaching-learning schema.

With regard to the state of the learner, teachers of physical education have been neglectful about initiating movement experiences for the range of students that can benefit most by them. Current emphasis in education is on early childhood education in all its forms. We in physical education have to realize the potential in those years that we are now neglecting. A concentrated effort to develop appropriate curricula for that population would have a profound effect on the movement capabilities of every participant. The effects on the remainder of our curriculum would also suggest a need for careful reexamination. Implications do exist for creating active-mobile life patterns for the children involved. We have yet to solve that mystery.

THE LEARNING PROCESS AND THE CONDITIONS FOR LEARNING

The learning process and the conditions for learning suggest many interesting avenues of study in the concept areas of reinforcement, motivation, mental rehearsal, transfer, retention and forgetting, practice and rest distribution, and whole-part learning. Examining movement education in terms of these seven concepts and their possible uses should shed light on its benefits.

What kind of learning environment permits the most appropriate use of the seven motor-learning concepts? The learning environment, or climate, is most closely related to the teacher's personal behavior, the content, and the method of presenting it. Hamachek's article [3] deals with teacher behavior, and Mosston's book, *Teaching Physical Education*, [7] analyzes the possibilities that exist when various styles of teaching are used. Knowledge of your students' abilities and of the proposed content that they are required to learn provides more information concerning the learning climate.

Reinforcement is part of the feedback model. Feedback includes correction, rewards, punishments, knowledge of results, partial reinforcements, and extinction. Teachers must understand the implications of the feedback mechanism in learning. Without feedback a student lacks the guidance that is necessary if learning is to take place. The results of a nonfeedback environment, or of a completely negative feedback environment, are nonlearning and negativism. In an environment in which the teacher is free to assist those who need him, the opportunity for individual as well as group feedback is greater than in an environment in which the teacher is busy controlling the entire class at once.

Feedback affects motivation by informing the student of his capabilities. A student who has a realistic picture of himself, realizing his strengths and weaknesses, knows what he can do; he will set his aspirations at an attainable level. Positive feedback allows the learner to set positive goals. If learning is to take place, motivation is necessary, and the total motivation complex is just that—*complex*. It is the result of one's total life environment and, as such, requires special attention from teachers. In providing appropriate learning experiences, teachers must plan for motivation before and during the experience and hope they have met the challenge significantly enough to allow for carry-over after class.

Mental rehearsal is a concept tied closely to conceptualization and verbalization. Some benefits accrue from being able to describe the movements that constitute the skill. Description enables the student to receive feedback himself by making it possible for him to understand a movement and its results. If the student can conceptualize and verbalize, he understands the movement. Thus many avenues that effect learning and retention are opened. If the student understands a movement, he can practice it after school with adequate knowledge to correct wrong responses. This procedure allows overlearning of the skill to take place, so that it becomes more and more reflexive with each repetition. With understanding, the student requires fewer trials to learn the skill, and overlearning results in less forgetting and longer retention. Understanding and the ability to analyze are among the benefits of mental rehearsal.

Transfer is a much-used concept of motor learning in movement education. It relies on the similarity of movements and thus focuses on the movement-pattern approach and the sequential breakdown of skills by degree of difficulty or whole-part relationships. Research shows that transfer depends on the previously learned skills and natural abilities of the learner, the difficulty of the task, and the extent of initial learning during a student-content interaction session. Thus transfer is closely related to retention, overlearning, mental rehearsal, and conceptualization, which in turn depend on both the practice and rest distribution and the feedback that guides the student to the correct response. If all these factors are combined in a positive, successful manner, we may expect higher levels of motivation, including a more positive self-image that manifests itself in higher levels of aspiration and a positive outlook toward life.

Retention and forgetting can be considered jointly with practice and rest distribution. A current teaching technique called interval training, which is concerned with amounts of practice combined with appropriate rest intervals, has many implications for learning. During the rest periods, mental rehearsal can take place; during the practice periods, control of the understood movements can be attained. The rest or nonactive periods are as important for learning as the active periods in certain instances. Techniques of mental rehearsal that ensure mental practice are many, the motor learning texts are full of examples. The amount of participation in and the amount of understanding about an activity determine its retention. The number of practice trials is the crucial issue in motor learning, performing, and retaining or forgetting. Physical education has to investigate this factor more closely. It is tied directly to the availability of equipment and facilities, as well as the learning environment that allows the student direct involvement with the equipment.

Because of its child-centered approach, movement education allows for more teacher-student interaction on a personal basis—a necessity for maximum feedback possibilities. It manipulates the subject matter from the simplest to the most complex. Its open-ended challenges encourage maximum involvement. Movement education begins at the base level, with content that is simpler than skills. It approaches movement by progressing from general to specific. It focuses on conceptualization, which is the foundation for self-practice, self-analysis, and mental rehearsal, and which enables overlearning and transfer to take place. Efficient transfer of subject matter and principles of movement enables the student to apply general movements over a wide range of skills or activities. The individualized teaching process permits each student to work at his own pace for the period best suited to him within the time block allotted for the class. Individual differences are honored within movement education, whereas in the traditional single-standard approach, to have a hereditary difference might be disastrous.

There are many more implications for the teaching of physical education in the movement-education approach. Some are yet to be discovered, others are hypothetical and still untested, and still others sound logical but lack proof. The concepts through which the investigation can take place are available. More grass-roots research is needed. Motor learning, or the study of motor activities and skills, remains a rich field for study in the field of movement education.

BIBLIOGRAPHY

1. Edward Bilodeau. *Acquisition of Skill.* New York: Academic Press, 1966.

2. Bryant J. Cratty. *Movement Behavior and Motor Learning.* Philadelphia: Lea & Febiger, 1964.

3. Don Hamachek. "Characteristics of Good Teachers and Implications for Teacher Education." *The Phi Delta Kappan.* February, 1969, pp. 341f.

4. Ernest Hilgard and Gordon Bower. *Theories of Learning.* New York: Appleton-Century-Crofts, 1966, pp. 564f.

5. Barbara Knapp. *Skill in Sports: The Attainment of Proficiency.* London: Routledge and Kegan Paul, 1964.

6. John D. Lawther. *The Learning of Physical Skills.* Englewood Cliffs, N.J.: Prentice-Hall, 1968.

7. Muska Mosston. *Teaching Physical Education.* Columbus, O.: Merrill, 1966.

8. Joseph B. Oxendine. *Psychology of Motor Learning.* New York: Appleton-Century-Crofts, 1968.

9. Robert N. Singer. *Motor Learning and Human Performance.* New York: Macmillan, 1968.

8

The Movement Movement
LAWRENCE F. LOCKE

The word *movement* has high currency and great popularity in physical education today. We are reminded of this every day, whether *movement* is used in the ubiquitous sense denoting a class of human behavior, or in one of the more narrow usages such as *movement education.* There are movement books, articles, courses, monographs, speeches, researches, school programs, and now—experts.

This plethora of new information and ideas comes from a variety of sources, including such diverse areas as clinical, perceptual, and learning psychology, neurophysiology, prosthetics, electromyography, physical therapy, and dance theory. In addition to these external sources there have been many contributions from within the physical education profession. For example, the concept of movement education has been a by-product of attempts to improve physical education programs for college women.

Efforts are already being made to generate miniature theories designed to draw together portions of this unruly collection of information. While most of these theories are tentative and represent no more than careful speculation, they have provided an important stimulus to unifying and holistic thought.

Where are we now? We are standing amidst a growing abundance of uncounted intellectual riches. The explosion of information has propelled words and concepts concerning movement into prominence and has generated a sense of great activity. The important question is, where are we going now? I propose to entertain three possible answers—to nowhere, to somewhere, or to several places.

By the first possibility, nowhere, I mean that nothing new or of lasting substance will result from the present interest in movement. This will be true if the interest is only a fad or if the word is only a substitute for older words that cover already familiar concepts. The sharing of a special language, an idea, or just a new word, can give people the illusion of novelty and substance.

The presence of new words is not a positive indication of new ideas. The activity that surrounds the word movement may be old stuff in new clothes, part of a cycle of professional interests having the same predict-

From *JOHPER,* January 1966. Reprinted by permission of the author.

ability as Halley's comet—and about the same impact on our professional lives.

In the professions, academic storms seem quite real when you are involved. In retrospect, they often turn out to be teapot tempests, without progeny. For example, physical educators in past years have become tremendously excited about such professional concerns as sportsmanship, posture, and creativity. None of these caused any perceptible changes in the way we operate, and at best, they evoke a yawn from today's membership. Many new ideas and issues disappear—not because they are developed or resolved—we just become bored with them!

Real or illusory, serious substance or accidental fad—the final judgment concerning human movement can only be made retrospectively. My own best judgment in this matter is that there is already enough genuinely new information and enough fruitful interdisciplinary exchange to ensure that movement stands for more than an intellectual hallucination.

Given this presumption—that we have the substance at hand to be going somewhere—the first possibility is that we are somehow all going there together. By this I mean that the word movement, as presently used, may be a symptom of the emergence of a new, unifying viewpoint. As diverse a group as Eleanor Metheny, Franklin Henry, Rudolph Laban, Bryant Cratty, Muska Mosston, and Alfred Hubbard might all be sharing some common ground. I do *not* simply mean that they are all observing the same phenomenon.

A simple analogy may clarify the point. "Psychologist" is a generic word that covers all people looking at the same class of events. A particular school such as psychoanalytic psychology, on the other hand, supplies lenses for observing that are ground to a particular prescription. The growing interdisciplinary dialogue concerning human movement could serve as unwitting midwife for a new theoretical framework concerning this dimension of man's behavior. It might provide a common lens for scientist, artist, and educator, just as psychoanalytic theory once provided a common viewpoint for clinician, experimentalist, and normalist.

My judgment would be that the satisfaction, excitement, and especially the increasing self-consciousness with which individuals of diverse backgrounds are consulting together on problems in human movement indicate that this alternative must be entertained as at least a possibility.

Another possible presumption is that our interest in human movement will lead us toward several independent ends. The most obvious candidates here are the development of human movement as an academic discipline and the development of human movement as an educational process.

Franklin Henry[1] has pointed out that there is ample precedent in the modern interdisciplinary sciences for the formation of a systematic body of knowledge around the focus of human movement. Such an academic discipline would direct the attention of psychologists, physiologists, anthropologists, sociologists, and historians to a phenomenon that now is only peripheral within their areas of concern.

The new concept of movement education also seems to have sound credentials for inclusion as an end toward which we might move. In so far as I understand them, the people interested in this area are centrally concerned with the substrate of capacities that make effective and efficient movement possible. Their crucial assumption seems to be that one can directly deal with, and perhaps manipulate, the substrate of capacities through the application of selected movement experiences. To a degree, this is a unique viewpoint concerning the role of movement experiences in physical education. Dance and sport are regarded only as specific agencies for acting out more fundamental movement capacities. While empirical evidence on this point is almost nonexistent, some recent work in neurology suggests at least that this is a worthy hypothesis.

These areas of professional ferment which relate to movement can bear fruit only as they begin to influence existing practices in physical education. As with fissionable materials, the critical mass either will or will not be achieved. If there is a significant sense of community and a sufficiently large body of new ideas, then it is inevitable that someone will decide that he does not like the status quo. A move to bring about change will occur. There will be a series of actions taken by a group of people working toward a particular end—by definition, a movement movement.

Scholars in the social sciences have worked out a natural history which we can fruitfully, if imperfectly, apply to such an eventuality. There are five stages. The first is marked by preliminary symptoms of discontent. These are of the same order as what some of you may have felt while trying to teach tennis to college students who are distressingly inept, considering their twelve years of physical education background.

Stage two is characterized by advanced dissatisfactions. This stage is marked not only by greater discomfort, but by localization of the problem and recruitment of other dissidents. The inclusion of topics concerning movement in the programs of professional conventions betrays just such a tendency to polarize issues and recruit sentiment.

---

[1] "Physical Education an Academic Discipline," Franklin Henry. *JOHPER,* September 1964, pp. 32-33.

When those who hold power in the area of concern are unable or unwilling to meet the emerging demand for change, the third stage is reached—an outbreak of action. It is easy to think of the great wars of revolution in this context but it must be remembered that there are other kinds of revolutionary outbreaks. At a certain point those interested in progressive education started a school, the city of Muskogee started a fitness program, and the University of Illinois recommended that all freshmen girls take a course called "Basic Movement."

The third stage is always accompanied by a great proliferation of symbols. In this regard it is interesting to note that we have recently acquired kinestruct, anthropokinetics, neurogeometrics, basic movement, homokinetics, ideomotor and kinesics. Words provide convenient handles for new abstractions, and perhaps give a sense of community through the sharing of a secret language.

Stages four and five are less meaningful to us at this point. The fourth stage is the move toward extremism. The moderates who are recuited along the way often find the complete and ultimate fulfillment of their objectives so abhorrent that they defect. One could speculate that just this is happening within the physical fitness movement today. A physical education program that is defined in practice as calisthenics, circuit training, and fitness testing repels people whose original interest was only in the introduction of vigorous activity into the program.

The nature of the fifth stage depends somewhat upon your point of view. Some ardent supporters of the movement strive to perpetuate the extremes achieved in the previous stage. Most people desire a synthesis that unites and draws upon the strength of both the old and the new.

If we accept this framework and the presumption that indeed we are headed somewhere, then we probably are now between stages two and three. Further events will depend upon factors such as effective leadership, clear statement of both dissents and beliefs, adequate communication, access to the power structure and development of process skills to carry out the new order. Few social movements generate all of these, and we would have to be surprised if human movement, by any definition, were to do so.

My feeling is that it would be tragic if the movements towards either of the two ends mentioned above were to abort at some stage short of full maturity. If the two can continue to evolve, and particularly, if the two can achieve a measure of rapprochement and functional interdependence, then we may at last find a firm base from which to define our role as a profession.

The emergence of human movement as the focus for an academic discipline will depend, I believe, upon the capacity of physical education graduate schools to attract and hold not only physiologists, but staff members who are competent in other biological and behavior sciences. This has not been accomplished, and until it is, the body of knowledge concerning human movement will remain uneven in its quality, depth, and breadth. An academic discipline must also inspire conscious, central loyalties. It is one thing to say that movement can serve as an adequate focus for a new interdisciplinary science, and it is quite another to produce a cadre of student-scholars whose persisting interest lies there and not in the pre-existing, allied sciences.

I believe that the future of movement education hinges upon four pivotal problems. Dissatisfaction with the present system must be crystalized, objectives must be developed that can be defined in terms of behavior, and empirically derived techniques must be produced that can be applied with some confidence to public school children. Finally, there must be access to the power that can cause change in the public school program. I judge this last point to be the keystone. It must be await the development of well-publicized, attractive pilot programs in public schools.

The possibility of an effective liaison between the two broad areas of movement education and the academic discipline of human movement is a special concern and presents several difficult problems. On the one hand the discipline could have no direct obligation to the needs of the practicing movement educator. Most people would agree that such a relationship would risk the possibility of stultifying a new science. On the other hand, it has been proposed that it would be a disgrace if the scientist did not help the practitioner to understand the body of knowledge and help him to discover relevant applications. Such a proposal ignores the distance between the average undergraduate student in physical education and the scientific specialist in graduate physical education which grows greater, and not smaller, with every passing year. They do not share a common language, a common view of what is significant, or a common level of intellectual competence.

If movement educators are to draw effectively upon the discipline of human movement, then some exceptionally creative methods of translation and teaching will be necessary.

Section 4
References

MOVEMENT EDUCATION BIBLIOGRAPHY

American Association for Health, Physical Education, and Recreation. *Idea Book in Physical Education for the Elementary School Teacher.* Washington: AAHPER, 1965.

_____. *This is Physical Education.* Washington: AAHPER, 1965, 1966.

_____. *This is Elementary Physical Education.* Washington: AAHPER, 1966.

Anderson, Marian H., Margaret Elliot, and Jeanne LaBerge. *Play with a Purpose.* New York: Harper and Row, 1966.

Andrews, Gladys. *Creative Rhythmic Movement for Children.* Englewood Cliffs, N.J.: Prentice-Hall, 1954.

Andrews, Gladys, Jeannette Saurborn, and Elsa Schneider. *Physical Education for Today's Boys and Girls.* Boston: Allyn and Bacon, 1962.

Arnold, P. *Education, Physical Education and Personality Development.* New York: Atherton Press, 1969.

Ashton, D. *Rhythmic Activities, Grades K-6.* Washington: NEA, AAHPER, 1964.

Barratt, M., *et al. Foundations for Movement.* Dubuque, Iowa: Brown, 1964.

Barrett, Kate Ross. *Exploration, A Method of Teaching Movement.* Madison, Wis.: College Typing and Printing, 1965.

_____. *A Procedure for Systematically Describing Primary Physical Education Lessons Implementing the Concept of Movement Education.* Unpublished doctoral dissertation. Madison, Wis.: University of Wisconsin, 1969.

Bilbrough, A., and P. Jones. *Physical Education in the Primary School.* London: University of London Press, 1964.

Bingham, Alma. *Improving Children's Facility in Problem Solving.* New York: Teachers College Press, Columbia University, 1958.

Blake, O. W., and Anne Volpe. *Lead-Up Games to Team Sports.* Englewood Cliffs, N.J.: Prentice-Hall, 1964.

Bortin, Helen. *Do You Move As I Do?* New York: Abelard, Schuman, 1963.

Braithwaite, Molly. *Medau Rhythmics Movement.* London: Associated Press, 1955.

Broer, Marion. *Efficiency of Human Movement.* Philadelphia: Saunders, 1966.

Brown, Camille, and Rosalind Cassidy. *Theory in Physical Education.* Philadelphia: Lea and Febiger, 1963.

Brown, Margaret, and Betty Sommers. *Movement Education: Its Evolution and One Modern Approach.* Reading, Mass.: Addison-Wesley, 1969.

Bruner, J. S. *Toward a Theory of Instruction.* Cambridge, Mass.: Belknap Press of Harvard University Press, 1966.

Cameron, W., and Peggy Pleasance. *Education in Movement School Gymnastics.* Oxford: Basic Blackwell, 1964.

Chatwen, Nora. *Physical Education for Primary Grades.* Ottawa: Physical Education Branch, Dept. of Education, 1967.

Citizenship Education Study. *Problem Solving.* Detroit: Wayne State University Press, 1967.

Clark, Carol. *Rhythmic Movement Activities for Kindergarten and Primary Grades.* Danville, N.Y.: Instructor Publications, 1969.

Clarke, H. H. *Nature and Extent of Individual Differences and Their Significance for Physical Education and Athletics.* Eugene, Ore.: Oregon School Study Council, University of Oregon, 1965.

Combs, A. (Chairman, 1962 ASCD Committee). *Perceiving, Behaving, Becoming.* Washington: Association for Supervision and Curriculum Development, NEA, 1962.

Cureton, T. K., and A. J. Barry. *Improving the Physical Fitness of Youth.* Monographs of the Society for Research in Child Development, Serial No. 95, Vol. 29, No. 4, 1964.

Dauer, V. *Dynamic Physical Education for Elementary School Children.* Minneapolis: Burgess, 1968

Davis, E. C., ed. *Academy Papers No. 1.* "Motor Learning and Performance." Tucson: American Academy of Physical Education, Dept. of Physical Education, University of Arizona, 1967.

Demeter, Rose. *Hop-Run-Jump.* New York: Day, 1968.

Detroit Public Schools. *Exploration of Basic Movements in Physical Education*. Detroit: Publications Dept., Detroit Public Schools, 1960.

Dickinson, Marie B. *Independent and Group Learning*. Washington: Dept. of Elementary-Kindergarten-Nursery Education, NEA, 1967.

Diem, Liselott. *Who Can*. Trumbull, Conn.: Physical Education Supply Associates, 1957.

Diem, Liselott, and R. S. Methner. *Corrective Gymnastics and Special Exercise Class in Schools*. Trumbull, Conn.: Physical Education Supply Associates, 1957.

Doll, R., ed. *Individualizing Instruction*. Washington: 1964 Yearbook, Association for Supervision and Curriculum Development, 1964.

Drehman, Vera L. *Head Over Heels—Gymnastics for Children*. New York: Harper and Row, 1967.

Dunn, Lois. "Motion." *Investigating Science with Children*, Vol. 4. Darien, Conn.: Teachers Publishing Company, 1964.

Edmundson, J., and J. Garstang. *Activities on Physical Education Apparatus*. London: Oldbourne, 1962.

Fabun, D., ed. "Communications." *Kaiser Aluminum News*, Vol. 23, No. 3. Kaiser Aluminum and Chemical Corp., 1965.

Freeman, R. *Movement Education for US*. Morristown, N.J.: YMCA, 1967.

Gell, Heather. *Music, Movement and the Young Child*. London: Australasian Press, 1960.

Gilliom, Bonnie. *Basic Movement Education for Children: Rationale and Teaching Units*. Reading, Mass.: Addison-Wesley, 1970.

Glass, H. *Exploring Movements*. New York: Educational Activities, 1966.

Godfrey, Barbara, and N. C. Kephart. *Movement Patterns and Motor Education*. New York: Appleton-Century-Crofts, 1969.

Hackett, L., and R. Jensen. *A Guide to Movement Exploration*. Palo Alto, Cal.: Peek Publications, 1966.

Hall, J. T., *et al. Fundamentals of Physical Education*. Pacific Palisades, Cal.: Goodyear, 1969.

Halsey, Elizabeth. *Inquiry and Invention in Physical Education*. Philadelphia: Lea and Febiger, 1964.

Halsey, Elizabeth, and Lorena Porter. *Physical Education for Children, A Developmental Program*. New York: Holt, Rinehart and Winston, 1963.

Halsman, P. *Philippe Halsman's Jump Book*. New York: Simon and Schuster, 1959.

Halverson, Lola. "Development of Motor Patterns in Young Children," *Quest,* NCPEAM and NCPEAW. Vol. VI, May 1966.

Hatcher, Caro, and Hilda Mullin. *More Than Words . . . Movement Activities for Children.* Pasadena: Parents-for-Movement Publications, 1969.

Heuser, Inge, and G. Spahn. *Come On–Join In.* Trumbull, Conn.: Physical Education Supply Associates, 1963.

Houghten, W. F. *Educational Gymnastics.* London: Inner London Education Authority, 1965.

Hudgins, B. *Problem Solving in the Classroom.* New York: Macmillan, 1967.

Hudson, L. *Contrary Imaginations.* London: Methuen, 1966.

Humphrey, Louise, and R. Jerrold. *Interpreting Music Through Movement.* Englewood Cliffs, N.J.: Prentice-Hall, 1964.

Hymes, J. *Teaching the Child Under Six.* Columbus, O.: Merrill, 1968.

Inner London Education Authority. *Movement Education for Infants.* London: ILEA, 1965.

Jordan, Diana. *Childhood and Movement.* New Rochelle, N.Y.: Sportshelf, 1968.

Kessler, Ethel and L. *Are You Square?* Doubleday, 1966.

Knapp, Barbara. *Skill in Sport: The Attainment of Proficiency.* London: Routledge and Kegan, 1964.

Laban, R. *Mastery of Movement.* London: MacDonald and Evans, 1960. Revised by Lisa Ullman. Bridgeport, Conn.: Educational Recordings of America, 1960.

_____. *Modern Educational Dance.* London: MacDonald and Evans, 1963.

Laban, R., and F. C. Lawrence. *Effort.* London: MacDonald and Evans, 1947.

Latchaw, Marjorie, and G. Egstrom. *Human Movement: With Concepts Applied to Children's Movement Activities.* Englewood Cliffs, N.J.: Prentice-Hall, 1969.

Lawther, J. *The Learning of Physical Skills.* Englewood Cliffs, N.J.: Prentice-Hall, 1968.

London County Council. *Educational Gymnastics.* London: LCC, 1964.

_____. *Movement Education for Infants.* No. 4208. London: LCC, 1964.

Marx, E. *The Ball Primer Book for Schools and Clubs.* Trumbull, Conn.: Physical Education Supply Associates, 1962.

Mauldon, E., and J. Layson. *Teaching Gymnastics*. London: MacDonald and Evans, 1965.

McCristal, K., and W. C. Adams, eds. *Foundations of Physical Activity*. Champaign, Ill.: Stipes, 1965.

Metheny, Eleanor. *Connotations of Movement in Sport and Dance*. Dubuque, Iowa: Brown, 1965.

———. *Movement and Meaning*. New York: McGraw-Hill, 1968.

Miller, Donna Mae, ed. "The Art and Science of Human Movement," *Quest*, Monograph II, Spring issue, April 1964.

Miller, Donna Mae, and E. C. Davis, eds. "Papers on Motor Learning and Performance." *Academy Papers, No. 1*. Tucson: American Academy of Physical Education, 1968.

Ministry of Education. *Moving and Growing*. *Physical Education in the Primary School, Part I*. London: Her Majesty's Stationery Office, 1952.

———. *Planning the Programme*. *Physical Education in the Primary School, Part II*. London: Her Majesty's Stationery Office, 1965.

Morison, Ruth. *Educational Gymnastics for Secondary Schools*. Liverpool: I. M. Marsh College of Physical Education, 1960.

Mosston, M. *Development Movement*. Columbus, O.: Merrill, 1965.

———. *Teaching Physical Education*. Columbus, O.: Merrill, 1966.

Mott, Jane. *Conditioning and Basic Movement Concepts*. Dubuque, Iowa: Brown, 1968.

Munden, Ivy. *Physical Education for Infants*. London: Ling Book Shop, 1953.

Munrow, A. D. *Pure and Applied Gymnastics*. London: Arnold, 1963.

Murray, Ruth L. *Dance in Elementary Education, A Program for Boys and Girls*. New York: Harper and Row, 1963.

North, Marion. *A Simple Guide to Movement Teaching*. London: Ling Book Shop, 1964.

———. *Composing Movement Sequences*. London: Marion North, 1961.

O'Quinn, G. *Gymnastics for the Elementary School*. Dubuque, Iowa: Brown, 1967.

Oxendine, J. *Psychology of Motor Learning*. New York: Appleton-Century-Crofts, 1968.

Pallett, Doreen G. *Modern Educational Gymnastics*. New York: Pergamon Press, 1965.

Polya, G. *How To Solve It*. New York: Doubleday, 1957.

Preston-Dunlop, Valerie. *Readers in Kinetography Laban: Motif Writing for Dance.* London: MacDonald and Evans, 1967. Four books: 1, *Introducing the Symbols;* 2, *More about Symbols;* 3, *Moving with a Partner;* 4, *Effort Graphs.*

Randall, Marjorie. *Basic Movement.* London: York House, 1963.

Rasmussen, Margaret, and Lucy Prete Martin. *Early Childhood—Crucial Years for Learning.* Washington: Association for Childhood Education International, 1966.

Raths, L. E. *Teaching for Thinking, Theory and Application.* Columbus, O.: Merrill, 1967.

Redfern, Betty. *Introducing Laban Art of Movement.* London: MacDonald and Evans, 1965.

Robinson, Helen, and B. Spodek. *New Direction in the Kindergarten.* New York: Teachers College Press, Columbia University, 1965.

Rowen, Betty. *Learning Through Movement.* New York: Teachers College Press, Columbia University, 1963.

Russell, Joan. *Creative Dance in the Primary School.* London: MacDonald and Evans, 1965.

_____. *Modern Dance in Education.* London: MacDonald and Evans, 1958.

Schlein, Miriam. *Shapes.* New York: Scott, 1952.

Schurr, Evelyn. *Movement Experiences for Children.* New York: Appleton-Century-Crofts, 1967.

Shipley, F., and E. Carpenter. *Freedom to Move.* Washington: NEA, 1962.

Shulman, L., and E. Keislar. *Learning by Discovery.* Chicago: Rand McNally, 1966.

Singer, R. *Motor Learning and Human Performance.* New York: Macmillan, 1968.

Smith, Hope. *Introduction to Human Movement.* Reading, Mass.: Addison-Wesley, 1968.

Souder, Marjorie, and Phyllis Hill. *Basic Movement—Foundation of Physical Education.* New York: Ronald Press, 1963.

Strang, Ruth. *Helping Children Solve Problems.* Chicago: Scientific Research Associates, 1965.

Tidgwell, Lois A. *Movement and Learning.* Mimeographed 12-page paper. Claremont, Cal.: Pitzer College, 1969.

Tillotson, Joan. *Syllabus of Workshop in Movement Education.* Plattsburgh, N.Y.: 1968.

Ubell, E., and Arlene Strong. *The World of Push and Pull.* New York: Atheneum, 1964.

Wann, K., Miriam Dorn, and Elizabeth Liddle. *Fostering Intellectual Development in Young Children.* New York: Teachers College, Columbia University, 1962.

Wessell, Janet. *Movement Fundamentals.* Englewood Cliffs, N.J.: Prentice-Hall, 1957.

Willee, W. W. *Small Apparatus for Primary School Physical Education.* New York: Cambridge University Press, 1956.

Wisconsin State Department of Education. *A Guide to Curriculum Building in Physical Education, Elementary Schools.* Curriculum Bulletin No. 28. Madison, Wis.: 1963.

MOVEMENT EDUCATION FILMS

Anyone Can–Learning Through Motor Development. Bradley Wright Films, color, 27 min, $240.

Apparatus Skills. Gabor Nagy, Filmfair Communications (10946 Ventura Boulevard, Studio City, Cal., 91604). Supervised by Craig Cunningham, University Elementary School, University of California at Los Angeles, 9-11 min, $120.

Balance Skills. Gabor Nagy, Filmfair Communications (10946 Ventura Boulevard, Studio City, Cal., 91604). Supervised by Craig Cunningham, University Elementary School, University of California at Los Angeles, 9-11 min, $120.

Ball Skills. Gabor Nagy, Filmfair Communications (10946 Ventura Boulevard, Studio City, Cal., 91604). Supervised by Craig Cunningham, University Elementary School, University of California at Los Angeles, 9-11 min, $120.

Basic Manipulative Activities. Ealing Film-Loops (2225 Massachusetts Avenue, Cambridge, Mass., 02140), 7-loop set, $160.65. (1) Yarn Balls, Hoops, Ropes, and Wands. (2) Rolling and Fielding. (3) Foot-Dribbling and Kicking. (4) Bouncing, Hand-Dribbling, and Catching. (5) Volleying in Different Ways. (6) Hitting in Different Ways. (7) Throwing and Catching.

Basic Movement. Hayes Kruger, color, super-8 cartridged. Ealing Film-Loops (2225 Massachusetts Avenue, Cambridge, Mass., 02140), 6-loop set, $137.70; $22.95 each. (1) Moving in Many Directions. (2) Moving at Different Levels. (3) The Force of Movement. (4) The Flow of Movement. (5) Movements: Large and Small. (6) Movements: Fast and Slow.

Basic Movement Education in England. Audio-Visual Education Center, University of Michigan. Sound, black and white, 19 min, $4.25 rental. Describes movement education from primary grades through teacher training. Basic movement is shown to be fundamental to gymnastics and dance.

Basic Movement Skills. Gabor Nagy, Filmfair Communications (10946 Ventura Boulevard, Studio City, Cal., 91604). Supervised by Craig Cunningham, University Elementary School, University of California at Los Angeles, 9-11 min, $120.

Being Me. University of California Extension Media Center (2223 Fulton Street, Berkeley, Cal., 94720), $75. Creative dance class for children, produced by Hilda Mullin.

Boys' Modern Educational Gymnastics. Wayne State University, $3.20 rental.

Fun with Parachutes. Documentary Films. Sound, color, 11 min. Visual presentation of selected parachute activities that add a new dimension to movement education.

Functional Fitness. Ealing Film-Loops (2225 Massachusetts Avenue, Cambridge, Mass., 02140), 6-loop set, $137.70. (1) Balance. (2) Arm and Abdominal Strength. (3) Leg Strength. (4) Flexibility. (5) Agility. (6) Coordination.

Hopping. Skipping. Throwing. Hitting. Absorptive Patterns. Preparatory Movement. Arm and Leg Opposition. Application of Force. Series of eight films on movement patterns done by Margaret M. Thompson, available from Audio-Visual Center, Purdue University, $10.00 each; $2.50 rental. (Audio tapes may be acquired from Margaret M. Thompson, Department of Health and Physical Education, University of Missouri, Columbia, Missouri, 65201.)

Movement Awareness. Patricia Tanner, color, super-8 cartridged. Ealing Film-Loops (2225 Massachusetts Avenue, Cambridge, Mass., 02140), 5-loop set, $114.75. (1) Shapes. (2) Leads. (3) Supports. (4) Weight Transference. (5) Flight.

Movement Education. Audio-Visual Department, Northern Illinois University. Black and white, 10 min, 1967.

Movement Education: Guided Exploration (U-6264). University of Iowa. Sound, black and white, 8 min, $1.65 rental. An eight-minute class focused on guided exploration of speed, fast and slow, with second grade children.

Movement Education in Physical Education (U-5610). University of Iowa. Sound, black and white, 17 min, $3.00 rental.

Movement Education in Physical Education. Hayes Kruger, Louise Duffy School (95 Westminster Drive, West Hartford, Conn., 06107). Black and white, 20 min, $20 rental. Demonstrates the methodology of the problem-solving approach, emphasizes the importance of a well-structured environment, and discusses the relationship to good traditional programing.

Movement Education in Rural Schools. Movement Education in First and Second Grades. Movement Education in Third and Fourth Grades. Three German Movement Education films. Charles Benton, Public Media, Inc. (1144 Wilmette Avenue, Wilmette, Ill.).

Movement Education: The Problem-Solving Technique. (U-6265). University of Iowa. Sound, black and white, 12 min, $1.65 rental. A twelve-minute class focused on solving the problem of composing a dance with fifth grade children.

Movement Education: Time and Space Awareness (U-6263). University of Iowa. Sound, black and white, 8 min, $1.65 rental. An eight-minute class focused on time and space awareness with second grade children.

Movement Experiences for Children. Uil G. Rabb, Instructional Media Distribution, Northern Illinois University. Black and white, 8 min, $2.70 rental.

Movement Experiences for Primary Children. Uil G. Rabb. Color, 15 min, $5.45 rental.

Movement Exploration. Documentary Films (3217 Trout Gulch Road, Aptos, Cal.). Sound, color, 22 min, $20 rental. Children four to ten years of age demonstrate exploring movement. Shows techniques of movement exploration; describes concept in action.

Movement Speaks. Wayne State University Systems Distribution and Utilization (5448 Cass Avenue, Detroit, Mich., 48202), Dr. T. W. Roberts, Director. $4.00 rental.

Project: Movement Education, Plattsburgh, New York. Dr. Joan Tillotson, Bailey Avenue Elementary School, ESEA Title III (Plattsburgh, N.Y., 12901). Sound, black and white, $1.00 rental. Film depicts program in operation in the elementary schools of Plattsburgh, N.Y. Many student activities with innovative equipment.

Sensorimotor Training. Barbara E. Schuelle, Director, Early Childhood Education Program, Dayton Board of Education (1302 Cory Drive, Dayton, Ohio, 45406). Shows a preschool preventive activity program in perceptual-motor development.

Space Exploration. Department of Health and Physical Education, Milwaukee Public Schools (5225 West Vliet Street, Milwaukee, Wis., 53208). Black and white, 15-16 min, 1966.

Wir Turnen am Lueneberger Stegel. Kebelman Filmgesellschaft (Duesseldorferstr. 58, Berlin, W. 15, Germany). $36.

STUDIES IN METHODOLOGY

The following list includes scientifically designed research papers dealing with teaching methodology and related considerations. Comparisons of methods are the most prevalent though analyses of methods and methodology on attitude development, skill development, social-emotional climate, personality, and speed of learning are also considered. Many theoretical proposals of methods also exist in the literature. Further investigation of the theoretical in a scientific manner is warranted.

Barrett, Kate Ross. "An Analysis of Exploration as a Method for Teaching Movement." Unpublished Master's thesis. University of Wisconsin, 1964.

Berendsen, Carol Ann. "The Relative Effectiveness of Descriptive Teaching and Structured Problem Solving in Learning Basic Tennis Skills." Unpublished Master's thesis. University of Washington, 1967.

Bookout, Elizabeth C. "An Observational Study of Teaching Behavior in Relation to the Social-Emotional Climate of Physical Education." Ph.D. dissertation. New York University, 1965 (microcard).

Church, K. "The Effect of Different Teaching Methods and Spot of Aim Techniques on Bowling Achievement of College Men." Unpublished study. Indiana University (mimeographed).

Deelman, Margaret. "An Investigation into the Effects of Two Different Programs of Physical Education on Certain Aspects of Behavior of First Grade Children." Master's thesis. University of Wisconsin, 1968 (microcard).

Djorup, H. E. "The Effects of Two Methods in Physical Education on Personality Adjustment," Ph.D. dissertation. New York University, 1943 (microcard).

Garland, Iris Lillian. "Effectiveness of Problem Solving Method in Learning Swimming." Unpublished Master's thesis. University of California, Los Angeles, 1960.

Graylee, Gayle. "A Comparison of the Effectiveness of Two Methods of Teaching a Four-Week Unit on Selected Motor Skills to First Grade Children." Master's thesis. University of North Carolina at Greensboro, 1965 (microcard).

Hall, Mary Frances. "A Study of Two Methods of Teaching Bowling to College Women of High and Low Motor Ability." Unpublished doctoral dissertation. State University of Iowa, 1958 (microcard).

Hill, Rose Mabel. "Educational Gymnastics for the Teacher of Physical Education." Master's thesis. State University of Iowa, 1962 (microcard).

Hofland, Synnova E. "Comparison of the Learning Curves of Two Classes Taught Bowling by Different Methods." Unpublished Master's thesis. University of North Carolina at Greensboro, 1960.

Howard, Shirley Ann. "A Comparison of Two Methods of Teaching Ball-Handling Skills to Third Grade Students." Ph.D. dissertation. State University of Iowa, 1960.

Keller, R. "A Comparison of Two Methods of Teaching Physical Education to Secondary School Boys." Ph.D. dissertation. University of Illinois, 1963 (microcard).

Kenzie, Leota P. "A Comparison of the Effectiveness of Two Methods of Instruction on the Performance of First Grade Children in Selected Motor Activities." Master ot Science thesis. University of Wisconsin, 1963.

LaPlante, Marilyn. "A Study of the Problem-Solving Method of Teaching Bowling." Master's thesis. University of North Carolina at Greensboro, 1965 (microcard).

Maltzman, I., *et al.* "Some Relationships Between Methods of Instruction, Personality Variables and Problem-Solving Behavior." *Journal of Educational Psychology.* 47: 71-78, 1956.

Pestolesi, R. A. "Critical Teaching Behaviors Affecting Attitude Development in Physical Education." Ph.D. dissertation. University of Southern California, 1968 (dissertation abstracts).

Russell, Marilyn R. E. "Effectiveness of Problem Solving Methods in Learning a Gross Motor Skill." Master's thesis, University of Washington, 1967 (microcard).

Scott, R. S. "A Comparison of Teaching Two Methods of Physical Education With Grade One Pupils." Master's thesis. Wisconsin State University, LaCrosse, 1965 (microcard).

Sheehan, T. J. "The Construction and Testing of a Teaching Mode for Attitude Formation and Change Through Physical Education," Ph.D. dissertation. Ohio State University, 1965 (microcard).

Spring, Marjorie. "A Pilot Study in the Teaching of Selected Activities in Apparatus and Tumbling to Children Enrolled in the First Grade with Emphasis on the Problem Solving Approach." Unpublished Master's thesis. Texas Women's University, 1964.

Van Allen, Martha. "An Investigation Using the Movement Exploration Approach in the Teaching of Selected Swimming and Diving Skills." D.P.E. dissertation. Springfield College, 1966 (microcard).

Workman, Donna Jo. "A Comparison of Basic Motor Skill Achievement after Two Types of Instruction." Master of Science thesis. University of Michigan, 1959.

Young, Earlaine. "A Comparison of Two Methods of Teaching Field Hockey to College Women." Master's thesis. Arkansas State College, 1965 (microcard).

Ziegler, Yvonne. "A Comparison of Two Methods of Teaching Gymnastics." Master's thesis. University of Wisconsin, 1965 (microcard).

SOURCES FOR MATERIALS USED IN MOVEMENT EDUCATION

Inclusion in the following list does not constitute endorsement of company or product. Sources should be investigated, and purchase should be determined on the basis of satisfaction of the customer. Many items listed, as well as others, can be made by children, faculty, workshops, etc. Some of the products listed should be installed by the manufacturer as safety and liability measures.

The J. E. Burke Company, New Brunswick, N.J. Playground equipment.

Childcraft, 155 East 23rd Street, New York, N.Y., 10010. Climbing ropes for primary children, doorway gym bars, hippity hop scotch, punching bag on stand, wheeled toys, Wibblers, tumble tub, Tunnel of Fun, Silly Cycles.

Childcraft Education Corporation, P.O. Box 94, Bayonne, N.J., 07002. Silly Cycles, Ride-A-Roller, Hop Ball, Wibblers.

Community Playthings, Rifton, N.Y., 12471. Blocks, pairs of stairs, rocking rowboats, slides, towers, "Variplay" triangle sets, wheeled toys, balance platforms and beams.

Cosom Corporation, 6030 Wayzata Boulevard, Minneapolis, Minn., 55416. "Saf-T-Play" plastic balls, bats, bowling sets, hockey sticks.

Creative Ideas Company, Tooties Division, 5838 West 142nd Street, Hawthorne, Cal., 90250. "Tooties," perceptual-motor development materials.

Creative Playthings, Princeton, N.J. Activity Dollies, balance blocks and boards, cargo nets, hoops, punching bags (suspended), puppets, rhythm instruments, rope ladders, stilts, tumble tubs, wheeled toys, unicycles.

Dick Dean of Dean Enterprises, P.O. Box 87, Pittstown, N.J. Parachutes and all supplies.

El-J-Plastics, Inc., 233 Robbins Lane, Syosset, N.Y. "Kick-A-Loop," similar to jingle jump.

Electro-Mech Industries, Inc., 825 New Hampshire Avenue, N.W., Washington, D.C., 20037. Orbitgames, Orbitwheel, Superhoop guidance system.

Fun and Fitness Incorporated, Box FF, Montezuma, Iowa, 50171. Playground and gymnasium apparatus.

Game-Time, Inc., Litchfield, Mich., 49252. Playground equipment, obstacle course, Punch-A-Ball, Loop-O-Ball.

General Sportcraft Company, Ltd., Bergenfield, N.J., 07621. Sport and game equipment, Pogo sticks.

I. Goldberg Company, Army Goods, 429 Market Street, Philadelphia, Pa. Parachutes.

Groiler Industries, Inc., 35-47 31st Street, Long Island City, N.Y., 11106. "Skippy," Hula hoops, other equipment.

Hadar Athletic Company, 1108 North 13th Street, Humbolt, Iowa, 50548. Tumble-Aid, black plastic TiniKling sticks, throwdown bases, plastic playground balls.

Harcostar Ltd., Windover Road, Huntingdon, England. Playbarrel, Polyethylene moulded barrel for children 2-10 years old.

Delmer F. Harris Company, P.O. Box 288, Department J, Concordia, Kan. Swedish climber, other apparatus.

J. W. Holden, P.O. Box 1484, 131 Washington Street, Providence, R.I., 02901. "Chinese" jump-ropes.

H. Hunt and Son, Ltd., Woodend Avenue, Speke, Liverpool 24, England; 33-35 Lewisham Way, New Cross, S.E. 14, London, England. Sherwood Junior "B" equipment.

Idea Development Company, 440 West Baseline Road, Claremont, Cal., 91711. "Toobers" (truck inner tubes), Huskylite plastic blocks.

The Learning Center, Elementary Department, Princeton, N.J. Educational toys and games.

Lind Climber Company, 807 Reber Place, Evanston, Ill., 60202. Lind climber.

Lojen Apparatus, Inc., Box 785, Fremont, Neb., 68025. Lojen miniature jumping stands, 5' turning bar.

The Mexico Forge, Inc., R. D. 1, Reedsville, Pa., 17084. Playground equipment, physical fitness course.

Mitchell Division, Royal Industries, 1500 East Chestnut, Santa Ana, Cal., 92701. Specialized flooring products for gymnasium and playground.

Elliot Morris, 678 Washington Street, Lynn, Mass., 01901. Bean bags and Bean bag boards.

Nissen Corporation, 930 27th Avenue S.W., Cedar Rapids, Iowa, 52406. Balance beams, horizontal bars, horses, mats, parallel bars, ropes, trampolines, parallel ropes.

Phillip's Ewing Bazaar, 1680 North Olden Avenue Extension, Trenton, N.J. Parachutes.

Physical Education Supply Associates (PESA), P.O. Box 292, Trumbull, Conn., 06611. "Stretch" ropes, Wevau balls, hoops.

Playground Corporation of America, 29-16 40th Avenue, Long Island City, N.Y., 11101. Playscapes, playground planning.

Portapit Corporation, P.O. Box C, Temple City, Cal., 91780. Skill development equipment, foam landing surfaces of varied sizes and shapes.

Porter Athletic Equipment, 9555 Irving Park Road, Schiller Park, Ill., 60176. Prudden "Gymster."

Premier, River Vale, N.J. Cage balls, mats, medicine balls.

School Equipment Corporation, P.O. Box 175, Foley, Mo. Horizontal bars, horses, "Turning Bar," walking beams, other apparatus.

F.A.O. Schwarz, Fifth Avenue at 58th Street, New York, N.Y., 10022. Complete line of toys, games, and equipment.

H. Severin, Winona Avenue, Box 141, Lincoln Part, N.J. Yarn balls.

Sterling Recreation Products, 7 Oak Place, Montclair, N.J., 07042. Southhampton and trestle tree apparatus, complete line of equipment, cargo net.

Switlik Parachute Company, Inc., 1325 East State Street, Trenton, N.J. Parachutes.

R. E. Titus Gym Scooter Company, Winfield, Kan., 67156. Gym scooters.

R. W. Whittle Ltd., P. V. Works, Monton, Eccles, Manchester, England. Portable physical education equipment for movement education—K to 6th Grade.

Wicksteeds of Royston, Ltd., Meridian Works, Barkway Road, Rouston, Herts, England. Build-A-Climb agility apparatus.

Wolverine Sports, 745 State Circle, Ann Arbor, Mich., 48104. Complete line of equipment.

PERCEPTUAL-MOTOR BIBLIOGRAPHY

American Association for Health, Physical Education, and Recreation. *Perceptual-Motor Foundations—A Multidisciplinary Concern.* Washington: NEA, 1969.

Anderson, J. E. *Growth and Development Today's Implication for Physical Development.* Estes Park, Col.: National Conference of Social Changes and Sports, 1958.

Ayers, A. Jean. *Perceptual Motor Disfunction in Children.* Cincinnati, O.: Greater Cincinnati District, Ohio Occupational Therapy Association Conference, 1964.

Ball, T., and Clara Lee Edgar. "The Effectiveness of Sensory-Motor Training in Promoting Generalized Body Image Development." *The Journal of Special Education,* Vol. 1, No. 4, Summer 1967.

Barsch, R. *Achieving Perceptual-Motor Efficiency.* Seattle: Special Child Publications, 1967.

_____ . *Enriching Perception and Cognition,* Vol. 2; *Perceptual-Motor Sequences,* Vol. 3. Seattle: Special Child Publications.

_____ . *A Movigenic Curriculum.* Madison, Wis.: State Department of Public Instruction, State of Wisconsin Bulletin No. 25, 1965.

_____ . *A Perceptual-Motor Curriculum.* Seattle: Special Child Publications, 1969.

Bender, L. *Psychopathology of Children with Organic Brain Disorders.* Springfield, Ill.: Thomas, 1956.

Benyon, Sheila. *Intensive Programming for the Slow Learner.* Columbus, O.: Merrill, 1968.

Chaney, Clara, and N. C. Kephart. *Motoric Aids to Perceptual Training.* Columbus, O.: Merrill, 1968.

Corder, W. D. "Effects of Physical Education on Intellectual, Physical, and Social Development of Educable Mentally Retarded Boys." Unpublished social project. Nashville: George Peabody College, 1965.

Cratty, B. J. *Development Sequences of Perceptual-Motor Tasks.* New York: Educational Acitivities, Inc., 1967.

_____ . *Exploring Perceptual-Motor Needs of Primary Level Children,* No. 606-7. New York: Educational Activities, 1967.

_____ . *Movement Behavior and Motor Learning.* Philadelphia: Lea and Febiger, 1964.

_____ . *The Perceptual-Motor Attributes of Mentally Retarded Children and Youth.* Los Angeles, Cal.: Mental Retardation Services Board of Los Angeles County.

_____ . *Perceptual-Motor Behavior and Educational Processes.* Springfield, Ill.: Thomas, 1969.

_____ . *A Program of Developmental Physical Education Activities for Educationally Handicapped Pupils.* Los Angeles, California: Los Angeles City Schools.

Cratty, B. J., and Sister Margaret Mary Martin. *Perceptual-Motor Efficiency in Children, The Measurement and Improvement of Movement Attributes.* Philadelphia: Lea and Febiger, 1969.

Cruickshank, W. M., ed. *The Teacher of Brain-Injured Children.* Syracuse, N.Y.: Special Education and Rehabilitation Monograph No. 7, Syracuse University Press, 1966.

Dayton Board of Education. *Basic Movement: Purpose, Content, Helpful Hints, and Lesson Sequence.* Dayton, O.: Elementary Education Bulletin No. 8, February 17, 1965.

Delacato, C. H. *Diagnosis and Treatment of Speech and Reading Problems.* Springfield, Ill.: Thomas, 1965.

Dunsing, J. (Director). *An Annotated Bibliography of Research and Theory Related to the Achievement Center for Children.* Lafayette, Ind.: Achievement Center for Children, Department of Education, Purdue University, revised yearly.

Dunsing, J., and N. C. Kephart. "Motor Generalization in Space and Time." *Learning Disorders,* Vol. 1. Seattle: Special Child Publications, 1965.

Ebersole, Marylou, *et al. Steps to Achievement for Slow Learners.* Columbus, O.: Merrill, 1968.

Espenschade, Anna S. "Growth and Development." *Expanding Horizons in Physical Education.* Report of the Fourth International Congress on Physical Education for Sports for Girls and Women. Washington: U.S. Government Printing Office, 1960.

Feelings and Learning. Washington: ACEI, 1963.

Francis, R. J., and G. L. Rarick. "Motor Characteristics of the Mentally Retarded." Madison, Wis.: U.S. Office of Education, Cooperative Research Project No. 152 (6432), University of Wisconsin, September 16, 1957.

Frostig, M., and D. Horne. *The Frostig Program for the Development of Visual Perception.* Chicago: Follett, 1964.

Fry, E. (Chairman, Perception and Reading Conference). *Perception and Reading Proceedings.* New Brunswick, N.J.: Reading Center, Rutgers, State University, March 20, 1967.

Gesell, A. *The First Five Years of Life.* New York: Harper and Row, 1940.

Getman, G. N. *How to Develop Your Child's Intelligence.* Leverne, Minn.: Announcer Press, 1962.

_____. "The Visuomotor Complex in the Acquisition of Learning Skills." *Learning Disorders,* Vol. 1. Seattle: Special Child Publications, 1965.

Getman, G. N., and E. R. Kane. *The Physiology of Readiness.* Minneapolis: P.A.S.S., 1963.

Harmon, D. B. "A Preliminary Report on a Study of Eye Preference, Certain Body Mechanics and Visual Problems." *Learning Disorders,* Vol. 2. Seattle: Special Child Publications, 1966.

Hayden, F. J. "Physical Fitness for the Mentally Retarded." Toronto: Metropolitan Toronto Association for Retarded Children, 1964.

Ismael, A. H., and J. J. Gruber. *Motor Aptitude and Intellectual Performance.* Columbus, O.: Merrill, 1967.

Ismael, A. H., N. C. Kephart, and C. C. Cowell. *Utilization of Motor Aptitude Tests in Predicting Academic Achievement.* Lafayette, Ind.: Purdue University, 1963.

Kephart, N. C. *The Slow Learner in the Classroom.* Columbus, O.: Merrill, 1960.

Kinsella, P. J. *The Place of Perception in Improving Reading Comprehension.* Boston: The A & M Reading Bulletin, Allyn and Bacon.

Let's Keep Them Straight: Body Mechanics for the Infant and Young Child. Los Angeles: American Institute of Family Relations.

Lowder, R. G. *Perceptual Ability and Social Achievement.* Winter Haven, Fla.: Winter Haven Lions Club, 1965.

McLeod, P. H. *Readiness for Learning, A Program for Visual and Auditory Perceptual-Motor Training.* Philadelphia: Lippincott, 1965.

Neuropsychological and Perceptual-Motor Theories of Treatment for Children with Educational Inadequacies. A comparison of the Doman-Delacato and Kephart theories. Harrisburg, Pa.: Commonwealth of Pennsylvania, Department of Public Instruction, 1966.

Piaget, J. *The Origins of Intelligence in Children.* New York: International University Press, 1952.

Piaget, J., and Barbel Inhelder. *The Child's Conception of Space.* London: Routledge and Kegan Paul, 1963.

Pitcher, Evelyn, *et al. Helping Young Children Learn.* Columbus, O.: Merrill, 1968.

Pontiac, Michigan, Schools. *A Guide for Elementary Physical Educators and Classroom Teachers, Manual of Perceptual-Motor Activities.* Johnstown, Pa.: Mafex Associates, 1965.

Radler, D. H., and N. C. Kephart. *Success Through Play.* New York: Harper and Row, 1960.

Roach, E. G., and N. C. Kephart. *The Purdue Perceptual-Motor Survey.* Columbus, O.: Merrill, 1966.

Rosborough, Pearl. *Physical Fitness and the Child's Reading Problem.* New York: Exposition Press, 1963.

Rowen, Betty. *Learning Through Movement.* New York: Teachers College, Columbia University, 1963.

Russell, R. *Programs of Special Classes for Children with Learning Disabilities.* East Orange, N.J.: New Jersey Association for Brain Injured, 1965.

Schilder, P. *The Image and Appearance of the Human Body.* International University Press, 1935.

Strauss, A. A., and N. C. Kephart. *Psychopathology and Education of the Brain-Injured Child.* Vol. III, *Progress in Theory and Clinic.* New York: Grune and Stratton, 1955.

Stuart, Marion F. *Neurophysiological Insights Into Teaching.* Palo Alto, Cal.: Pacific, 1963.

Thompson, Margaret M. *A Study of the Relationship Between Performance in Selected Motor Skill and Mental Achievement of Children of Elementary School Age.* Unpublished doctoral thesis (typewritten; microfilmed). Ames, Iowa: State University of Iowa, 1961.

Valett, R. E. *The Remediation of Learning Disabilities.* Palo Alto, Cal.: Fearon, 1969.

Van Witsen, Betty. *Perceptual Training Activities Handbook.* New York: Teachers College Press, 1967.

Wheeler, J. C. *Perceptual-Motor and Body Management Programs.* Dayton, O.: Board of Education, Dayton Public Schools, 1966.

ELEMENTARY PHYSICAL EDUCATION BIBLIOGRAPHY

American Association for Health, Physical Education, and Recreation. *Children and Fitness, A Program for Elementary Schools.* Report of the National Conference on Fitness of Children of Elementary School Age. Washington: AAHPER, 1960.

_____. *Children in Focus, Their Health and Activity.* 1954 Yearbook. Washington: AAHPER, 1954.

Anderson, Marian H., Margaret Elliot, and Jeanne LaBerge. *Play with a Purpose.* New York: Harper and Row, 1966.

Bancroft, Jessie H. *Games.* New York: Macmillan, 1955.

Boyer, Madeline Haas. *The Teaching of Elementary School Physical Education.* New York: Pratt, 1965.

Bucher, C., and Evelyn Reade. *Physical Education in the Modern Elementary School.* New York: Macmillan, 1965.

Canadian Association for Health, Physical Education, and Recreation. *The Physical Work Capacity of Canadian Children.* Toronto: CAHPER, 1968.

Clarke, H. H., and F. B. Haar. *Health and Physical Education for the Elementary School Classroom Teacher.* Englewood Cliffs, N.J.: Prentice-Hall, 1959.

Corbin, C. *Becoming Physically Educated in the Elementary School.* Philadelphia: Lea and Febiger, 1969.

Fabricius, Helen. *Physical Education for the Classroom Teacher.* Dubuque, Iowa: Brown, 1965.

Fait, H. F. *Physical Education for the Elementary School Child.* Philadelphia: Saunders, 1964.

Farina, A. M., *et al. Growth Through Play*. Englewood Cliffs, N.J.: Prentice-Hall, 1959.

Fleming, R. S., ed. *Curriculum for Today's Boys and Girls*. Columbus, O.: Merrill, 1963.

Fraser, Ellen D., Joan Bransford, and Mamie Hastings. *The Child and Physical Education*. Englewood Cliffs, N.J.: Prentice-Hall, 1956.

Garrison, Charlotte, and A. Sheahy. *At Home With Children: The Guide to Pre-School Play and Training*. New York: Holt, 1943.

Geri, F. *Illustrated Games, Rhythms and Stunts for Children: Primary Grades*. Englewood Cliffs, N.J.: Prentice-Hall, 1955.

Goome, Alice. *Children's Singing Games*. New York: Dover, 1968.

Halsey, Elizabeth. *Inquiry and Invention in Physical Education*. Philadelphia: Lea and Febiger, 1964.

Hartley, Ruth, *et al. Understanding Children's Play*. New York: Columbia University Press, 1952.

Harvey, Sister Ann. *Rhythm and Dances for Pre-School and Kindergarten*. New York: Schirmer, 1968.

Hindman, D. A. *A Complete Book of Games and Stunts*. New York: Prentice-Hall, 1958.

Humphrey, J. H. *Elementary School Physical Education*. New York: Harper, 1958.

————. *Child Learning Through Elementary School Physical Education*. Dubuque, Iowa: Brown, 1965.

————. *Readings in Physical Education for the Elementary Schools*. Palo Alto, Cal.: National Press, 1958.

Humphrey, J. H., and Virginia Moore. *Read and Play*, Champaign, Ill.: Garrard, 1962.

Humphrey, Louise, and J. Ross. *Interpreting Music Through Movement*. Englewood Cliffs, N.J.: Prentice-Hall, 1964.

Jones, Beti-Havard. *Bean-Bag Activities*. Lynn, Mass.: Elliott-Morris, 1966.

Jones, Edwina, Edna Morgan, and Gladys Stevens. *Methods and Materials in Elementary Physical Education*. New York: World, 1950.

Joynson, D. C. *A Guide For Games*. London: Kaye and Ward, 1969.

Kirchner, G. *Physical Education for Elementary School Children*. Dubuque, Iowa: Brown, 1966.

Kraus, R. *Play Activities for Boys and Girls*. New York: McGraw-Hill, 1950.

Kulbitsky, Olga, and F. Kaltman. *Teachers Dance Handbook* (Grades 1-6). Newark, N.J.: Bluebird, 1960.

Larson, L., and Lucille Hill. *Physical Education in the Elementary Schools.* New York: Holt, 1957.

LaSalle, Dorothy. *Guidance of Children Through Physical Education.* New York: Ronald Press, 1957.

Latchaw, Marjorie. *A Pocketbook of Games and Rhythm Activities for Elementary School.* New York: Prentice-Hall, 1956.

————. *The Evaluation Process in Health, Physical Education and Recreation.* Englewood Cliffs, N.J.: Prentice-Hall, 1962.

Latchaw, Marjorie, and Jean Pyatt. *A Pocket Guide of Dance Activities.* Englewood Cliffs, N.J.: Prentice-Hall, 1958.

McNeiley, S., and Elsa Schneider. *Physical Education in the School Child's Day.* U.S. Dept. of Health, Education and Welfare, Office of Education, Bulletin No. 14, 1953.

Miller, A., and Virginia Whitcomb. *Physical Education in the Elementary School Curriculum,* 3rd ed. Englewood Cliffs, N.J.: Prentice-Hall, 1969.

Monsour, Sally, *et al. Rhythm in Music and Dance for Children.* Belmont, Cal.: Wadsworth, 1966.

Moustakas, C., and Minnie P. Berson. *The Young Child in School.* New York: Morrow, 1956.

Murray, Ruth Lovell. *Dance in Elementary Education, a Program for Boys and Girls.* New York: Harper and Row, 1963.

Nagel, C. *Play Activities for Elementary Grades.* St. Louis: Mosby, 1964.

Nagel, C., and Fredricka Moore. *Skill Development Through Games and Rhythmic Activities.* Palo Alto, Cal.: National Press, 1966.

Neilson, N. P., and Winifred Van Hagen. *Physical Education for the Elementary Schools.* Cranbury, N.J.: Barnes, 1954.

O'Keefe, P., and Anita Aldrich. *Education Through Physical Education Activities.* St. Louis: Mosby, 1959.

Pearson, C. E. *A Classroom Teacher's Guide to Physical Education.* New York: Teachers College, Columbia University, 1958.

Prudden, Bonnie. *Fitness From Birth to Six.* New York: Harper and Row, 1964.

————. *Is Your Child Really Fit?* New York: Harper and Row, 1956.

Richardson, Hazel. *Games for the Elementary School Grades.* Minneapolis: Burgess, 1961.

Saffran, Rosanna B. *First Book of Creative Rhythms.* New York: Holt, Rinehart and Winston, 1963.

Salt, E. B., *et al. Teaching Physical Education in the Elementary School.* Cranbury, N.J.: Barnes, 1942.

Schneider, Elsa. *Ten Questions on Physical Education in the Elementary Schools.* Washington: U.S. Dept. of Health, Education and Welfare, 1957.

Schurr, Evelyn L. *Movement Experiences for Children.* New York: Appleton-Century-Crofts, 1967.

Stuart, Frances, and J. Ludman. *Rhythmic Activities,* Series 1. Minneapolis: Burgess, 1955.

Vannier, Maryhelen, and Mildred Foster. *Teaching Physical Education in the Elementary Schools.* Philadelphia: Saunders, 1963.

Young, Helen L. *A Manual-Workbook of Physical Education for Elementary Teachers.* New York: Macmillan, 1963.

PLAY BIBLIOGRAPHY

Alschuler, R., and C. Heining. *Play: A Child's Response to Life.* New York: Houghton Mifflin, 1936.

Aries, P. *Centuries of Childhood.* New York: Knopf, 1963.

Axline, V. M. *Play Therapy: The Inner Dynamics of Childhood.* Boston: Houghton Mifflin, 1947.

Bowen, W., and P. Mitchell, eds. *The Theory of Organized Play.* New York: Barnes, 1923.

Boyce, E. R. *Play in the Infant's School.* London: Methuen, 1921.

Caillois, R. *Man, Play and Games.* New York: Free Press, Macmillan, 1961.

Carlson, B., and D. Gingland. *Play Activities for the Retarded Child.* Nashville: Abingdon Press, 1961.

Curtis, H. S. *Education Through Play.* New York: Macmillan, 1915.

Davis, J. F. *Play and Mental Health: Principles and Practices for Teachers.* New York: Barnes, 1938.

Dulles, F. R. *America Learns to Play.* New York: Appleton-Century-Crofts, 1940.

Fraser, Ellen D. *The Child and Physical Education.* Englewood Cliffs, N.J.: Prentice-Hall, 1956.

Gerber, Ellen W. "Learning and Play: Insights of Educational Protagonists." *Quest.* Monograph XI, Winter issue, December 1968, pp. 44-50.

Groos, K. *The Play of Animals.* New York: D. Appleton, 1901; translated by E. L. Baldwin, 1913.

Gulick, L. H. *Philosophy of Play.* New York: Scribner, 1920.

Hartley, R. E. *New Play Experiences for Children: Planned Play Groups, Miniature Life Toys and Puppets.* New York: Columbia University Press, 1952.

_____. *Growing Through Play: Experiences of Teddy and Bud.* Columbia University Press, 1952.

Hartley, R. E., and R. M. Goldenson. *The Complete Book of Children's Play.* New York: Crowell, 1957.

Herron, R. E., *et al. Children's Play, a Reseach Bibliography.* Champaign, Ill.: Motor Performance Laboratory, Children's Research Center, University of Illinois, 1967.

Holbrook, D. *Children's Games.* Bedford, England: Gordon Fraser, 1957.

Holmes, B. M. *Organized Play in the Infant and Nursery School.* London: University of London Press, 1937.

Huizinga, J. *Homo Ludens: A Study of the Play-Element in Culture.* Boston: Beacon Press, 1955.

Jackson, L., and K. M. Todd. *Child Treatment and the Theory of Play,* 2nd ed. New York: Ronald Press, 1950.

Kawin, Ethel. *The Wise Choice of Toys.* Chicago: Chicago University Press, 1965.

Kepler, Hazel. *The Child and His Play.* New York: Funk and Wagnalls, 1932.

Kraus, R. G. *Play Activities for Boys and Girls.* New York: McGraw-Hill, 1957.

Lambert, Clara. *Play: A Child's Way of Growing Up.* New York: Play Schools Association, 1947.

_____. *Play, a Yardstick of Growth.* New York: Play Schools Association, 1948.

Lee, J. *Play in Education.* New York: Macmillan, 1922.

Lehman, H., and P. Witty. *The Psychology of Play Activity.* New York: Barnes, 1927.

Leland, H., and D. Smith. *Play Therapy With Mentally Subnormal Children.* New York: Grune and Stratton, 1965.

Lowenfeld, N. *Play in Childhood.* London: Gollancz, 1935.

Menninger, K. *Love Against Hate.* Chapter 7, "Play." New York: Harcourt, Brace and World, 1942.

Mitchell, E. D., and B. S. Mason. *The Theory of Play.* New York: Barnes, 1948.

Palmer, L. A. *Play Life in the First Eight Years.* Boston: Ginn, 1916.

Piaget, J. *Play Dreams and Imitation in Childhood.* New York: Norton, 1951.

Pickard, Phyllis M. *The Activity of Children.* London: Longmans, Green, 1965.

Rainwater, C. E. *The Meaning of Play*. Chicago: University of Chicago Press, 1915.

———. *The Play Movement in the United States*. Chicago: University of Chicago, 1922.

Rogers, J. *The Child and Play*. New York: Century, 1932.

Rogerson, C. H. *Play Therapy in Childhood*. London: Oxford University Press, 1939.

Sapora, A., and E. Mitchell. *The Theory of I··y and Recreation*. New York: Ronald Press, 1961.

Shoemaker, R. *All in Play; Adventures in Learning*. New York: Play Schools Association, 1958.

Slovenko, R., and J. A. Knight, eds. *Motivation in Play, Games, and Sport*. Springfield, Ill.: Thomas, 1967.

Spath, Martha. *Education in Play*. Kirksville, Mo.: Simpson, 1966.

Sutton-Smith, B. *The Games of New Zealand Children*. Berkeley: University of California Press, 1959.

Thorburn, Marjorie. *Child at Play*. London: Allen and Unwin, 1937.

Tudor-Hart, Beatrix. *Play and Toys in Nursery Years*. New York: Viking, 1966.

Van Alstyne, Dorothy. *Play Behavior and Choice of Play Materials of Pre-School Children*. Chicago: University of Chicago Press, 1932.

Winnicott, D. W. "Why Children Play," in *The Child, the Family, and the Outside World*. Middlesex, England: Penguin, 1964.

Wolfe, A. W. M., and E. L. Boehm. *Play and Play Things*. New York: Child Study Association of America, 1930.

ADDITIONAL SOURCES OF INFORMATION

The American Academy of Physical Education, Department of Physical Education for Women, University of Arizona, Tucson, Ariz., 85721.

American Association for Health, Physical Education, and Recreation (AAHPER), 1201 Sixteenth St., N.W., Washington, D.C., 20036.

Association for Childhood Education International (ACEI), 3615 Wisconsin Ave., N.W., Washington, D.C., 20016.

The Canadian Association of Health, Physical Education, and Recreation (CAHPER), 703 Spading Ave., Toronto 4, Ont., Canada.

The Center for Programmed Instruction, Inc., a nonprofit educational organization, 365 West End Ave., New York, N.Y., 10024.

Center for the Study of Motivation and Human Abilities, Ohio State University, Columbus, O.

Educational Methods, Inc., 64 East Van Buren St., Chicago, Ill., 60605.

Learning and Physical Education Newsletter, John N. Drowatzky, ed., Division of Health and Physical Education, University of Toledo, Toledo, O., 43606.

Learning Research and Development Center, 160 North Craig St., University of Pittsburgh, Pittsburgh, Pa., 15213.

Microcard Publications, School of Health, Physical Education, and Recreation, University of Oregon, Eugene, Ore., 97403.

Movement Education Newsletter, Vera M. Johnston and Lois Tidgwell, eds., 701 Locust Ave., Long Beach, California, 90813.

National College Physical Education Association for Men (NCPEAM), 203 Cooke Hall, University of Minnesota, Minneapolis, Minn., 55455.

National Laboratory on Early Childhood Education, 805 West Pennsylvania Ave., Urbana, Ill., 61801.

The Physical Education Association of Great Britain and Northern Ireland, Ling House, 10 Nottingham Place, London, W.1, England.

Physical Education Newsletter, Arthur C. Croft Publications, 100 Garfield Ave., New London, Conn.

The Physical Educator, Phi Epsilon Kappa Fraternity, 400 Meadows Drive, Suite L-24, Indianapolis, Ind., 46205.

Quest, National College Physical Education Association for Men and Women, David C. Bischoff, School of Physical Education, University of Massachusetts, Boyden Hall, Amherst, Mass., 01003.

The Society for Research in Child Development, Inc., Publications Office, Child Development Publications, University of Chicago Press, 5750 Ellis Ave., Chicago, Ill., 60637.

Stanford Center for Research and Development in Teaching, School of Education, Stanford University, 770 Welch Rd., Palo Alto, Cal., 94304.

Wisconsin Research and Development Center for Cognitive Learning, University of Wisconsin, 1404 Regent St., Madison, Wis., 53706.